2850

D0331452

"Find You the Virtue"

Other books by Irving Massey:

The Uncreating Word
The Gaping Pig

Translation:

Stello, by Alfred de Vigny

Edition:

Posthumous Poems of Shelley

Find You the Virtue

Ethics, Image, and Desire
in Literature

Irving Massey

**"Find you the virtue, and I'll find
the Verse."**
　　Pope, Epilogue to the *Satires*

The
George Mason
University Press

Cover photo from the Cathedral at Orvieto.
Copyright by Carlo Bavagnoli.
Used by
permission of Mr. Bavagnoli.

For Ann

Mi natura dedit leges

Cornelia

Contents

Acknowledgments

I SHOULD LIKE TO THANK SUNG-WON LEE FOR HIS EXPERT assistance with the references for this book, as well as for serving as my (sometimes unheeded) scholarly conscience. Without the encouragement of Herman Rapaport and Charles Molesworth I might never have brought the work to completion. I should also like to acknowledge, with thanks, permission to republish chapters that have appeared in a different form elsewhere: chapters 1, 3, and 6 in *Georgia Review* (Fall, 1978; Summer, 1980; and Fall, 1983, respectively), and chapter 2 in *Jewish Dialog* and *Midstream* (Spring, 1978, and Summer, 1983). The Kunsthistorisches Museum in Vienna has allowed me to reproduce Parmigianíno's "Conversion of St. Paul." The reference staff at Lockwood Library and the secretarial staff of the English Department at SUNYAB provided sustained and generous cooperation. Summer grants from the University gave me free time to work on several chapters, and a subvention from the Julian Park fund helped defray costs for technical necessities. Robert Waterhouse and Cheryl O'Neill kindly assisted me with the bibliography and index.

Introduction
Ethics, Images, and Several Other Things

> [In] the spectrum of colours . . . language already
> reigns. . . . The image . . . turns against primordial
> intimacy. . . . Just put black against white . . . , and
> all the decisions of ethics begin stirring, all the
> foliage of words starts hissing.
>
> Yves Bonnefoy

TOO BIG A TOPIC, SOME WILL SAY. BUT THE TOPIC IS BIGGER
than even my title suggests. To talk about ethics is necessarily
to talk about a number of things. As the ethical has asserted
its unavoidable connections to other subjects, I have found
myself forced into additional areas. On the other hand, despite
Pope's challenge:

Find you the Virtue, and I'll find the Verse,

some would deny that ethics has any role whatsoever in the discussion of literature; and Pope's assertiveness can be read as a sort of whistling in the dark, in that dark place where rhymes have become nugatory as virtues have grown scarce. Besides, does one even need verses where one can find virtues? Sartre, for one, would deny any connection between the two. "It is stupid to confuse the moral with the aesthetic." The Good requires being in the world, the Beautiful detachment from the world, imagination, negation. The real is never beautiful.[1]

Of course, recent aesthetics has not been excessively concerned with beauty: we now speak of "The no longer fine (i.e., 'beautiful') arts" ("Die nicht mehr schönen Künste").[2] But accepting Sartre's vocabulary for the moment, one might go farther and say that the Good is so much a matter of commitment to being in the world that it is not even accessible to language, let alone to art. Who wants to talk about ethics? We feel instinctively that it is a sterile topic. Aristotle himself, at the end of his own *Ethics,* admits that ethical theory is ineffectual in practice, and that "passion is not amenable to reason but only to force" (10.9).[3] Ethics is act. There is a long tradition, from Aquinas to Walter Benjamin, that maintains that the Good cannot be represented; there is no Image for the good. Either it is, or it is not. It cannot both be and not be at the same time, as it would have to, in order to maintain a position within the ambiguous ontology of the image.

Can one, then, imitate virtue?[4] And should one, for that matter, write about vice? (This is not an idle question.)[5] Maybe there is not even a language for the Good, since language, like image, is at least partly a form of representation. Or, at least, since the Fall, as Benjamin would have it, language, no longer pure creative Name, is tainted, and is unable to carry the force of the Good as such.[6] It must be admitted that the present book too reveals an occasional prejudice against the language of literature, attacking fiction as representing hostile impulses (chapter 1), and at another point poetry (chapter 2) as a vector of death. The question even arises whether literature as such, which must accept pure negativity as one of its possible poles, can claim a place within a consistent ethical scheme.

What, then, is literature good for? I can distinguish several purposes that literature serves, though they may be incompatible, or work only at different times. One is play. Another is the communication of solidarity or shared humanity between author and reader[7]—though I doubt that literature can work as a didactic instrument to improve individual conduct (see below, chapter 3) or help in dealing with life.[8] A third possible value of literature can be found in its provocative effect. I should like to consider this third possibility at greater length.

Literature engenders ideas that we would never have without it;[9] it teases into thought because it teases beyond thought. Schelling calls it "the only true and eternal organ and document of philosophy...."[10] As a source of the new, literature helps us to transform and revitalize our world. After all, originality has at times been thought of as the key attribute and the peculiar contribution of art to the domain of the human. Conversely, it is a mistake to think of art as a stationary object to be admired. Art refers only to the future, to what must be conquered by each person. Art tells you what it is possible for mankind to have: not what it has. There is no "treasure" to bank on. One may find in art an instigation, or a challenge, but really the only effect it can have is to strike one a glancing blow on its way to another destination.

There can be no doubt, though, that, at least along one of its faces, literature is an intellectual thing. It is a way of asking whether life is worth living, quite without respect to those violent interventions from external circumstances (such as war or Holocaust) which may make life seem unendurable. Writing turns everything to the purposes of this personal meditation. In that meditation, life and death are regularly at stake, in forms that may actually be life-threatening and even life-dissolving, although these are not the same life or the same death that is threatened by physical danger. The removal of threat to the body does not do away with the threat engendered in the mind. Kundera's "The Angels," for example, jams one up against the internality of death in a way that is both devastating and enticing: it seems to prove that the only important thing is the dismantling of the self; that the only place where anything interesting can begin to happen is in the space of an accepted death. Tamina's life drags along aimlessly after the death of her husband until she begins to experience her own death from within. The stifling conditions of the external world, simultaneously brutal and juvenile, are translated into the hideously attractive crowd of children that seduces her, engulfs her, and eventually watches her drown in the Lethe that surrounds this island of the damned.

It is because so much of literature is occupied with meditations of this sort that it is foolish to blame Sylvia Plath (as has been done) for using the image of the Nazi to describe her father. As René Char says, "art knows nothing of History, but helps itself to its terror."[11] In a sense, it doesn't even matter what material literature uses, whether the most violent or the most etiolated; it's all for a meditation. Of course, there can't be a literature "about" certain events, such as, say, the Holocaust; but the reason why there can't is not only that the Holocaust cannot be encompassed by literature; it is also that literature is always about the inner life of the author, though not necessarily in any personal sense. But that "violence from within" may not even protect us from a "violence from without,"[12] so great can be the difference between the two registers of experience; the first may merely lead us to ignore the second, as though that were a violence of an inferior order.

As an intellectual act (the aspect of the literary act that I have just been considering), literature is also a meditation about the relation of image to abstraction. To extend the discussion to politics, I might cite Jean-Joseph Goux's opinion that even the battle between Hitler and the Jews was really a battle over images: the cult of images pitted against that which cannot be metaphorized, against the Jewish faith in the unrepresentable.[13] I shall return to the association of the image with violence; but in the meanwhile I find that I have edged toward a fourth possible conception of literature, beyond its uses as amusement, as confirmation of fellowship, or as provocation to thought. There is at least one obviously different possibility. Maybe literature is actually about violence, as René Girard, for one, would say. The very notion of image implies imitation; and imitation, in turn, implies suppression of action and coercive authority relations. Even Sartre saw the image as a kind of "possession."[14] In Lyotard's *Discours, Figure,* image, or, as he calls it, *figure,* is always associated with basic, originary violence. (This attitude may seem a little surprising in an author who is very much on the side of images and opposed to strategies, whether Freudian or semiotic, for reducing them to concepts). The rejection of images, on the other hand, can also be construed as a form of violence, in which the patriarchal father forbids the son access to the mother even in the sublimated version of the image. (Goux argues that all images are essentially female).[15]

In any event, literature certainly records violence; it also enables us to indulge our propensity for violence in a sublimated form,[16] or it suggests that man's life is inherently violent. Not amusing, nor consolidating of human bonds, nor intellectually intriguing, it can jolt us, if we pay close attention to it, with a vision of uncompromising, not merely "tragic," ferocity and terror. In this view, if we take heed of what it says, we shall necessarily be sadder; wiser we may not be, for wisdom implies the possibility of either accepting or acting on knowledge, and such knowledge as this can neither be accepted nor used to change the world. Freud says: "perhaps . . . you . . . will fall back upon the argument that it is surely very improbable that we ought to concede so large a part in the human constitution to what is evil. But . . . are you ignorant of the fact that all the excesses and aberrations of which we dream at night are crimes actually committed every day by men who are wide awake? . . . And now look away from individuals to the great war still devastating Europe: think of the colossal brutality, cruelty and mendacity which is now allowed to spread itself over the civilized world. Will you venture, even in these circumstances, to break a lance for the exclusion of evil from the mental constitution of humanity?" (*General Introduction to Psychoanalysis,* lecture 9; cf. Plato, *Republic* 9.571–72).

But even this knowledge, at its worst, is not the worst. The "intolerable truths" of man's basic hopelessness and depravity are not so intolerable as the *This Way for the Gas* truths of Tadeusz Borowski's Holocaust tales, the kinds of truths that would make literature altogether obsolete in any of its functions. The idea of man's evil is not so difficult to endure as the practice of it; the theory may even be an evasion of the fact. Robert Nozick finds realities such as the Holocaust and the Gulag so difficult to contemplate that he deliberately excludes their consideration from his chapter on the foundations of ethics in *Philosophical Explanations* (Cambridge: Harvard University Press, 1981), p. 402. Unavoidably, the present book has to be considered as written under the aegis of Maurice Blanchot's *L'Écriture du désastre,* where Blanchot asks: "How can we make thought into something in which to preserve the Holocaust, when, in the Holocaust, everything, including the preserving thought itself, went lost?" Inevitably, the truth will always be worse than anything that can be said about it.[17]

It will be remarked that the last two conceptions of literature to which I have referred (literature as producing an encounter with the new, experientially or intellectually, and literature as demanding that we confront truths we would otherwise avoid), have little to do with the beauty that Sartre was at such pains to distinguish from the real (see above, p. xii). It has also been suggested that beauty, even if it is a feature of art, is not the luxury that Sartre seems to assume it is. Frances Ferguson argues that beauty is an entrapment:[18] it would follow that to experience something as beautiful is to experience oneself as weak. In another context, Wilhelm Worringer speaks of beauty as the symptom of a crucial ignorance. Coming from Egyptian art, he says, one sees Classical sculpture as "the productions of a more childlike, more innocent humanity, that has remained untouched by the great dread. The word 'beautiful' will suddenly appear to him quite petty and insignificant."[19]

But even a literature not tainted with beauty may be tainted with image. As such, it would still be barred by Sartre's criteria from participation in reality, no matter what acknowledgments of painful truths it might require. The image immediately provokes confrontations with the problem of responsibility and with a whole range of partly ethical issues, from the role of metaphor in argument to the idealization of sexual love.

Before following any of these lines of connection between ethics and image even a short way, though, I should probably make a feint toward a definition of the ethical, at least vis-à-vis the unethical. (I shall return to this subject in my last chapters). An ethical act is merely returning one's happiness to the universal. But an unethical act I take to be one that, without sufficient reason, reduces, whether by physical or emotional deprivation, someone else's ability, or desire, to survive. In other words, it is essentially physical, even though it may consist of neglect, insult, or sexual betrayal, rather than theft or physical injury.[20] Nevertheless, in Western tradition, unethical acts seem to group themselves loosely in the broad categories of the sexual and the violent, even though, of course, Dante, or any other moralist, for that matter, could readily divide the subject into many more elements.[21]

My use of the word *image* in this book has been, in general, practical and conventional, as has my use of the word *ethics.* For the most part, I use *image* to suggest something visual, something that can be pictured, though in a few cases (notably in chapter 7) it is closer to another of its common meanings: "trope," "figure of speech," or "something imagined rather than real."

Those transgressions which have to do with sex are associated with the image; I would hazard a guess that the other forms of violence may be associated with the word.[22]

All of the above does not yet broach the question whether literature is good or bad for people, a matter on which I offer some opinions in the section on Tolstoi and Chekhov. But I have said that books like Tadeusz Borowski's *This Way for the Gas* negate literature, make us think that it is for nothing at all. I would stop somewhat short of that conclusion with respect to the confrontation between literature and violence. Literature may be a carrier of violent impulses; but at least in one of its forms it represents a stepping aside from the overwhelming violence of the world. In this situation, which defines the final area in which I wish to investigate literature's uses, namely, parable, the question is not, what are the ethical implications or applications of literature, but what literature, if any, is generated by ethics? Implicit in this approach, however, is a premise that will at first seem arbitrary: the premise that there has been an assault, that an invasion is actually under way, so that ethics is not an abstract problem but a burning issue; that the evil powers and the evil people are upon us, and that this is no time for amusement, casual companionability, meditation, or sublimated hostilities. Ethics is a critical problem because we are in a state of emergency, or catastrophe, when right and wrong, good and bad, are all that matter. Ethics is important not because we want to find out what it is, but because it is being violated right now. When the machete is entering the face there may not be time for literature, but there is always time to know that one is being done a wrong.

This sense of urgency that abruptly imposes substantiality upon our topic, overwhelming one with its three-dimensionality like a northern landscape in which sea and sky rush upon a fugitive shoreline, may indeed limit literature.[23] But, after all, what happens in emergencies is what really happens in life: and, as I have said, when the blade is upon one, there is time to think only of what is happening, how and why it is happening. There is no comforting distance, no chance for recollection in tranquillity, or for meditation. There would seem to be little room for literature under such conditions. Yet if, as I have suggested, literature always implies a question about whether life is worth living (I would prefer not to use Camus's formulation, but it's right) then it must start from a state of imbalance, in which everything is up for grabs; perhaps it is, in fact, all about emergency, about that space that leaves no space or time; if so, the absence of any orienting possibility, of tranquillity or meditation, except a meditation upon death, would be, if anything, its precondition. Still, the only form of literature that seems to flourish on the soil of apparent, visible emergency is (for reasons to which I shall return later) the parable, where literature is a way of dealing with crisis.[24]

The presence of the rampant enemy, of the overwhelmingly selfish and brutal, who take joy in whatever they can seize and whose pleasure is in no way predicated upon the minimizing of others' suffering, is not an invention. They are among us; you or I may be those very people; at least there is much of them in all of us. But the feeling that they are now actually abroad, that the barbarian instinct is incarnate and real, that it is not just potential, or maybe even tolerable, is probably a Jewish feeling. (It may be that my own call for a more humble ethics, in my final chapter, is just an attempt to evade this feeling by generalizing the problem). That recurrent panic, often apparently gratuitous and quite without context at the time when it arises, even though always justified in the long run, is usually identified as a Jewish symptom. And we may as well recognize that at the outset of this book. The urgency of ethics, or call it the paranoia of the pogrom, is something that in the West has long been marked as a Jewish concern. And in close association with it goes the suspicion that images, representations, literary or visual, are also tied up with violence; that they are misleading; that they are criminal evasions of obligation. Hence the topic, ethics and image in literature.

But to return to a matter that I was considering earlier: why parable should supply a particularly appropriate, if brief, literary escape for the Jewish condition is not at all obvious. I shall offer, for lack of a good answer, an obvious one. Parable does not set literature, or image, apart from life. It is open to life, and above all, to argument, at either end; it feeds directly into and out of life and quibble. It is the decisive denial of the independence of art from the kind of reasoning that experience requires of us. It represents the rejection of the whole idea of literary autonomy: the parable is that form "in which artistic mastery is proved by the final abolition in it of all elements of art."[25]

Isaac Babel provides a good example of how a Jewish writer, engulfed by violence, gets trapped in parable. Babel deals with the dilemma of having to exist in a world that pivots on brutality, and of falling into its rhythms without coming to partake of its ethos. There is nothing that these apparently cruel people who surround him genuinely hate but a peace-loving man. Babel must learn to ride a Cossack horse, to look a Cossack horseman, without having been a Cossack. What am I doing here, in the midst of the grand world of myth and novel,[26] war and revolution? his brief accounts seem to ask. The quizzical moral stance is isolated amid motiveless, metonymic action; it occupies its tiny, motionless spot of ground in the thoughtless epic torrent that sweeps over and around it. Quietly it steps out of the diachronic to ponder and survey.

Of late, an increasing number of non-Jewish scholars, such as Blanchot, Girard, Goux, Bucher, have realized that these matters, impacted in Jewish history, condensed in Jewish experience and parable, are not only the parochial obsessions of an obstreperous minority. The Jewish roots of Marx and Freud have also become increasingly obvious, and, with them, the relevance of basic Jewish concerns for our conception of both society and personal psychology. Whether we want to or not, Gentile, Arab, or Jew, we recognize that, in the history of this minute fragment of humanity, issues come to focus that are crucial for all of us. Maurice Blanchot's words, often quoted of late, are apt:

Why have all misfortunes, finite, infinite, personal, impersonal, contemporary, eternal, always had beneath them, and why have they always reminded us of, the historically dated, but undatable, misfortunes of a people already so reduced that it seemed virtually erased from the map, yet the history of which overflowed beyond the history of the world? Why?[27]

It is as if Jewish experience were the field in which certain human battles are fought, over and over again; it is the crucible of our making, our thought, and our unmaking. The dim lineaments of lurking violence, of the lynch mob or pogrom, only faintly perceptible to the naked eye when the social order appears stable, are revealed by Girard and identified as the very founding operation of society. Goux clarifies the links of Mosaic law to Marxist economic theory, and connects the figure of Moses to both Freud's iconoclasm and his preoccupation with incest. And Gérard Bucher has defined the true nature of Jewish assimilationism. I offer here a brief development of Bucher's ideas.

It is easy for Jews to make of Judaism a negative thing, to say that if the rest of the world did not identify them as Jews, they would cease to exist, and, with their identity, their tribulations. But Bucher argues, quite rightly, that behind this plausible eagerness for self-effacement lies the desire to join the lynch mob, because it is too hard to go on rejecting the impulse to blind, unconscious violence, and, with it, the impulse to its necessary concomitant, iconophilia. It would be easy enough to stop being a Jew if one could be something else; but, in the absence of any alternative but this one, one prefers to remain what one is, unsatisfactory, inadequate, and only half-Jewish as that always is.[28] It would seem, then, that the desire for assimilation is not merely a natural desire to "belong"; it is also a positive desire for idolatry, a rejection of one's mission, a desire to *give up*.[29] It is closer to the truth to say that the unassimilated Jew defines the Gentile world rather than vice versa;[30] it is not anti-Semitism that creates Jews. Jews are not defined as those whom Gentiles reject, but as those who have themselves rejected the Gentile combination of group violence and exaltation (Bucher again).[31]

In view of these concerns, I have attempted, in some parts of this book, despite the danger of introducing a confusing element into its thematics, to take up some problems in literature and ethics in a Judaic context. In particular I have tried to rehabilitate the image, despite its traditional Jewish associations with idolatry, in the setting of dialogue, in which we move past literature as such to the general exchange process that expresses the bonding of humanity (to the extent to which it may still be susceptible to such bonding).

Unable to end on that theme, however, and forced to confront still more general problems that subsume both violence and ethics, I have had to extend my conclusions and also to recast certain chapters of this book. The hovering question that is still present, when all the rest has been said, is whether there is any way to accommodate desire to ethics, even in a literary context. That unresolved issue remains an uneasy qualifier in much that I have written.

Within the overarching ethical preoccupations of this study, however, several subordinate processes occur. Some of these will be recognized by previous readers of my work; others are specific to the present volume. Among the former are a tendency to speculate on silence and the latent elements of thought, which remains an abiding inclination even when I am entirely unaware that it is there. If, in my first book (*The Uncreating Word*), words resolve into ecstasy, in the second (*The Gaping Pig*) into despair, then in the present one they tend to disappear into the ethical act. The confident idealism of the first book, and the agonized sense of distortion in the second, at one point led me to consider my present undertaking as an effort to provide a middle ground, a sort of mountain or rather a plateau for my reasoning. Age is, of course, an infallible antidote to such Dantesque fantasies of having made the circuit of human possibilities and seen all the major stations on the human journey; nevertheless, it seems true that I have throughout been struggling to create some sort of ethical center, no matter how inadequate, for my thinking, and that that is where my main commitment lies, rather than in either demonism or transcendence.

The practical ordering of the book produces a roughly binary division. The first chapters are not primarily directed toward social ethics; an ethics of particularity is their underlying concern. They argue in defense of dissociation and a tolerance of disorder. The specific is preferred to the general, and the unpremeditated to the foreseen. What is favored is fidelity to a visual or a linguistic impulse, adherence to the quiddity of human relations, commitment to the next word written rather than to previous words reread, and finally an engagement with the concrete experiences of human life rather than with systems, whether retrospective or supernatural. The second part of the book (beginning with chapter 5) recapitulates these themes with greater emphasis on the relations between men and women, where the question of desire complicates the ethical: it begins with that paradoxical love story, "The Frog King, or Iron Henry." In keeping with the general motif of the first part, the opening chapter considers the possibility of moving freely, yet responsibly, between two worlds, the world of words and the world of images, without requiring total interdependence between the two.

1

Words and Images: Harmony and Dissonance
(Poetry and the Responsibilities of Language)

> The image, says Husserl, is a "fulfillment" (*Erfüllung*) of meaning. The study of imitation has, on the contrary, led us to the conclusion that the image is a degraded meaning, sunk to the level of perception.
>
> Sartre, *L'Imaginaire*[1]

IT IS DIFFICULT TO WORK ONE'S WAY BACK FROM CONSIDering the kind of writing in which subject matter is dominant, as, for instance, in the parable, to what may seem to be mere questions of technique. To resolve experience into "words and images" can appear tantamount to eliminating experience altogether. One might say that language functions as it was meant to only as long as it is totally unconscious, buried under the Niagara of experience. All else is metalanguage, which is not language but reflects a different process.[2]

Language, however, has a way of slipping back into metalanguages,[3] which are unethical in the sense that they are

1

uncommitted, and one of the ways it has of doing that is by falling back on pictorial values—not merely images, but what is sometimes called spatial form. Language can move from continuous responsibility into mere self-conscious order through one of two procedures: by freezing, becoming an impasse to itself, in a reactionary self-approval which, at its worst, is what we call idolatry; or by becoming enmeshed in a self-questioning, reflexive mode of operation that proceeds as though it could reach behind the sources of thought, though in fact all it can grasp is those structures which it has invented for itself to grasp.

But only a saint can be held to the ultimate standards of commitment; all of us dream, and dreams, apparently necessary for our survival though they are ultimately exploratory, start off as narrative, which is the essential element of fiction, and rely on focal images; all of us take pleasure, be it a guilty pleasure, in resting and looking back, creating pictures to see and fantasies (imaged or intellectual) to believe. Nevertheless, some force within us breaks the mirror, and we find ourselves with our head sticking through the frame, looking out beyond the fragments of what had seemed necessary convictions. I would hardly contest the value of the larger musical forms; yet in music, too, it sometimes happens that a composer tries to exploit the spontaneity of a melody, first freezing it by repeating it (see chapter 3, text above n. 10), then, in an attempt to recapture the legitimacy of the initial inspiration, putting it in the service of a structured form. (It is to the credit of Schubert that he always failed when he tried this device; he consequently succeeded in much greater things). Architectonic structures can create the illusion of having reached a stable conclusion, simply because they produce the necessity for a retrospective overview. (This possibility may explain the frenetic assertiveness in the last movements of quite a few symphonies—say, the Brahms first—the kind of solution that Beethoven's piano sonata op. 109, for instance, explicitly rejects, in an ending that is, by implication, also a criticism of many musical "conclusions").

Even the framing of a question may imply the comfortable certainty that an answer is necessarily available, as long as we have made sure that the terms in which the question is couched haven't shifted their meaning in the answer. Of course, some would hasten to remind us that without this assumption no reasoning would be possible, and a fortiori, no conception of personality. It was pointed out by Reid, in response to Hume's sensationalism and atomism, that one couldn't even have a sentence if the same person weren't there to start and finish it. Yet the fact is that the same person *isn't* there; and one might argue that meaning is produced in a sentence by the very fact that discrepancies exist between its start and its finish.

It is something of this errant quality of language, its redeeming elusiveness, that I would like to talk about in the following chapter, though it may seem, as I have said, by comparison with the introduction, to be devoted to matters of mere technique. Yet the fidelity of language to its generative principles is also an ethical concern, perhaps not less so than its trustworthiness in describing its objects. An aspect of ethical responsibility that I have not dealt with is the responsibility of language to thought itself; and I should like to explore the ways in which even metalanguages (in the particular sense in which I have been using the term) may escape, at least partially, from the contracting hand of retrospect, the bond of certainty, and move freely in accordance with the responsibilities of thought.[4]

What is my problem? I can try either to answer that question or not. I may even have to resist trying to answer it. There is a strong aesthetic, even sensual, pleasure in compos-

ing a well-formed argument. It is fun, but it obscures the
processes of thought. Thought is spasmodic. It does not sit
back, relax, look around, and take stock of itself. Writing may
do that, but thought does not. Writing tends toward pattern.
It tends to impose on thought a spatial, harmonious graphic
design, with a clearly defined border; it tends to make it into
a picture. (As Walter Benjamin puts it, writing "wants to be a
picture"[5]). In its substitution of pictorial values for intellectual ones, it seduces us by the "shape" of an argument, the
artful distribution of materials within it for maximum effect,
all the rhetorical devices that turn out, in some way, to be
geometrical or graphic, to derive from an aesthetics of space.

It is appealing to spread one's materials out and to collate
one's notes on topics and subtopics, secure in the knowledge
that some overarching idea is going to emerge at the end of
the process — some idea that is going to pull it all together, to
give order to all one's jottings. Once they are all on the table,
they cannot help but begin to hang together by subtle threads,
the spiderweb (or dustweb) of the mind. One will find out
what one has been thinking about, identify one's problem,
and solve it. But a syllogism is only a picture. Thoughts
themselves come one at a time. They do not push us toward
any all-inclusive generalization, and certainly not toward
pattern. There is no stopping point from which we can take a
view all around and state "This is complete."

That is not, of course, to say that thought should have no
relation to visual experiences; vision constitutes much of the
subject matter, the content, and even the form of thought. Yet
a thought has more in common with a glimpse than with a
view. Each act of vision is detached from other acts of vision;
we do not see continuously. We see one thing, and then
another. There is a closure in each experience of sight. The
essential nature of a thought is also to be isolated. It may
connect in our minds with one other thought, but really a

valve shuts it off from thoughts before and after. I quote from Robert Musil's *Young Törless:* "Our thoughts and feelings don't flow along quietly like a stream, they happen to us, which means they befall us, fall into us like rocks. . . . If you watch yourself carefully, you realize that the soul isn't something that changes its colors in a gradual transition, but that the thoughts jump out of it like numbers out of a black hole. Now you have a thought or a feeling, and all of a sudden there is a different one there, as if it had popped up out of nothingness. If you pay attention, you can even notice the instant between two thoughts when everything is black. . . . For our life is nothing but . . . hopping over thousands of death-seconds every day."[6] The things we add in the spaces between thoughts to give them the appearance of continuity are not actually part of the thoughts themselves, but they and the thoughts they join can all be made to look like a seamless web if the interpolated elements are skillfully introduced among the others.

The process of writing leads one to assume that one has actually accomplished something because one has put something down on paper; that it is meant to stick, to become permanent, instead of simply being replaced by the next idea that comes along. It creates the illusion of finality. Because paper lasts longer than sound, we think our ideas should last, like the paper they are written on. When talking, we present something as provisional: we don't expect it to become a truth for ever; it is only part of the tumult of ideas that constantly pass through our heads and those of others. When we write something down, and then realize that sooner or later it must necessarily be replaced by another idea, whether our own or that of another, we are disturbed, as though we had expected our thought to share in the fixity of the visual form to which we had transferred it. When we stop writing we are puzzled to find that we have to go on thinking.

But the mind is not like a field of grain, but like a forest fire, or like life itself: an idea flares up only to be destroyed as flame erupts from another crest. A thought is only that which makes necessary another thought.

By themselves thoughts do not go anywhere. They may be parts of a series, but never of a set. A thought is an image, with some words attached to it or preceding it: an aperçu. The sense of purpose in our thoughts is strictly a teleological afterthought, table-top or after-dinner thinking. As Schelling says, "Organization as such is succession hampered...,"[7] and "everything that organizes an individual is external to him."[8]

But one must be careful not to confuse the spatial with the visual as such. We can sense shape, closure, even in nonvisual media. Is form in music visual? It is, in at least some sense, spatial.[9] A similar kind of aesthetic spatialization takes place when we try to create a "well-formed" argument; we are trying to produce a sensed pattern that we relate to by obscure potential energies in our bodies;[10] yet we are not trying to produce a seen image. The well-formed argument is a spatial pattern; the true thought is like a seen image.

The natural movement of the mind is from image to image. To think, we must let the process of association prevail, not the rules of rhetoric. Even scientific realizations, often thought to be inductive in nature, arise from a single image or observation rather than from an accumulation of examples; this is the meaning of the fable about Newton and the apple.

In fact, it is difficult to say what thought consists of, besides images. And why should we not reason in images, when our perceived images, as Kant and Wittgenstein pointed out, are full of reason?[11] Hannah Arendt concluded that we have no access to that other dimension of thought, to pure thought or thought proper, have no way of talking about it (*Thinking*). All the more of a mystification is it to pretend that we can proceed in that dimension alone, when we can't even say what it is. The Nominalists (John Holkot, Nicholas of Autrecourt) had the same problem, and the attack on abstractions has been renewed by a group of psychologists at McMaster University.[12] What thought seems to consist of, by and large, is an image with a few words preceding or attached to it, a comment on an image. One can't simply detach the comment and pretend that it came from nowhere.[13] "A whole essay might be written on the Danger of *thinking* without images." Coleridge prefers to have "*Images* the symbol of Things, instead of resting on mere words. . . . "[14] But no image has an intrinsic meaning. You attach an interpretation to an image. It may have invited you to interpret it, but it doesn't supply its interpretation. Image and meaning are discontinuous.

The divergence of image from language, that is, the separateness of image and concept, has been conveniently summed up in split-brain experiments that seem to show, at least in males, the dominant hemisphere mediating concepts, the other mediating images and music, with only uncertain communication between the two areas. I wish to consider some problems in the relation of meaning to imagery, in the light of our sharpened awareness that there may be significant disparities between the two functions. Those who will feel more at ease if our topic is set in a more familiar context of psychological speculation can easily assimilate split-brain theory, the neurological opinion that there may be a separation of image from language processes, to a now popular Derridean thesis: namely, that no psychological symptom has a stable antecedent or an interpretation inherent in it, but that every interpretation is something superadded, externally attached to the symptom.

W. G. T. Mitchell's book on Blake, *Blake's Composite Art* (Princeton: Princeton University Press, 1978), argues that in Blake's illustrated works, the poems and the illustrations do not necessarily support each other.[15] What I intend to examine here is the divergence of concepts from images within ordinary, unillustrated literary works. There are intermediate examples, an extraordinary one being Calvino's *The Castle of Crossed Destinies,* in which the would-be narrators are struck dumb, and the action has to be deduced from the sequence in which tarot cards are presented. Even here, though the cards are made to speak, they do so with much ambiguity and effort, and in the end, of course, one cannot be sure what they really say. They illustrate my first principle, which is that no image has a sense self-evident to everyone; there is no fixed meaning that we can deduce from it. Explanation follows later, and is always gratuitous.

And yet, paradoxically, thought itself requires us to ignore this truth. We rely on images, at least on images from the natural world, to bring us meaning. There is a transitory locking-on of meaning that takes place in metaphor, a fixing of an essence by a vehicle. Without that fixing, meaning can never take shape for us. The surface of reality shimmers with meanings for us. That is what we mean when we say that things are beautiful: they mean something. And words appear together with those meanings. A vehicle doesn't need any word to make it clear. But a "tenor" can emerge only in tandem with a word.

Yet meaning isn't always available to us, for metaphoric perception isn't always available to us. In this respect, as in some others, the erotic state is privileged. Love sees double, depression single. When one is in love, a thing strikes the senses *initially* as that which it is not (arm rather than branch, jingling coins rather than rattling leaves, etc.). Connotative perception precedes denotative perception. Perhaps the tendency to perceive in metaphors is a secondary sexual characteristic of *homo sapiens,* and may even have survival value for the species. Certainly, if, as Aristotle says, the best

metaphors make the best poetry, poetry produces the universals with which we think, and thinking is one of the means by
which our species survives, then metaphors may be of some
assistance to love in maintaining our species in existence.
Freud, in the book on jokes, maintains that when we are
happy we can allow our minds to revert to their natural play-
fulness, to the irresponsible associations that release us from
bondage to the literal. I have said elsewhere that "Common
as love is essence,"[16] and this too is true; we have access to the
experience of essence—but only and precisely to the extent
to which love makes it available to us—through the capacity
to perceive in metaphors.[17] Love permits the latent comparisons in us to ripen, complete themselves, rise to the surface,
and be put to use.

When emotional energies have been throttled, the function of metaphors and images, and therefore the thinking
process itself, can be damaged. When Christopher Smart
says, "There is no rose for minds in grief, / There is no lily
for despair," he means not only that there is no way for the
unhappy man to experience the rose and the lily, but that
there is no way for the unhappy man to know or *think* them.
Knowing is a subspecies of metaphor. Rose and lily are love
and purity; in a state of love we see them double: as that
which they are, and as that which they represent or mean.
The unhappy man, since he has no access to metaphor, has
no access to meaning. As Wordsworth says, "where he [man]
has no pleasure he has no knowledge" (preface to the *Lyrical
Ballads*).[18] It may be said that perception itself depends on
love. "In order to see anything—a leaf or a blade of grass—
you have, I think, to know the keenness of love" (John Cheever,
"The Fourth Alarm"). And in order to see others, of course,
as well; the unhappy man can recognize others only in terms
of his own denials.

So when I say that no image has a meaning built into it,

that is, "no image speaks for itself,"[19] I should perhaps at the same time add the complementary truth, at least with respect to images derived from the natural world: namely, that it is only through speaking images that we can think at all. The image-thought is the basic instrument of the mind. But an image will speak only if it chooses to; we cannot force it to yield us a meaning. In itself it is hermetic, not subject to interrogation. Images embody a principle of irreversibility, a directional signal. Their responsibility is to the future; they are prospective and exploratory acts, not givens meant to be imitated or iterated in a nonimagistic medium.[20] For that matter, truth itself may be considered a form of organization, a plan, not a template.

But what is a mental image to begin with, in contrast to a physical picture or an object? The majority opinion of philosophers in the twentieth century is that it simply doesn't exist. They seem determined to drive it out, or to reduce it to an epiphenomenon, something not to be taken seriously. Not only the psychologists of the Warburg School, but Ryle, Wittgenstein, and Sartre inveigh against the mental image; Freud is suspicious of images. The general opinion seems best summarized by Sartre, who argues that the mental image is simply a thought, and not a very good thought at that.[21] Misrepresenting Husserl, he comments: "The image, says Husserl, is a 'fulfillment' (Erfüllung) of meaning. The study of imitation has, on the contrary, led us to the conclusion that the image is a degraded meaning. . . . "[22]

In the eighteenth century (a period as much preoccupied as our own with the relation between words and images) Diderot had suggested that images do at least one thing for the mind that other forms of thinking cannot accomplish: they represent the simultaneity of thought, whereas syntax distributes thought, which is atemporal, over time. Jeffrey Mehlman has reviewed some of the relevant passages from the *Lettre sur les sourds et muets* in the fine essay, "Cataract: Diderot's discursive politics, 1749–1751."[23] As a rule, "language drags endlessly after the mind"; but, in poetry, "discourse is no longer merely a linkage of energetic terms presenting thought ... but, as well, a tissue of hieroglyphs heaped one on another, portraying it. I would say, in this sense, that all poetry is emblematic." As Mehlman puts it, "The virtual wads of hieroglyphics are thus intended to redeem — or deny — time, to stem the temporal flow of discourse in its incompatibility with the timelessness of mind." Thought is atemporal; sentences are always temporal. "Our soul is a moving scene that we are ceaselessly trying to paint: it takes us a long time to render it faithfully; but it exists in its entirety and all at once...."

The image, then, rescues us momentarily from time: it provides an exit through the walls of discourse, an escape into the realms of simultaneity: until the course of the sentence resumes (and syntax begins to dominate again) we are out of time. I do not feel moved to dispute this conception of the image as such, but I do disagree explicitly with the conception of language from which it derives, and which is standard from St. Augustine to Kenneth Burke.[24] I have no desire to eliminate or even to reduce the distinction between thought and language, but I do wish to assert that language has no need to go outside itself, to image, in order to produce something worthy of the thought process that is invested in it. In accordance with the general tendency of this chapter, I shall here argue that there are in fact two kinds of meaning, each adequate to its own purposes, not only a single kind, awkwardly reflected in an inappropriate medium, from which we must seek the temporary relief of images. I locate the temporal and spatial dimensions of language, respectively, not in syntax and imagery, but in what I call prospect and retrospect. As long as we are moving with a sentence, listening to it, we are following a meaning that is dissolved in the sentence, and that is a truly temporal meaning. Being truly temporal, this experience of meaning is unconscious. Temporality is the unconscious. (Life, too, like a sentence, is lived unconsciously, and its "meaning" in retrospect is another thing.) There is no way to be conscious of the words in a sentence and still grasp the meaning of that sentence. As Valéry says, "You will find that we understand others as well as ourselves only as a result of the *speed with which we pass over words.* One must not linger over them, on pain of seeing the clearest discourse disintegrate into enigmas, into more or less ingenious fantasies."[25]

When we think back over a sentence that we have read, after we have unconsciously understood its temporal meaning (and said to ourselves, "Ah! So that's what he meant!"), we have derived from it a spatial or retrospective meaning. I would add that poetry blocks that second, or retrospective response; it functions by preventing us from thinking backward, from reversing ourselves, and by preventing us from paying conscious (i.e., retrospective) attention to what is being said. Perhaps, (as John Dings has suggested to me), spatial, retrospective organization has the advantage of setting things behind one, so that one can forget them. But this poetry does not allow. The unfallen language, the paradisal language of poetry is, then, paradoxically, purely temporal. This may help to account for the fact that we do not visualize lines of poetry; not because language is, as in Lessing's or Diderot's model, sequential, but because it is temporal. "Images will never, after all, be anything but things, and thought is a movement."[26] We do not visualize because we are not conscious and because we do not stop over words. Submerged in the flow of meaning as it takes its course, we have no eyes. (For this reason nonsense poetry is easier to accept than we might expect it to be: we don't "image" the words in normal poetry any more or any less specifically than we "image" the words in "Jabberwocky"). Some of the best lines in poetry seem grotesque or ridiculous when we try to "look" at them:

> Thy light alone, like mist o'er mountains driven
> (Shelley)

or

> With rocks, and stones, and trees
> (Wordsworth)

or

> O wert thou in the cauld blast
> On yonder lea, on yonder lea
> (Burns)

In fact, in a good passage (I think of Dorothy Wordsworth's *Recollections of a Tour Made in Scotland,* passim) much goes by without producing any sensory impression whatsoever; reading is like going into a well-arranged room, where you notice nothing in particular, only the sense of well-being it creates. One stops to notice and specify only when there is some hitch in the continuity, something that doesn't quite work.

There is, consequently, no *mot juste:* there are only *mots justes.* (Cf. Bergson: "We don't start by learning to speak in words, but in sentences. A word always anastomoses with those words which accompany it . . . "[27]) The reason why a poem can't really be summarized or translated is not that it uses "right" .words for which there are no substitutes, but because its meaning resides in a flow, in the interconnectedness that prevents us, precisely, from ever asking "What did that mean?" It suppresses the reversal reflex, and instructs us that any meaning obtained in retrospect is of a radically different nature from the meaning gained in prospect.

The experience that gave rise to this insight occurred during a Ph.D. examination that I was attending recently. My attention wandered while the candidate was talking about *Paradise Lost;* but, although I had not noticed what he was saying, I realized that it sounded right. When my attention snapped back, I repeated his sentence to myself and thought— aha! so that's what he meant! (The sentence concerned the Garden of Eden's being possible because Adam and Eve had not yet fallen, rather than vice versa.)

In other words, I had understood that the sentence was a good sentence before I "understood" the sentence. A judgment of meaning and an evaluation of form had both taken place while the sentence was still lodged in what is sometimes called the "immediate memory." The realization then dawned on me that there is an understanding of meaning— dissolved in the entire length of a sentence, gleaned from word to word, and obtained more or less unconsciously— which is quite different from the snapshot, timeless meaning that we consciously draw out of a sentence in retrospect.[28] As I later wrote to a friend, seeking light on the matter: "In poetry, we must understand in the first, time-bound sense: what is more, the attempt to understand in the second sense frequently produces a distortion of meaning that makes it impossible to tell what we are responding to in a line in the first place. . . . Poetry often works by . . . blocking the retrospective extraction of a meaning that can be grasped outside the duration of the sentence. . . . Are there, in fact, two radically different kinds of meaning: one sentence-bound, time-bound, and grasped, largely, unconsciously; and another, timeless variety?"

There may, then, really be an "Eden" in language; a poetic understanding that takes place in the flow from word to word ("the poetry consisting mainly in the fluidity of thought rather than objects of thought"[29]), and that is different from the retrospective prose understanding. (The dimension in which this first understanding transpires would also be a place of full linguistic responsibility and therefore, in that sense, an ethical place). We are constantly doing two readings at once; the first, of which we are not conscious, swirls ahead of the second. The mind works at maximum speed and in slow motion at the same time. (Cf. *Hamlet*, 5.2.30–31: "Ere I could make a prologue to my brains, / They had begun the play.")

What may happen in practice is that the eye moves forward, picks up key words or salient details in the text, then drifts back to consolidate. The true sentence is made up of these salient details, not of the syntactic unit, and it can span several sentences.

In any case, the sort of thing that happened to me during that examination is an effect deliberately cultivated by Shelley, with his disjunctive syntax, his inversions, his flip, glib rhymes—all of which make one *not* notice meaning in the second sense in order to preserve it for the first. I think of the last stanza "written in dejection," with its extraordinary dispersal of meaning:

> Some might lament that I were cold,
>   As I, when this sweet day is gone,
> Which my lost heart, too soon grown old,

Insults with this untimely moan;
They might lament—for I am one
　　Whom men love not—and yet regret,
Unlike this day, which, when the sun
　　Shall on its stainless glory set,
　　Will linger, though enjoyed, like joy in
　　　memory yet.

I think, too, of "The Zucca," beginning,

Summer was dead and Autumn was expiring,
　　And infant Winter laughed upon the land
All cloudlessly and cold;—when I, desiring
　　More in this world than any understand,
Wept o'er the beauty, which, like sea retiring,
　　Had left the earth bare as the wave-worn sand
Of my lorn heart, and o'er the grass and flowers
Pale for the falsehood of the flattering Hours.

An unsuccessful line of poetry—such as (ironically) the fourth, above—is one that can be understood.

In the sonnet on "The Floure and the Lefe," Keats describes the process of reading:

This pleasant tale is like a little copse:
　　The honied lines do freshly interlace
　　To keep the reader in so sweet a place,
　　So that he here and there full hearted stops.
　　And oftentimes he feels the dewy drops
　　Come cool and suddenly against his face,

And by the wandering melody may trace
Which way the tender-legged linnet hops.

The "honied lines," the lines of the poem, like the twigs of
the copse, or like limed twigs meant to capture birds, catch at
the reader in a way that is evident to both him and us. Yet
when he is stopped, "here and there" in the copse, he does
not seem to know just what has brought him to a halt at those
particular moments. For behind the visible lines of the poem,
which one might deal with or even choose to resist, moves
the unconscious meaning or "wandering melody," against
which we are defenseless, and which can be traced only by its
effects on us.

It is only the cup of soup that fills us that should be
counted. In the Russian version of a universal folk tale, a
hungry peasant buys a large dish of soup, but after gobbling
it down he is still hungry. He buys a bowl of soup, but that
doesn't fill him either. He buys a cup of soup, and that
finally fills him. "Fool that I was!" he says to himself. "I
should have bought the cup of soup in the first place!" This
is true poetic thinking. We take the outcome. What has come
into us along the way we cannot take account of.

In "Space as an Image of Time" Rudolf Arnheim comes to
much the same conclusions as Diderot on temporal-spatial
relationships in meaning.[30] We must "convert sequence into
simultaneity, time into space. . . . [A]ny organized entity, in
order to be grasped as a whole by the mind, must be translated into the synoptic condition of space." The question for
me, though, is whether we *should* try to grasp all things in
this way (see my opening remarks on spatial form). Arnheim's
position is orthodox: memory may allow us either to per-
form an entire symphony over again in our mind or to
survey its pattern, but "surely," he says, "this second ability is

the more admirable one. It is less mechanical.... [I]t enables us to overcome the instant mortality of time...."

In the essay "Writing and Reading," E. D. Hirsch, Jr., also comes out eventually in the same place.[31] Hirsch is interested in the temporality-simultaneity problem too, especially as it bears on literature. His review of recent experiments in the area of sentence processing and memory models makes a useful introduction to that difficult subject.[32] From Hirsch's point of view, the component of understanding that occupies the ground that I have called "unconscious" is the suspended series of interpretations awaiting determination by the conclusion of a clause. The potential meanings remain in solution until an actual meaning has been achieved (p. 119). At that point, after closure, memory sets in—but, according to the latest evidence, the storage of meaning obtained from such a clause is nonsyntactic and perhaps even entirely nonlinguistic in nature (p. 122). Valéry arrived at precisely the same memory model for language in 1939 (see the *Oeuvres* [Paris, 1965], 1:1325).

All of these observations lead to questions about the experience of reading prose fiction that remain, at least at the present stage of our understanding, largely unanswerable. I shall here confine my comments to the more manageable if not entirely representative area of poetry. Hirsch maintains that our memory of literary texts is, like our memory of other utterances, basically synoptic and semantic. I would argue, *contra* Hirsch, that our memory at least of poetic texts *is* unlike other linguistic memory, and that whereas meaning may be memory in psychological terms, it is not memory in literary terms (if memory is taken to be the timeless schema of meaning that remains in our mental reservoir). In poetry— perhaps in all literature—meaning is necessarily and continuously timeful. We always try to remember the exact words of a poem, and we are dissatisfied unless we have recalled

those exact words. The reason is not (as Hirsch suggests) that
the words, though merely "surface features" of language,
pertain in some special way to the semantic content of the
poem that goes into storage, but the opposite: it is that they
have never gone into semantic storage at all. They must be
retrieved whole because they could not be subjected to summation; like traumata, they have never been understood,[33]
so there is no timeless essence of them, no retrospective
"meaning," to retrieve. A line of poetry can only be mem-
orized: it cannot be remembered. Hirsch says that "large
dimensions of textual meaning may be non-temporal in
character, whereas language is unremittingly temporal." There
is also, I would add, a kind of meaning that is unremittingly
temporal: namely, poetic meaning.

I began this long digression on temporal vs. atemporal
meaning with the remark that Diderot found in the image-
functions of poetry a way of reflecting the simultaneity of
thought in the otherwise sequential and discursive medium
of language, whereas most twentieth-century philosophers
have subordinated images to language, or interpreted images
as a subspecies of language. In spite of these contentions, we
are now aware that image functions do have a certain independence, if only in the sense that one half of the brain is
more actively involved with the perception of images than
with language. Some interaction of the two processes is, of
course, usual. In a nightmare, we may sometimes feel panic-
stricken by an interruption in the communication between
these activities. The worst dreams are those in which we can't
scream, can't relieve ourselves by breaking into the world of
language. We feel suffocated, not so much because we can't
breathe as because we can't speak. It is as if, in order for us to
survive, the imaging part of our minds must have access to
the verbal part.

But to return to the role of the image in thinking: I can

accept Sartre's formulation—that an image is only a kind of thought—subject to one proviso. It is only to the extent that an image is not recognized as fully embedded in the associationist matrix from which it springs, only to the extent that its independent origin is not fully understood, that it can be a successful thought.[34] For the fact is that the roots of every image do go down into that associationist matrix, and that at that level, the root-level, the image has nothing to do with the argument that it may be used to advance. "Images just want to go their own way, they don't care about anything."[35] But energy—a kind of libido, if one wishes—does attach itself to images: images are energy-storage nodes,[36] at which an increased potential accumulates; when the current of thought begins, they discharge their force, like boosters, adding strength to the current and helping it to define its direction. But part of them must stay behind, at the associative level, a level at which they do not exist for the purposes of thought or for problem-solving.

I shall give a personal example of the way in which thought moves from an imaging activity, which is virtually dream, to problem-solving. For a long time, my sense of what happens when either interpreting texts or dealing with more general literary problems was dominated by the image-phrase *unpacking a series*. One morning, before waking up (when I was trying to keep my thoughts in a fluid state, so that I could at the same time observe and understand what was happening in my own mind), I caught the meaning of that phrase which I had been using, with the attendant feeling of being taken aback at discovering what is "unpacked." The phrase was not so general and featureless, not so much of a dead metaphor, as it now sounds. It referred to a large crate, made of plywood and lined with tinfoil, that stood in my attic. I had used the crate for packing china and glassware when moving from Cambridge to Montreal, and then again from

Montreal to Buffalo. I remembered the feeling of surprise
that I had when greeting each object, recognizing it as it
emerged from its unidentifiable lump of newspaper. That tea
crate, with objects wrapped in newspaper, that had to be
individually unwrapped, was what I had in the back of my
mind when I used the phrase *unpacking a series. Like a dream,
that crate was pure uninterpreted image.* The newspaper-wrapped
objects were already close enough to interpretation for their
relevance to the problem-solving (i.e., series-unpacking) function of the metaphor to become conscious. The tea crate,
though, remained in dream.

We use dreams to solve problems, but part of the dream
remains back there in the mind, remote from words; unspoken,
unrecognized, and unthanked. There are three levels, then:
the part of the image that remains completely unrecognized,
the part that is halfway to consciousness, and the language
that describes the part that is halfway to consciousness. The
language, where it has broken through the surface, is our
first clue, the first thing that we are aware of, that enables us
to work our way back to the other two levels, but only by a
deliberate effort; the third or bottom one often can not be
reached at all. The word *unpacked,* (to repeat a phrase),
punctured the membrane between image and language: it
was the first stratum of the image that got named. An image
seems to struggle toward a linguistic surface, stage by stage.
What Shakespeare's associations with "unpacking" were when
he had Hamlet say, "[I] must, like a whore, unpack my heart
with words," we shall probably never know.[37] But the expression does signal to us that the play will never get back again
from language — it will remain mired in "words, words, words"
(2.2.191); as I shall try to show, it can never connect image
(what is seen) to words (what is known).

Thinking consists of a constant alternation between image-
making and word-making. We narrow our eyes when thinking,

partly because of the effort but partly also to see what is happening in our dimly lit inner theater. But in dreams there are disconnections between images and words: the shuttle does not incessantly flit back and forth between them. In a dream, the image reel can go one way and the sound track another, each pursuing its own course. Often in dreams we hear words that do not come from anyone represented in the visual content of the dream, and the words may be completely unrelated to the visual materials.[38] The effect is like that of some of Blake's plates, in which the pictures do not seem to illustrate the verse: it contradicts the dictum (Benjamin, *Über Haschisch*, p. 116), "Quod in imaginibus, est in lingua." Or, to reverse the formulation, as J.-F. Lyotard puts it: "Here lie the sin and the pride: in wanting to have the text and the illustration together" (*Discourse, Figure*, p. 10).

The sound-image discrepancies in dreams, though, may just be symptomatic of the general looseness in linkage between mental systems. Frequently, what we think we are about to do is different from what we actually do. I am intending to play an F on the piano; perhaps I even hear the F I am about to play, but my finger goes for a D. Any ordinary slip of the tongue may give us a clue to a deeper process. I am about to have a foot operation, but I also have to arrange to bring my car in for repair. I try to think of the things on my car that ought to be checked, and decide that the arch supports need attention. It requires a deliberate violation of my own language—a waking from my dream, so to speak—to force the right word upon myself and begin to talk of shock absorbers, to give domination to the image (automobile), to destroy the harmony that prevailed between word and image as long as they were allowed to exist in their separate registers. Could it be that the language in dream carries our emotional concerns, whereas the images reflect our practical situations? Certainly, images are easier to remember: perhaps dreams assign to images things that need to be dwelt on. At any rate, we fall asleep by allowing our words to move with freedom among and around our images, instead of being subordinated to them as they are in our waking life: the words to the accompaniment of which we fall asleep are gradually joined by a dance of images in the background that for once do not (to our relief) exact congruence between themselves and the language passing through our minds, but let us think what we want.

John Ashbery's poem "No Way of Knowing" describes "waking up / In the middle of a dream with one's mouth full/ Of unknown words. . . ."[39] Yet, he says, that waking amid those unknown words "takes in all of" the previous and possible experiences of life, whether as lived or as dreamed. What were, or what are, these experiences?

> Colors and names of colors,
> The knowledge of you a certain color had?
> The whole song-bag, the eternal oom-pah refrain?
> Street scenes? A blur of pavement
> After the cyclists passed, calling to each other
> Calling each other strange, funny sounding names?

"It" (the awakening with one's mouth full of unknown words) "is both the surface and the accidents / Scarring that surface," both the curiously inviolate envelope of dream language and the weals of images rising upon it, like the tracks of water insects in the moonlight.

The way in which words and images drift apart is strikingly illustrated in Wordsworth's "Resolution and Independence." Lewis Carroll, in "The White Knight's Song," had the good sense to accentuate the disjunction instead of trying to disguise or rationalize it. Carroll, in fact, virtually produced a new charter for poetry by insisting on allowing the disruptive forces to show, by insisting that they were the poem. Wordsworth pretended to tie his images and his ideas together with a moral; Carroll untied the rope. What the poet is seeing—the disquieting images of the huge stone, the seabeast, the cloud—has nothing to do with what he is saying—"How is it that you live," or with his moral at the end. Nor does what he is seeing have anything to do with what he is hearing, which makes equally little sense: as he himself admits, "nor word from word could I divide." No wonder that he asks his questions over and over again. The scene, he tells us, is like something experienced in a dream; which means precisely that what is seen must shock by its incongruity with what is known.

In *Hamlet*, what can be modeled or visualized is also contrasted with what cannot be pictured: and language refuses to mediate. But anyone who has read Jean-François Lyotard's classic essay on *Hamlet*, "Jewish Oedipus," will approach the theme of the disjunction between image and thought in that play with caution.[40] Lyotard draws a gleaming complex of strands from the Greek stage to Freud and back into the Renaissance; the whole web waisted through the ring of *Hamlet*. Hamlet's commitment to the obedient ear rather than the rebellious Oedipal eye is the expression of an attachment to the father's word that keeps him in a permanently subordinate and unfulfilled position. Freud's own task is to circumvent that role—the role of being "good," of displacing desire permanently, of fated allegiance to the father—and, by the understanding of Hamlet's condition, to advance beyond the necessary obedience of the ear, to the act. All these problems, in turn, are reflected in the many facets of representation. Such are, in barest outline, the themes that Lyotard deals with.

My own effort must be more limited. Without as yet attempting to account for the fact, I should like to point out that from the very beginning of *Hamlet* there is difficulty in connecting image to word. At first the ghost is seen but will not speak; then, at the end of the first act, he speaks, repeatedly and disturbingly, but from beneath the feet of the actors: he cannot be seen. In between, when he is both visible and audible, in his tête-à-tête with Hamlet, he only perpetuates the initial dilemma: what he has communicated is a secret not to be repeated. The sense of confusion falls over the action once more as all are sworn to silence, and we realize that what is seen in Denmark and what is known must separate again; our momentary hope for a reconciliation of the visible with the intelligible has been dashed.

The first dumb-show of the ghost, followed by his attempt to talk out the meaning of his return, prepares the way for similar sequences later in the play. In the actual dumb-show, there is a repeat, as in the ghost's appearances: first we have it without language, then with language. But initially we have just the scene, the visual image alone, and we get a good look at it. It draws the eye all the more powerfully because it focuses, paradoxically, on the ear, the instrument of the very sense that has been excluded from the action. Almost no one, as yet, has heard of what has happened. The rupture of seeing from hearing is complete. And where words cannot take their normal course, poison must flow in.

Hamlet's effort in presenting the dumb-show is to reconcile image with language. The silent image has been demanding that he say what he only sees: but he "can say nothing" (2.2. 596). Now he wants to make the truth visible, in the hope that it will speak for itself. He does make it visible, but it still does not speak; as Hamlet himself has told us, dumb-shows are inexplicable (3.2.13–14). They are a kind of sleep-walking. What has not been articulated remains as sleep; it cannot be

acted upon. Despite Hamlet's own eagerness to explain the
action of the play — like a puppet-master (3.2.256–57) or, as
Ophelia says, like a chorus (3.2.255) — nothing gets explained.
Dumb-show, speaking-show, and Hamlet's commentary all
together have no effect; and we can tell beforehand (3.2.80ff.)
that they will not. We are not in the least surprised when,
instead of taking prompt action after Claudius betrays himself through his response to *The Mousetrap,* Hamlet instead
begins a leisurely, amused dialogue with Horatio, as though
what had just transpired concerned him in only the most
casual way.

In fact, Hamlet seems to have accepted the futility of this
effort at reconciliation of the visible with the known early in
the play. I take his first reaction to his father's ghost as
critical. Initially, he had spoken with the greatest respect and
admiration of his father, for all his faults. (1.2.188); before the
confrontation with the ghost, Hamlet still seems a man very
much capable of unqualified love; when he says to his mother
(1.2.76), "I know not *seems,*" he does not seem to be exag-
gerating; we take him at his word. But a ghost is something
that can only be seen as seeming.

After his encounter with his father in ghostly form, as has
been often observed, Hamlet appears as a man whose capacity for affection (except for the oblique friendship with
Horatio) has been drained out of him. His behavior, beginning with his manner toward the ghost under the stage,
becomes infected with a jaunty sarcasm that conveys his
hopelessness about relationships, about the possibility that
people, or even words and things, can connect to each other.
Hamlet is alone. Nor are the other characters in much better
case. Affect does not take hold. People in this play slide past
each other; nobody confronts anyone else head-on for long.
Even the murders all take place by accident or indirection.
The Oedipal pattern itself is an expression of this elision of

relationships. Everything, including the concluding duel, is a "play." We are becalmed on a sea of "words, words, words," which will never allow the characters to reach the shore of experience. Only in play or in plays is it possible to "suit the action to the word, the word to the action" (3.2.19–20). Words and images unite in feeling only in the imagination: only "in a fiction, in a dream of passion" (2.2.578), as in the player's speech on the death of Priam. Even in the first of Ophelia's mad songs, we have to leap across a chasm between image and meaning.

> How should I your truelove know
>   From another one?
> By his cockle hat and staff
>   And his sandal shoon.

But the image that the speaker has of her lover has long been detached from his embodiment; he has changed from a real man into an idea in her head without her having been apprised of the substitution.

> He is dead and gone, lady,
>   He is dead and gone,
> At his head a grass-green turf,
>   At his heels a stone.
> (4.5.23–26,29–32)

Ophelia's words, in turn, seem to have a kind of domino effect on those who hear her speak, stirring them to invent a meaning for the chaotic images that she presents them with:

"Her speech is nothing, / Yet the unshaped use of it doth move / The hearers to collection. They aim at it / And botch the words up fit to their own thoughts" (4.5.7–10). As for Hamlet, all he can do (as he too truly says) is, like a whore, unpack his heart with words (2.2.614)—like a whore, whose love is only playing, and whose anger issues in helpless profanity, in more words. No words relate to the event; all words are superfluous ("Free me from the words I cannot use."—William Moebius, "Ode X").

Even when we have what looks like a true confrontation, in the truest of possible places, Ophelia's grave, it turns out to be a contest of language again; Hamlet, disgusted by Laertes' bombast, offers to outrant the ranter. There seems to be no way of getting out of confinement to words in this play, except by getting out of language, and out of life, altogether.

Detached from love, Hamlet has only his thoughts to work with. "There is nothing either good or bad, but thinking makes it so" (2.2.244–45) conveys more than its apparent flippancy. Because of his abstraction, Hamlet is not really capable of double vision, of seeing connotatively. He is full of puns, but he does not see in metaphors. The clouds can have any shape at all; it is all a game to him, whether it be camel, weasel, or whale (3.2.392f.); the world does not catch him with its double beauty and fix a meaning for him. He cannot accept the connectedness that allows reality to produce its meanings for us. ("A man's life is no more than to say 'one' " [5.2.74] refers not only to time.) He can think of the relation between seeing and saying, even when what is to be seen is Ophelia's beauty, only as a dirty joke:

> Ophelia: Will he tell us what this show meant?
> Hamlet: Aye, or any show that you'll show him. Be not you

ashamed to show, he'll not shame to tell you what
it means.

(3.2.153–56)

It seems only suitable that in a world such as this, when all
has been shown, the rest should be silence.

Conversely, Hamlet has no tolerance for the involvement,
or self-projection into the seen, which, in its simplest form, is
expressed as a sexualization of the environment. Himself
condemned to single vision, he rejects the erotic perspective
of the maids who "nickname God's creatures, and make your
wantonness your ignorance" (3.1.144), the same maids who are
implicitly reproved by Gertrude for their coldness, for turning
life to death, as they name the "long purples, / That liberal
shepherds give a grosser name," and in which the mad Ophelia
has draped herself, "dead men's fingers" (4.7.171–73).

Ophelia drowns. Unable to keep her world together, she
has fallen back on the language of flowers, where meaning is
presumably already in the object.[41] But that strategy has not
helped either. When she is drowning she does not even know
that she is drowning; her thoughts and her real situation are
unrelated. Singing, she appears to be genuinely afloat; what
we know and what we see are out of touch, as she is with
herself. But the film of words will not long sustain her. Voice
goes one way, image another. The event itself will be as silent
as the skulls in the graveyard where she will be buried—
sketches, or caricatures, of once highly vocal men, but, as
things merely to be looked at, having nothing to say for
themselves, and about which there is not much to say.

In the end, the poison goes from the ear to the mouth, and
through the blood, from drink and sword, from everywhere.
In the *logomachia* of which so much of Hamlet's life has
consisted, the potent cock, the poison, speaks loudest of all:

"The potent poison quite o'ercrows my spirit" (5.2.364); he it
is who has the last word. The cock whom the poisoned
Socrates had said he owed to the God of health comes back,
from the first act, to announce the eternal dawn of death.

"High on a stage" the bodies are to be placed to view; we
will have yet another dumb-show. They are to be seen, and
then talked about—explained. In the harshest of ironies,
Fortinbras can even proclaim that Hamlet's corpse will pipe
up for itself: "The soldiers' music and the rites of war / Speak
loudly for him" (5.2.410–11).[42] Fortinbras's martial flourishes
will stamp out silence and strike the angels dumb. The presumably more appropriate discourse of Horatio will follow;
still, words will be used to interpret, to account for, what is
seen. But only a critic would try—not the playwright. The
bodies are there; that is all we know. As in the case of the
Grecian urn, the rest is for us to make fantasies about; the
images are silent. We need a whole myth to persuade ourselves that the riddle of the Sphinx can be answered; but, in
the end, all we have discovered is man, confronting the
image again. What the character Hamlet was unable to do
because he was too self-preoccupied to love (namely, find
meaning in the things he sees) the play *Hamlet* demonstrates
cannot be done in principle. That is the play's tragedy for us.
Hamlet's tragedy is one thing, sufficient for him; the tragedy
that the play makes its spectators suffer through is another.
We realize that what has not been furnished gratis by love
cannot be achieved by thought, as what is available to the
understanding in the progressive mode of language cannot
be grasped in retrospect.

We, or Horatio, may continue trying to interpret what
happened to Hamlet; but Shakespeare chose to go no farther.

2

The Ethics of Particularity: Literature and the Monad

"THE SENSE OF THE INDIVIDUAL IS THE ONLY GOOD." THERE has been, in the past few years, a noticeable preoccupation with the concept of particularity in literature, as though many who write on the subject had taken this remark of William's in *The Name of the Rose* to heart. Three excellent articles on *Hamlet* alone approach the play with individuality and / or particularity as their principal concern;[1] and Paul Fry's book-length study of literary criticism, *The Reach of Criticism* (New Haven and London: Yale University Press, 1983), argues that the kind of commentary that works with particular observations and insights is, on the whole, more successful than systematic criticism that proceeds from generalizations. The possible reasons for this widespread interest in particularity of both personality and detail I will not go into here, but I find what seems to be an oversight in recent studies of the topic: they tend to make only passing reference to Leibniz, whose work is, after all, the fountainhead of thought on this whole subject in modern times.

I will, accordingly, place some concepts of Leibniz at the center of my own remarks, using *Othello* and Ashbery's "Self-Portrait in a Convex Mirror" as my principal examples, though recurring to *Hamlet* in an extension of previous remarks of mine on that play. But before launching into interpretive commentary, I should like to consider the question of how an observed particular is formed in the first place. The philosophical problem of defining generals and particulars is obviously beyond the scope of this essay as well as of my competence; but it should at any rate be possible to observe, in a purely subjective mode, the germinating of a significant particular in one's own mind and experience, to watch what is happening as something specific becomes unique, and then permanent.

During periods of depression, I have sometimes had the habit of walking in Buffalo's Delaware Park. A willow tree hangs over the lake. I sometimes stop under the tree, look out through the overhanging branches, and hope that the tree is going to do something for me. On one occasion, when it did, I wrote down a comment about the experience. I repeat it here, with a partial gloss.

"In the version of process philosophy, or Bergsonism, to which I have been committed, the ethical bonds to time and act; some defect of right haunts the pictures of the past. Yet what is love, if not an acceptance of the pictures of the past, present made continuous? It lifts the baskets of the willow, and they remain in air; they become then-forevers. Through the surge of vision that moved them, all absence that might ever have been in them is obliterated."

The thought contained in the first sentence doesn't require much commentary: it may be found among my remarks in chapter 1 about the nature of poetry as forbidding retrospective reading, visualization, or summation, and about *Hamlet*, in which the possibility of prospect (and therefore, as I argue in the present chapter, of poetry) is undercut from the beginning. In the second sentence of the passage, "Yet what is love, if not an acceptance of the pictures of the past, present made continuous?" attention moves to the willow tree itself. The "picture" of the willow tree, that is, the presence of the willow tree as I have seen it in that moment, becomes continuous — that is, permanent — if the willow tree strikes me in the right way, in what might be called the mode of love. Once it has become continuous, though, it has in fact become a "picture of the past." The moment that has been made permanent subsequently rises from the past. (Wordsworth has made all this familiar to us.)

To continue: "It lifts the baskets of the willow, and they remain in air." The baskets of the willow are the interwoven twigs as the wind lifts them; I see them for a moment hanging in air, as baskets. The wind that has lifted the baskets of the willow is the surge of feeling that is the response to what is happening. "And they *remain* in air"; as the wind suspends them, contrary to the force of gravity, contrary to common sense, so the feeling suspends them, makes them hang permanently. They remain seen forever in that suspended position: they have become "then-forevers."

"Through the surge of vision that moved them, all absence that might ever have been in them is obliterated." Things as we usually look at them are full of absence; they are steeped in absence; often they might as well not be there. The purging of that nothingness, of the potential for nothingness in the things that we look at, takes place through that act of vision which lifts the willow twigs and makes them "then-forevers." The need that lifted them has made them real for the first time. (Cf. Martin Buber, *I and Thou,* part 1).

When we become engaged in an experience in this way, it becomes different from any other possible experience. That once, which becomes *only* but is then forever, was still a once.

Leibniz thought of ones. Right goes with unrepeatable. We could go through *Hamlet* this way, unthinking of repetition.

But all things are *not* different from all other things except as we make them so. Unperceived, in neutral site, they may very well be alike (Leibniz's "Identity of Indiscernibles?"). Yet whether they be the same or different, they clearly become different when we strike them into being, or are ourselves stung into flushing them out of cover, into being; flush, eventually flesh (as in Hopkins, "Brim, in a flash, full.") What we experience, if genuine, is once: there are no generals.

There are no two women: there is one woman and one woman, and finally there is only one woman.[2] Custodians of the particular, we know no twos. The clock has gone mad: it has struck one four times (Coleridge, *Notebooks,* 1, entry 915). Only clocks can fail to recognize that one is once. For Leibniz, only God can give a complete description of a "once," of an individual, a "complete notion" of an individual, because it would entail a description of the entire universe. Lovers have a shortcut to that description.

Universals, individuals: on the specificity of experience I find Bataille congenial.[3] Things just do not repeat themselves, unless we are passive to them: if they exist for us fully, we do not experience them under the aspect of sameness or uniformity. Categories have something of the fraud about them. For this reason some passages in Freud make me uncomfortable. The "pure" sexual passion we assume behind the individualized forms of it that we know in real life is a myth: it is always contaminated with consciousness and individuality. It's a mere illusion, will-o'-the-wisp, or *Ding an sich.*[4] The Freudian unconscious, composed of de-particularized, imageless categories, circles round to join the Viconian unconscious—they meet in the porch of the unstated universal, the speechless antechamber to all particularity.[5] (And, since we still have no satisfactory explanation of how categories come into being — though Hegel, in the *Logic,* thought he had — we may as well account for that whole area by calling it "the unconscious").

Even more obscure than the way in which categories or group concepts are formed is the way in which the palpable particularity of experience gets into language, to the extent to which it does.[6] Language is not (contra Heidegger)[7] entirely made up of individuals;[8] but it is engaged in a constant effort to take account of individuals. Individuals are not the notorious Inexpressible; they are the border territory where language struggles to come to terms with the all-important unique, for example, that which distinguishes the individual man or woman from sex as such, if there be such a thing as sex as such. The rest of language is a record of that effort. The unique neither desires not rejects expression; but language does desire to, or need to, take hold of that particular thing.

Why would we need language at all, if not to say something that is not yet language? The creation of language is repeated every time we say something — some part of that which is greater, more inclusive than language, and which makes language necessary (and possible).

Herman Rapaport asks, of the Cheshire cat's separated head, and the Queen's (mother's) decapitating fury in Carroll's *Alice:* "isn't it clear that what is at issue here is nothing less than what Freud calls the castration complex ... ?"[9] It is certainly so. But at the same time, there is something mistaken about pretending that all the individual experiences of life, in their variety and personal-ness, can be summarized. The problem is that there is too great a variety of experiences, not that experiences fall of their own accord into large classes that are unavoidably repeated. In the effort to find an individual, one learns that that which can be repeated is the least important, the least real. After all, the characteristic of the human is the creation of an unrepeated thing, something that cannot be duplicated. Literature itself is the changing of the relative, or interchangeable, into the irreplaceable. Why treat what is most characteristic of humanity—that is, that which evades the class or summary—as a mistake? Maybe "castration," in fact, is the forcing of us to accept class concepts, categories; perhaps this is what some women can do to some men: force them to generalize. To become aware that they are bound to a weak language, a language that is mere generalization, especially futile in their attempt to deal with the non-linguistic element in the female (the "in-fans," nonspeaking "child" Alice).[10] Silence, in this context, remains the preserve of the female; language as generalization becomes the province of the rejected male.

I come back to *Hamlet*, again à propos the general vs. the individual, sameness and difference. In chapter 1 I attempted to deal with this problem in relation to reading. Difference would be associated with forward or nonretrospective reading, nonsummarizing reading (poetry); sameness, with summarizing, retrospective reading, or, in *Hamlet*, with the Ghost (classification).[11] The diachronic experience of uninterrupted difference would be perfect sexuality; in it the pure springing feeling, like a field full of grasshoppers, knows no pause and seeks no retrospect.

Hamlet himself struggles, vainly and briefly, to be the summer's singer, the bearer of difference, the news in Denmark; but he is caught between two kinds of sameness, paternal and maternal, noise and silence.[12] The play is warped in a middle ground that permits no leveling. Even Hamlet's return to silence at the end, although it resolves some issues, and is mediated by his mother's drinking the poison meant for him, is not quite a "union" or reunification with her. The ghost himself is symptomatic of this intermediacy, or indeterminacy, of the play, in which every effort to achieve articulation (hence also song or poetry) is deflected, and finally short-circuited to one end of the polarity, to silence.

The particular, the individual, the language of sexuality, potent language, has no place here. Only the poison speaks with the powerful language of love. For the most part, what we get is a hollow language. To the extent that the ghost dominates the play, it is confederate with the language of comparison, of "as," which is also the ghostly language of "as if." We start with "like"—"like the king that's dead." "Looks it not like the King?" "Most like." "Is it not like the King?" " 'Tis strange" (i.e., unlike itself). (1.1.41,43,44,58,64).

When we start with *like*, we start out alienated from the variety of being, or (in Leibnizian phrase), from the sequence of discernible nonidentical events. It's the language of indirection, and caught up in reduplication from the start—ghosts are categories, categories are ghostly. Both the names Hamlet and Fortinbras have gone before, and are trapped in classes: they too must be "as," now, and not just themselves. The language, from the very beginning, is eroded by indefinites, prepositions, periphrases, words that will do anything except allow something to be called what it is. Even the ghost isn't himself: he is only "together with" his form (1.1.47). Marcellus is not himself, only like himself (1.1.59). Words like *such, so, in, some, to, Why, What,* and *Who* undercut line after line (1.1.60–79), until we are in the right frame of mind to accept the uncertainty principle about reality as a whole; we no longer care whether anything is true; "At least the whisper goes so" (1.1.80).

Is there another language in the play, besides the language of comparison? Clearly there has been the potentiality of another language, but it has received short shrift. Hamlet's chances for lyric freedom are aborted. "Anon, as patient as the female dove / When that her golden couplets are disclosed, / His silence will sit drooping" (5.1.309–11). These are the couplets of birth and poetry, not the repetition that haunts the play with the mephitic cloud of categorization. Hamlet falls into silence brooding over the eggs of love, his own testicles, his stillborn poetry.[13] These couplets are not the redundant vacuity of Osric and his "golden words" (5.2.136); Osric, another one who ought to be a ghost, whose only "semblable is his mirror, and who else would trace him, his umbrage" (5.2.123–25). The golden couplets are what allow for the same not to be the same, the dissonant harmony of metaphor and creation, the two, each precious in its singularity that reflects value on the other, not the sterile twinning of a Rosencrantz and Guildenstern.

The remaining language of the play, though, is not reassuring. Identity rests on uncertain grounds; we can neither fix it in the confidence of knowledge nor release it to the confidence of love. "To thine own self be true" (1.3.78) becomes "Lord, we know what we are but know not what we may be" (4.5.42–43); Ophelia accordingly doubles, becoming herself and a picture of herself, "Divided from herself and her fair judgment, / Without the which we are pictures" (4.5.85–86). Claudius accuses Laertes (not without reason) of being "like the painting of a sorrow" (4.7.109). In the graveyard scene, even the dead are beside themselves: every lady, though she "paint an inch thick, to this favor she must come" (5.1.213–14); semblance within (skull), semblance without (paint). "To know a man well were to know himself" (5.2.145–46), but neither seems possible. Finally Hamlet himself might as well have been Hamlet's ghost. "Was't Hamlet wronged Laertes? Never Hamlet." Hamlet from himself was "ta'en away" (5.2.244–45).

The ghost, then, is the symptom of the play's condition, undercutting, disqualifying immediacy and difference. Collusive with categories, with backward reading, it connects things insidiously with a futile past and a mock-ordered present. But repetition liquidates even itself: the ghost's appearance to Hamlet in the closet scene, presumably intended to revive the son's vengeful anger, actually attenuates Hamlet's resolution: "Do not look upon me, / Lest with this piteous action you convert / My stern effects. Then what I have to do / Will want true color—tears perchance for blood" (3.4.127–30).

So ends Hamlet's struggle to articulate his identity, to make a song: silent, he rejoins the universal categories of the pilgrim and the shrouded corpse (4.5.25–35), still without having had his say. Actor and audience are both mutes. "You that look pale and tremble at this chance, / That are but mutes or audience to this act, / Had I but time—as this fell sergeant, Death, / Is strict in his arrest—oh, I could tell you— / But let it be" (5.2.345–49). Perhaps "the potent poison" is the best thing one can have anyway, though: and, as I have said, it certainly speaks louder than words, whatever those words might have been (5.2.364).

Silence has another role in *Othello,* a role that relates to Desdemona's as woman, but it cannot be an entirely different one. Desdemona's voice is stopped too. Perhaps she cannot speak for herself, and should not have been expected to. (Here I anticipate some of the themes in Part II of this book). It is her invitation to Iago to praise her, to give her an identity, speak for her, give her even a ventriloquial voice, that first moves her into his domain—and all this she does, inappropriately, before it is clear that Othello has been saved from the storm at sea. (Desdemona's disclaimer of merriment in 2.1.123 doesn't excuse the poor taste of her query in 2.1.118: "What wouldst thou write of me if thou shouldst praise me?") And for all her chaste innocence, it is she who lets slip the rock-bottom truth about the relations between men and women, in some sense justifying Othello's jealousy, and validating the grounds of jealousy as a whole:

I called my love false love, but what said he then?
Sing willow, willow, willow.
If I court moe women, you'll couch with moe men.

(4.3.55–57).

But "All that's spoke is marred" (5.2.357). It is not suitable for Desdemona to speak; conquered, presumably, by Othello's eloquence, hers is the part of silence. She is not to speak: more, she cannot speak. No one can really speak, but least of all a woman whose role is, speechless, to arouse jealousy in men, so relegating *them* to "speeches," to language. "Alas, she has no speech" (2.1.103), which Desdemona says of Emilia, she had better say of herself. But even Emilia, when she finally speaks up, as though for Desdemona, can only say, "So speaking as I think, I die, I die" (5.2.251).

Who is Desdemona? In herself, she is nothing. She has no content. It is not only that she is unformed: that her hand "has felt no age nor known no sorrow" (3.4.37). In principle she cannot be anything. Her awkward attempts at explaining her motives, at describing herself, just express her helpless inability to do justice to her own identity, to give herself fullness of being. "Why, what art thou?" / "Your wife, my lord, your true and loyal wife" (4.2.33–34). She sews, sings, talks (4.1.198–201). Colorless, self-withdrawing, she retreats into an implausible innocence that serves only to make her condition as a cipher more apparent. Is there any woman who would commit adultery "for all the world"? (4.3.68). "I do not think there is any such woman" (4.3.84). The point is, rather, is there any woman who would give such an answer? Her banter with Iago and Cassio is out of character mainly because Desdemona is to have no character. Like all sacrificial victims, she must be pure; but, as the special kind of sacrificial victim that she is, what she must be pure of is attributes, other than the attribute of innocence itself. It will be left to Othello to confer a character upon her.

The case is even clearer than it is in *Swann's Way*, where Swann must bestow a character upon the nondescript courtesan, Odette, who doesn't need the individuality that he attributes to her. Desdemona does need the identity that Othello can give her; her inept, pathetic strugglings to be *something* are necessarily unsuccessful not because she lacks courage, desire, or will, but because one cannot be oneself. Only someone else can fulfill one as an individual. One cannot be the possessor of one's own individuality.

Will Othello retreat from love to a prior chaos? (3.3.92). It is too late for that choice. All unbeknownst to himself, for all his supposed coolness, Othello has taken on the responsibility of the lover. What is that responsibility?

Othello puts an end to all possibility of speech for Desdemona. He stifles her, so that his adoption of responsibility for her identity can be shown to be total. For in love, one takes on completely the burden of the individuality of the beloved: that is the lover's responsibility. She is the unrepeatable individual, the proof that Leibniz was right, that each monad is unlike all others. But by virtue of that very fact, she is, like the monad, impenetrable, inaccessible, refusal incarnate. She is the windowless monad (*Monadology* #7), though at the same time she is the palpable evidence of the constantly renewed creative power in God, from whom monads are born, "so to speak, by continual fulgurations of the Divinity from moment to moment . . . " (#47). The lover is in contact, in an almost physical sense, with some numinous principle that is above the caliber of ordinary experience, yet underlies and undergirds all ordinary experience. The beloved is the incarnation of the incommensurable, the one who will fit in no class concept, who is not exchangeable. The lover is the custodian of that person's uniqueness.

Only the lover can do justice to the individuality of the beloved, not she to herself. Desdemona's importance, to herself, by herself, is inexpressible. It is fumbled for, in inappropriate ways, when she is joking with Iago and Cassio, trying to get a *prise,* a sticking-point, a foothold, in the conversation with, and on the personalities of, the people around her, and it never amounts to anything. It never expresses her. (For all Othello's supposed eloquence, he too remains unexpressed except through the murder; he too is afflicted with a sort of mutism, stiffness or nonspeech, a nonaccess to communication, of which his blackness is the symbol).

Desdemona, then, is at last, and mercifully, silenced. Her murder is a symbolic gesture by which the futile struggle to give her individuality in herself is abandoned, and the enterprise left in the only hands in which it can have success. She remains a figure for the speechless, though not (like Hermione in *The Winter's Tale*) an image, painted as well as mute (2.1.109). She can stop groping for words. Her suffering of inexpressibility is taken over by her lover, in its mirror-image. What pains the lover? It is the burden of the awareness of the individuality of the beloved (which no one else can know, and which even she cannot grasp). The sense of the beloved's individuality becomes overwhelming, in violation of all categorized experiences, and of the full knowledge that she is, by all that we call "standards," commonplace, classifiable, just like anybody else. Love is the defiant experience of individuality, which can never be known abstractly. The lover is tormented by the experience of uniqueness, a uniqueness that remains as imperceptible to the perplexed bystander, the nonlover, as the ghost of Hamlet's father was to Gertrude.

As the custodian of Desdemona's individuality, which she herself cannot know or fulfill, Othello has the responsibility of identifying, experiencing, and sealing that essence—*for her.* It is not his own identity, but hers, that he seeks to forge in her murder. As early as the second act, Othello (arousing Desdemona's objections) associates perfection with death (2.1.191–96). The "sacrifice," *not* murder, that he had intended, is the completion of his knowledge of her, within which she should have been completed, though at the expense of a body (5.2.5): mere flesh turned "monumental alablaster" (5.2.65). The permanence of the perfection achieved is again articulated when he kisses her sleeping: "Be thus when thou art dead, and I will kill thee, / and love thee after" (5.2.18–19); for, surely, "I would not kill thy soul" (5.2.32).

Parallel to Desdemona's inability to possess herself as herself is Othello's inability to possess her as himself, in his own person. In order to relate to her fully, he must project himself into another man. In such a sense does Cassio, then, become the unwitting custodian of Othello's identity, an adequate embodiment of Othello's insufficient self: for the self, in this case the male sexual self, is, to itself, necessarily insufficient. The satisfaction Othello cannot have directly with Desdemona he can obtain by imagining her topped by another man. (Jealousy is the ultimate aphrodisiac). As Ed Snow, among others, has pointed out, Othello is always living his life as a story anyway;[14] this is just one more way of imagining his life, of making it adequate by fictionalizing it.

To digress briefly from the subject of identity and uniqueness, I should like to consider the question of Othello's jealousy, in particular of the voyeuristic or scoptophilic element in it (3.3.365 and 400ff). Somewhat as the quality of a love relationship can be intensified by the imagined death of a loved one (cf. Wordsworth's "Lucy" poems[15]), so erotic love may be intensified by our picturing the beloved with someone else: in both cases, loss is somehow made into gain. Othello's eager but agonized imaginings no doubt represent a form of voyeurism; but the question remains: is voyeurism, or scoptophilia, simply a perversion?[16] We are all aware of a certain loss when we move from looking at our beloved to the act of copulation itself, which necessarily interferes with looking; we can never see ourselves in the round when we are making love—so that, to some extent, we actually have to imagine what we are doing while we are doing it. Not only that. Even under ordinary circumstances, much of our pleasure in sex is derived from identification with the sexual pleasure of our partner; it is only a short step to identifying with that pleasure apart from ourselves. Still more—some of the values of watching are actually more intense than our own participation can be: we can project ourselves imaginatively into the experience of other participants more completely than we can experience those feelings when we are ourselves actors, distracted by our own actions and by our personalities, unable to concentrate on what is happening in its primary force. In fact, the idea of the image is based on the fact that watched sex, especially the sexual actions of someone whom we love, is in some ways more intense than sex enacted by ourselves.[17] This is the presumption that gives power to numerous situations in Shakespeare that would be futile if we did not all experience it as true. (Not only Othello re Desdemona, or Posthumus re Imogen in *Cymbeline* [2.5.14–24], but Leontes re Hermione, [*TWT* 1.2.190–207], Lear on women in general [*KL* 4.6.119–24], even Hamlet on his mother, passim). Jealousy is in some respects stronger than love, and is therefore also in some respects more satisfying.[18] And jealousy, with its images more powerful than any acts, is the avatar of the image in general. The image is based upon the visualization of sexual acts. The reason why there has always been so much worry and dispute about the image and about the imagination is that imagined or seen sex can be sex raised to a higher index, more powerful and, of course, more obsessive than sex enacted. This is equally true if we identify with the sexual experience of the beloved, or our imagined self, or of our rival, but especially of the beloved. These perverts in Shakespeare are not peculiar people; they are, as usual, just ourselves.

To return to the issue of quiddity or uniqueness in *Othello* that preceded my digression on scoptophilia: I had been saying that the lover becomes the custodian of the beloved's monadic specificity, sealed in this case through the physical sacrifice of the beloved's body. Leibniz may seem an unlikely spokesman for the idea of the *Liebestod*, but there is a sense in which his unrepeatability principle,[19] as combined with his monadic conception of identity, is in fact central to the psychology of literature. Uniqueness is, after all, one of literature's primary concerns; in Ashbery's phrasing, the "painful freshness of each thing being exactly itself" ("Voyage in the Blue").

Leibniz tends to lead us, though, in two directions at once.[20] His notorious optimism is at the same time a radical pessimism: this is the best of all possible worlds, alas! The unrepeatability principle has us driven from one perception to another by a relentless appetite (*Monadology* #15), from one flash of light to the next, the sparkling semen of eternity; but these perceptions, and especially the ideas, that are "a sign of something divine and eternal" (*New Essays,* Introduction), operate by the mechanical release of innate forces already formed within us. Ethics too works for Leibniz like a machine (*Monadology* #89). And the marvelous uniqueness of every monad (#9) is counterbalanced by its curse of isolation (#7); despite Leibniz's assurances to the contrary (#8), it is sometimes hard to see how any entity as isolated as a monad could even be compared with another in order to establish its difference. Again, though the reality of the percipient is supposedly located partly in his/her "harmony with other percipient beings,"[21] it is an even more perplexing undertak-

ing to establish intersubjectivity on persuasive grounds in
Leibniz than in a system of pure idealism such as Schelling's.

There is a countercurrent, then, in Leibniz's thought,
that can turn one back from the rippling flow of process,
through which the world is always new and fresh ("On the
Ultimate Origination of Things"), to a grim autism, static
beyond all stasis. Hamlet's lyrical velleities and impulses
to love might (had his circumstances not made his effort
to fulfill that promise nugatory), in principle, have fulfilled themselves; he might have escaped the ghost of retrospect and equivalence. (We shall pass over the possibility
that circumstances had nothing to do with the outcome,
but that a substratum of self-disqualification lay beneath
the effort itself; as Alan Williamson says of the line in
Ashbery: "the secret sweetness before it turns to life," "In
Ashbery, the greater part of the sweetness invariably dies
when it turns to life."[22]) And although, in *Othello,* the monad
is unable to express itself through itself, it could at least
display its energy in transfer, as Desdemona's identity flees
to Othello's keeping. But on a Leibnizian hypothesis, we are
always faced with the danger that things will turn inward
upon themselves, and if we confront the hardest implications
of the *Monadology,* as, I think, John Ashbery, consciously
or otherwise, has done, we will move no farther. The remaining struggle can only be within. Process must be suspended. Not only may we be unable to capture the infinite
variety of experience: on a consistent Leibnizian premise, we
may not be able to get out of ourselves at all, even enough to
know ourselves, much less the changing world. It is not
surprising that Wallace Stevens could not decide whether
Leibniz was an ally or an enemy of poetry ("A Collect of
Philosophy").

If we think back to the lines from "No Way of Knowing"
that I have quoted before (chapter 1):

> waking up
> In the middle of a dream with one's mouth full
> Of unknown words takes in all of these:
> It is both the surface and the accidents
> Scarring that surface

we can see that what Ashbery is speaking of is not just a comfortable solipsism or self-reflexivity. It's not just that we can't know other people's minds, or even that all our knowledge is only part of ourselves. It is that our own consciousness is caught up in the knowledge that it has no way of knowing itself, that is, that it has no outside. The image we have is that of a sleeper struggling to get out of his own skin, trapped in an unconscious consciousness. "There *is* no way of knowing" (emphasis mine). "No one can get in or out." ("Monads have no windows, by which anything could come in or go out." *Monadology* #7). There is a surface, and there is something beneath that surface, disturbing it; but, paradoxically, there is nothing outside that surface; all that is outside it feeds back into a place within, so there is no vantage point from which knowledge can be achieved, from which we can interpret the dream. We are always the dreamer struggling to awake, even if only enough to enable us to question our own language.[23]

At each moment, our consciousness carries the weight of the primeval monad in it. Who will tell us where to turn next? There is no place to take hold. Desdemona finds in Othello the shattering mirror of her soul, the only way to make her be. But we walk around with the heavy knowledge that something in us has never awakened completely and never will awake, something that is ourselves, and that has no way of knowing, struggle as it may. Father of monads for his century, Leibniz preaches the arousal of their stony cores

from bondage to sleep: but are we sure that it can happen?
"Although many substances have already come to great
perfection, yet owing to the infinite divisibility of what is
continuous, there always remain in the abyss of things parts
that are asleep, and these need to be awakened and to be
driven forward into something greater and better . . . " ("On
the Ultimate Orgination of Things"). Shelley hoped to see
Leibniz's desire fulfilled:

> Demogorgon: Ye elemental genii, who have homes
> From man's high mind even to the central stone
> Of sullen lead;
>
> . . . .
> A confused voice: We hear: thy words waken Oblivion.
>
> *Prometheus Unbound* 4.539–41,543

But something remains that is beneath awakening.

That necessarily mute struggling thing turning over in its
sleep that is at the same time the thing that we see is what we
revert to, stunned by the heavy hand, the blow in the face of
"Self-Portrait in a Convex Mirror." But that hand is also
ourselves, the "central stone" in us. The hand knocks us out,
knocks us out of the picture and back where we belong, back
into the only dimensions that we are fit to inhabit, out of the
hubris of "consciousness," back toward the condition of the
sleeping, struggling monad. As Desdemona prepares to
exchange her life for her basic condition, sleep encroaches
upon her:

> but the sands are hissing
> As they approach the beginning of the big slide
> Into what happened.
>
> *(Self-Portrait,* p. 81)

Whatever happened, "It happened while you were inside, asleep" (p. 74).

> Emilia: How do you, madam? How do you, my good
>   lady?
> Desdemona: Faith, half-asleep.
>
> *(Othello,* 4.2.96–97)

Everything we are has a strong element of the monad's torpor in it, even though "Something like living occurs" *(Self-Portrait,* p. 73). This particular poem is saturated with it, the poppy, almost as thoroughly as Keats's "Ode on Melancholy," and like much else in Ashbery. To multiply quotations is wasteful where the title tells so much. But another Parmigianino painting Ashbery might have spoken of, though clearly he chose not to, conveys a different message. John Erwin has pointed out, brilliantly, the focus of the companion picture that hangs beside the "Self-Portrait" in the Kunsthistorisches Museum, Vienna, to which Ashbery makes no reference: "The Conversion of St. Paul."[24] The horse's rump glows like a sphere of light, a convex mirror from which St. Paul has been entirely ejected (somewhat as the viewer had been from the "Self-Portrait"), suspended over him and twinned with the blaze in heaven above. But this time deposed consciousness swirls back into its global belonging through the intricately ribboned reins, the horse's arching neck and fine-drawn head; fingers, reins, and head connect the monad back to the Oversoul through a cloud, a streak, to the dense core of lightning. Here is Confused Consciousness[25] (the painter's, the blinded Paul's) in its extreme realization, in which the mirror is no longer a symbol of the monad's entrapment, but the throwing of the self back into what it should be and what it ultimately can be: namely, the changing record, at once conscious and unconscious, of a seminal vitality (see that horse! studded with stars) that courses through the universe, self-enwrapped, but never the same. Each spot on that horse's coat is Difference; each separate forehoof, hung in air. One might well call the picture, "Conversion of the Mirror," or, "The Mirror Redeemed."[26]

I guess one of the things I'm saying is that sleep, whether the monadic sleep into which we get thrown back, as in the "Self-Portrait," or the sleep to which we revert spontaneously and of our own accord, is all right after all.[27] The eternal speechless pupa in us is deserving of some trust. It has its own possibilities, as "The Conversion of St. Paul" makes clear. It sets a kind of limit on us, and a prolonged confrontation with it is bound to produce an Ashbery; there is no way of knowing, and we have to face that fact and know it. But, apart from the special kind of redemptive potential that Parmigianino shows can be available to the deposed consciousness, ordinary sleep is also the source of dreams, and without dreams we would not have even what little knowledge we do have, nor much of our capacity for registering change. We must respect our monad's sleep, its dreams, and its struggle. Even the hole left when the dreams have run out is itself a dream.

"The Conversion of St. Paul" (Die Bekehrung Pauli").
Original in the Kunsthistorisches Museum, Vienna.
Reproduced by permission of the museum.

the source of dreams
Is being tapped so that this one dream
May wax, flourish like a cabbage rose. . . .
                    "The forms retain
A strong measure of ideal beauty," because
Fed by our dreams, so inconsequential until one day
We notice the hole they left. Now their importance
If not their meaning is plain. They were to nourish
A dream which includes them all, as they are
Finally reversed in the accumulating mirror.
They seemed strange because we couldn't actually
    see them
And we realize this only at a point where they lapse
Like a wave breaking on a rock, giving up
Its shape in a gesture which expresses that shape.
The forms retain a strong measure of ideal beauty
As they forage in secret on our idea of distortion.[28]
Why be unhappy with this arrangement, since
Dreams prolong us as they are absorbed?
Something like living occurs. . . .
            Ashbery, "Self-Portrait in a Convex Mirror," p. 73

Something like living; both more and less.

3

Escape from Fiction: Literature and Didacticism

(In Homage to Walter Benjamin)

UNCERTAIN AS THE VALUE OF WORDS ALWAYS IS, THE WORDS (to quote Leibniz) in which our "confused consciousness" has to be conveyed, it is all the more apparent that, unless words come naturally, they had better not come at all.

Words can be forced from us, by need, or by love; sometimes, fortunately, the two can even coincide. But to take a stance from which one inflicts words on others, as in the writing of an essay such as this, is presumptuous, even violent. It presupposes self-satisfaction and a certain coarseness. It infringes on the fragility of our texture.

Is an author, Flaubert, Chekhov, Tolstoi, also guilty of such violence, of forcing language, or of imposing it on us? I don't know, for I am not (*pace* the late Roland Barthes) an author. I think all three may have felt some such guilt, since all of them moved often toward the fable, away from discursive literary forms. The fable compensates for the self-willed character of fiction. All fiction, in fact, aspires to didacticism. This is not to say that the narrative impulse as such is necessarily hostile and guilt-ridden (for that matter, experience itself is inherently narrative in texture), but that there are certain frequencies within it that are laden with anxiety and its attendant overtones of hostility, for which an author might well feel the need to make amends.[1] In any case, I propose to explore in some detail the truism that there is guilt attached to writing, and to see how that fact prepares the way for the didacticism that is an element of most literary fiction. Didacticism, or the claim to be didactic, is often thought of as merely a disguise for immorality in literature; I suggest that it may be a genuine compensation for the strains of aggression and weakness that authors themselves feel to be inherent in the act of producing fiction. After all, writers are not necessarily good people, even if (as Shelley claims) at the particular moment of composition they may be in contact with the essence of the good. Nor does their profession as such require virtue of them, for it allows them to hover on the border between the vulnerability of honesty and the invulnerability of make-believe.[2]

I began this chapter with a simple paradigm in mind. I intended to deal first with a "normal" story: that is, one in which the reader arrives at a moral interpretation at the end, deducing from the action and the treatment of character certain ethical principles implicit in the text. Second, I intended to deal with a story that declared its moral explicitly at the beginning, leaving nothing for the reader to "discover." The third story was to exemplify the rejection of moral interpretation, the refusal to accept the famous dictum in *Alice* that "Everything's got a moral: you just have to find it."

The three stories are, respectively, Chekhov's "Ward 6," Tolstoi's "The Death of Ivan Ilyich," and Flaubert's "The

Legend of Saint Julian the Hospitaler." I shall still attempt to follow my outline, but with some changes in order and emphasis. The reason for the alterations is that the integrity of the whole model I was trying to use was unexpectedly threatened by Tolstoi's fictional structure, and I shall have to cope with the far-reaching, not to say universal issues that it raises before I can consider going on. Briefly, the points I shall make are these: (1) during the last two centuries, there has been a change in the moral responses expected of a reader: we are no longer invited to enjoy the sufferings of sinners; (2) there are, in every reader, two readers: one anxious, hostile, and potentially sadistic; the other stronger and open to criticism; (3) there are, in every writer, two writers, one of whom is gone before the other has arrived; or, to put it differently, one of whom is there to receive the work before the other has delivered it; (4) in the problem-solving process, whether it be the solution of an equation or the struggle to complete a metaphor, an answer that was implicitly present beforehand comes to consciousness. In the case of the mathematical problem, the answer may be said to be "remembered," in the Platonic sense, having always been there; in the case of the metaphor, the answer, having been obtained recently, may be said to have been discovered; in the case of fiction, the answer (or outcome) to a story may be said to be postponed.[3]

I shall begin with the historical issue. Medieval readers, even eighteenth-century readers, were not infrequently permitted (or were actually enjoined) to take satisfaction in the sufferings of sinners. Not only does Dante's Beatrice remain untouched by the torments of the damned; Dante himself, by the time he has descended to the frozen pit of the Inferno, is quite capable of kicking a sinner in the face and, by way of apology, tearing out his hair (Canto 32). In the next canto he breaks a promise to wipe the frozen tears from Alberigo's eyes, "e cortesia fu in lui esser villano"; this, too, is evidence of true

courtesy, of moral progress. Similarly, we should be in violation of Pope's entire intention in the "Epistle to Dr. Arbuthnot"
if we refused to take pleasure in the verbal pillorying of
Sporus. The pillory and the public execution were, after all,
accepted institutions; had they aroused only revulsion in the
public, they would have disappeared sooner than they did.

It is by no means clear that we, too, have license to enjoy
the sufferings of the wicked. In our ostensibly secular times,
we seem to be preoccupied with redemption to the point
where we cannot admit the presence of unredeemable evil in
others, perhaps for fear of having to acknowledge its presence in ourselves. Yet even the modern reader has a way of
expressing his hostilities toward fictional characters, while
escaping guilt. This process is called interpretation. As a
rule, it is a collusive undertaking between the author and the
reader, in which the protagonist is put through a great deal
of suffering that, in the end, the author and the reader
"understand" to be justified. In "Ward 6," we and Chekhov
emerge triumphant at the end of the action with the verdict:
"Ragin—guilty!" (Kafka, in making causeless guilt the theme
of his novels, is making the very nature of fiction—not only
some hapless protagonist—his subject.) But "The Death of
Ivan Ilyich" does not conform to this pattern, which allows
us to eat our moral cake, and, if we choose, have it too.

Tolstoi cheats the reader of his prey by giving away the
moral right at the beginning of the action. "The story of Ivan
Ilyich's life was of the simplest, most ordinary and most
terrible." When the moral is prematurely revealed, the reader
is on his own. He is not being invited to join in the unfolding
of a little plot against the character. He is left to carry on the
story single-handed, to work out mechanically the brutality
bequeathed to him by the author. Consequently, he will
necessarily sympathize with the character whom he is being
forced to abuse. By accepting the task of continuing this

story about a dreary functionary and social climber who dies from climbing on the furniture, he has exculpated Tolstoi from his authorial guilt and assumed that guilt himself. He has been made good against his own will.

But is it reasonable to accuse Tolstoi of manipulating the reader, just because he declares his moral at the beginning? What is wrong with a moral story, even with one that presents its maxims openly? Shall we discard our fables and parables? Surely not. But fables and parables are not fiction; they consist of materials governed by a moral, rather than of materials from which a moral may or may not be deduced. In a fable, it is perfectly clear on whose side we are supposed to be, and sentimental identification with the fool or the wrong-doer is never open for consideration. Although we may not change our own behavior, we feel free to condemn that of others. But are we expected, or allowed, to enjoy Ivan Ilyich's cancer, or whatever it is that is killing him? Surely not, by ordinary ethical standards. We are, then, caught up in a fiction that is attempting to play by the rules of fable, and the result is a paradox. The reader tries to suppress his sense of contradiction throughout the story rather as Ivan Ilyich tries to suppress the awareness of his pain. But, unlike the pro-tagonist, the reader is never really let off the hook. He is caught within a circle of hostility that keeps recentering him. Not being invited to accept Ivan Ilyich's distress casually, as he would be in a fable, and not finding an accomplice in the author, as he should be able to do in any self-respecting piece of fiction, he begins to feel responsible for what is happening to Ivan Ilyich, little as he may relish the job of putting him through his agony. This is neither fiction nor fable; it is a device for tormenting the reader.[4]

Whether Tolstoi has actually succeeded in exculpating himself, in freeing himself from the various kinds of guilt that seem to be associated with the writing of fiction, is a question that I will return to. But that he deprives the reader of one of his usual options is fairly obvious to me. What, exactly, are these options? This question brings me to the second point in my introduction to this chapter. Reading functions in two ways. We read with both the healthy and the anxious parts of our minds. Our anxiety works itself off in hostility, in satisfaction taken from the suffering of the characters.[5] We experience the lessons of the book as worked out in *them*. Our better or stronger selves, on the other hand, recognize the lessons of the book as directed against ourselves, and face them; it is only to the extent that we allow the accusations against us to escape their aim at the reader and to glance off into fiction that they are absorbed by the other characters. In other words, the moral is effective only when we don't need it. When we do need it, we are too anxious to listen, and use the text to reduce our anxiety by projecting our suffering on others. Perhaps it is only in this last instance that it is even appropriate to talk of "catharsis," the achievement of emotional balance through art, and so on.

A reading of *Lear* offered by Harry Berger in a lecture at Buffalo is a case in point. The lecturer took Edgar to task for his repeated mistreatment of his father in the play, concluding that Edgar is hardly the unqualified hero he is often taken to be. It is certainly true that Edgar, both in his role as Tom o'Bedlam, and as Gloucester's entertainer at the foot of the imaginary cliff, shows little mercy to his helpless father. Surely Gloucester has been punished enough without being subjected to the cruel innuendos of Edgar's "mad" speeches, or even to the equivocal appeal, "Do but look up," after his fall. The question is not whether the shock therapy Edgar applies to his father is justified, appropriate, excessive, or too late to be anything but cruelty. If literature has any lesson, it is that there is never enough punishment. What may be too much for Gloucester is not enough for us. Lear's words to Gloucester are, if anything, even more excruciating than Edgar's. "Dost thou squiny at me? No, do thy worst, blind Cupid; I'll not love."

Edgar and Lear are not torturing a helpless victim; they are jolting a complacent spectator. As we say to ourselves, repeatedly, "Surely Shakespeare has gone too far," we realize, over and over again, that it is not Gloucester who is the prime target of all this cruelty, but ourselves. All of us are guilty, if not of Gloucester's crime, then of some equivalent. Only the ideal (i.e., nonexistent) reader does not need these lessons; or, to put it differently, does not need to read. With our stronger selves, we recognize the remorseless justice of Lear's words; with our weaker selves, we share in the satisfaction of baiting Gloucester. (We then add insult to injury by "interpreting" what has happened as resulting from the character's problems.) The author himself, by implication, must be moralist and sadist at once.[6]

As I have been saying, it is the peculiarity of "The Death of Ivan Ilyich" that Tolstoi attempts to deprive us of a choice of roles, or even entirely of one role. As readers, we expect to be free to identify now with the sufferings of the character, now with his tormentors. In this particular case, we are confined to the first role, with its continuous moral responsibility; we will not, in a state of emotional distress, find the gruesomeness of *this* story less unpalatable, as we should, according to the principle that violence in literature provides an anxious reader with sadistic relief.

Tolstoi, then, manages to put the reader under extraordinary pressure, by declaring a moral while still trying to write not parable but fiction. This sleight-of-hand is carried out under the pretense that the story adds nothing to the moral; in fact, that it is not a story at all. (At times, as in "Hadji Murad," Tolstoi seems to be trying to make his fiction into nothing more than the motto to an emblem: in that story, the thistle.[7])

It annuls its fictionality in order to justify its moral. (I shall return to this subject later.) Perhaps all fiction does indeed aspire to didacticism, or at least tries to gainsay its own fictionality, because of some sort of guilty conscience. But in this case there is something more: there is an attempt to negate the duality of language itself; as G. C. Spivak puts it, to do away with the double structure maintained in allegory and "to deny the inevitably truncated nature of signification. . . ."[8] Tolstoi's effort to erase the boundary between the literal and the moral suppresses a principle of allegory rather than exemplifying it, as precept and example become indistinguishable.

If there is no fiction here, only a moral that has somehow taken on the flesh of experience, there should be no pauses for pleasant relaxation, and no time out to plan an escape. Yet the tale does have one notable digression, if one can call it that: the introductory chapter, which comes after Ivan Ilyich's death. Here everything seems casual, incidental, supplementary: yet all the rest, the "serious" part of the story, is, after all, only flashback. Now Tolstoi obviously had many good reasons for beginning his story after its end: whether he was planning to show the redemption of Piotr Ivanovich, a guest at Ivan Ilyich's funeral, through the example of the latter's wasted life;[9] whether he simply thought he could produce a more dramatic effect by proceeding in reverse rather than in chronological order; or whether the intent was to increase the didactic impact by presenting us with the corpse in the first chapter and by following that display immediately with the explicit statement of the moral. But, in some sense, artists always begin at a point after the ending. The unconscious process of dredging up a meaning of which they are themselves not yet aware occupies a time that is not yet the time of realization, and when the realization is upon them the story is already over. (This is a psychological fact, not a matter of the technical capacity for foresight that some

artists, such as Mozart, possess to an astonishing degree.)
They are at the end before they are at the beginning: or,
rather, they are present at the end, but not at the beginning.
Such an observation has some relevance for this particular
work as well as for the creative process in general, for it is
only, of course, when his own "story" or fiction is over that
Ivan Ilyich himself can emerge into realization (or what I
later intend to call the time of metaphor), the relaxation that
he so urgently needs to learn.

There is a strong philosophical context for this conception
of the artist as one who is always beyond his own position, in
the debates over the nature of the self between Fichte on the
one hand, and Novalis and Schlegel on the other (see below).
As I myself experience the process, the gesture that the
audience loves to follow, the gesture for which we enjoy art,
is that movement in which the player (I tend to think in
terms of improvisation at the keyboard) or the poet becomes
entirely *other:* when he is secure enough to *surrender* what is
being produced, to give it up entirely, to become his own
auditor. Otherwise what one is playing/writing remains stuck,
part of it anxiously held back and part of it making gestures
toward escaping. It is as though one has to be in position to
catch the ball one has himself thrown, to be entirely out of
oneself (not in the usual sense in which the artist is said to
"lose" himself in his work; it's rather that one finds oneself,
greets oneself, from out there, or rather greets whoever or
whatever it is that has sent out that sound, those words). In a
word, people don't "lose themselves" in expression—they
become their *other.* The recognition of this process is itself an
integral part of artistic production. It helps explain, for
instance, why a musical phrase is often repeated in the development of a melody—the composer is trying to appropriate
the creative gesture and assure himself that it is his own. The
repetition permits him to hold his production briefly, and

for that moment to occupy a position intermediate between that of composer and auditor.

But if the artist is the catcher who, out there, receives his own creation, if he is pure audience, he is really, by definition, no longer there when the work is created. He is away from the work in the very instant of its creation, by virtue of, and as a function of, the act of creation: "away" in a positive sense, but still away, free from it. To create is to be free to receive the act of creation, to be free from the act (i.e., struggle) of creation, or, for that matter, free of *any* act — to be free from self as actor.

After all, then, who is left to be grateful for a creative act, but God? The creator himself is no longer there by the time creation has taken place, so he can't really *have* it (in time); the audience (of which he then becomes one) has it in a different, reduced, borrowed sense; only God has it permanently, as the full sound with which it was pronounced. Perhaps this has something to do with the necessity of Ivan Ilyich's being dead before the story can begin.

I have said that people don't "lose themselves" in expression — they become their other. The exact nature of that *"other"* is a recurrent problem in philosophy, but the version of the second self that corresponds most nearly to my own is the one developed by Novalis and Friedrich Schlegel. Fichte had posited a sub-self that detached itself unconsciously from the self to constitute what we then identify as the natural or outside world. This detached self becomes an unconscious, and pervasive, limitation to what one might call the productive self. Self-limitation, being unconscious, is no longer in our own hands. But, Novalis objects, "The possibility of self-limitation is the possibility of all synthesis, of all marvels. And a marvel inaugurated the world."[10] The true self-limiting self is to be respected; and it must be understood, as Schlegel points out, "not as a mere pale reflection of the self, but as a real self; no non-self, but a counter-self, a Thou."[11] The cultivation and recognition of the counter-self in this sense is, for these writers, a characteristic preoccupation of art.

In the case of Ivan Ilyich, too, the development of the second, reversed or redeemed self is clearly as much an aesthetic as a moral process. Ivan Ilyich is not condemned for any egregious evil, but really for lack of imagination; that is what is so "terrible" about his life. He is, in his own way, a kind of *"coeur simple."* If there is nothing special about his experiences, why should he deserve such a special redemption? It is not that the greater sinner is more greatly saved, but the duller sinner: the sinner against the imagination. Ivan Ilyich's struggle at the end of the story toward the recognition of an implicit moral truth that has to reach his consciousness is very much like the struggle to "solve" a metaphor, to find the other term that is lacking but lurking in the first half of a comparison, the half that is waiting to receive it and be redeemed by it.

Problem-solving in general is like metaphor-forming: both depend on the bringing to consciousness of something that is already implicitly there. But the implicit elements of a metaphor are of recent vintage; they cannot be attributed to a kind of absolute memory, as the solutions of abstract or mathematical problems can be. Plato's exiling of metaphor and poetry can be understood as merely a special expression of his devotion to the absolute memory, to problems for which solutions have always existed. It is not so much that metaphors are intrinsically untrustworthy, or misleading, as that they are Johnny-come-latelys to the problem-solving process, because their second term (solution) must always be newly identified for the occasion. They belong, at best, in the province of the immediate memory. They also escape the domain of the true or permanent memory in another way: since their elements cannot be exhaustively described, those elements cannot be clearly identified in the stock of preexistent solutions to all possible problems; lacking a criterion, we would not know whether we had found the absolute "solution," the correct counter-term or vehicle, for a metaphor, even if we had in fact found it. Apropos of Plato, I recall Walter Benjamin's observation that the Platonic dialogues are really the supplanting of one art form by another, not the rejection of art as such: the usurpation of tragedy's role by what Benjamin calls *Trauerspiel,* literally, "the sadness-game."[12] Although Benjamin associates *Trauerspiel* intimately with the allegorical mode in its displacement of myth, I am inclined to think of metaphor as the primary target of the Platonic strategy; the goal of its replacement by allegory would be to confine art to a form in which there are only preexistent, *remembered* answers. Benjamin also points out the inherent sadism in the allegorical mode, with its imposition of meaning on a helpless, deteriorated world that has no voice of its own; while I relate fiction, with its special invitation to interpret, to the sadistic or "bad" reader. (Both allegory and fiction are, then, in some sense "bad.")

How much time does it take to think of the answer to an abstract problem? Obviously, there is something wrong with the question when put in these terms: one is tempted to answer, with Grace Paley, that time is only what made a monkey of us all. But in fact there is a difference in the time involved in the two (abstract and metaphoric) processes. In the case of the metaphor, the clock starts running from the moment the uneasiness is felt that announces that a metaphor is coming or is struggling for release, for both terms of the metaphor are there from the beginning (one conscious, the other unconscious). In the case of the abstract or the physical problem, there may be any number of false starts, in which none of the elements of the eventual solution is present; and when the answer is found, it has no recent history: it is simply here, now. The time of metaphor is a simultaneity of the conscious and the unconscious stretched over actual historical time, brief as it may be; the time of abstraction is a nontime, in which a solution that has always been there is discovered, or "recognized," instantaneously, after a period of exploration that may have taken minutes or millennia.

These two forms of time have their counterparts—I am inclined to say, their negative counterparts—in fiction and allegory, respectively. I have always wondered how Freud thought it possible to distinguish information about ourselves that we have, but suppress, from information about ourselves that we have not found the means to articulate. It may take a long while for someone to realize that he is uncomfortable because he is cold, or because he is hot; and the threshold of realization is not crossed without some effort, even in simple cases such as these. There is very little about ourselves that comes to consciousness automatically.[13] In any case, I guess that the first or "Freudian" instance—that in which we do know something more or less unconsciously, but do not allow it to reach the threshold of recognition—is roughly the equivalent of fictional time. It is a time of postponement, a time of delayed awareness that usually ends in a painful reckoning. It is a time of the refusal of awakening, and therefore the opposite of metaphor, which is an effort to bring latent knowledge to the surface. Reasoning along analogous lines, we can see allegory dealing with the same materials as what we may, broadly speaking, call science: namely, the discovery in the known of that which was not yet known, but turns out to be a necessary (i.e., preexistent) fact. The difference is that it is only after it has thrown itself entirely into the present, solved a present problem, that science would claim to have reached into the storehouse of preexistent truths, whereas allegory carries its bag of touchstones with it. Although it claims to work from permanent truths, it is

deeply dependent on history.[14] And where science will risk
time, an indefinite amount of real time, to reach the point at
which it makes contact with truth, allegory only manufac-
tures time, creates the appearance of a time of exploration,
whereas it in fact artificially maintains a fixed distance between
its illustrations and the axioms that will eventually account
for them. "The intention of allegory is so opposed to that
which seeks the truth . . . " (Benjamin, *Ursprung,* p. 403). Fiction pretends not to know anything: allegory claims to know
too much. Like fiction, it prevents or postpones the achievement of knowledge.

Of course, this diatribe against allegory is largely heuristic,
and deliberately exaggerated; besides, the science-allegory
axis serves to balance my exposition but is not material to my
case, as the metaphor-fiction combination is. Tolstoi's attitude toward metaphor in his story is complex, and serves to
complicate further the questions of fiction and of morality
with which he is also dealing. On the one hand, the world is
not "supportive," as it is supposed to be in normal fictional
metaphors: it will not cater to or illustrate our illusions, nor
will it justify the pathetic fallacy. The furniture lets Ivan
Ilyich down, quite literally: he falls, and sustains the injury
that eventually kills him, while hanging a curtain in the
house he has bought. When he gets sick, he cannot even rest
his legs on a chair, but has to have the human support of the
servant Gerassim's shoulders. In one sense, Tolstoi has eliminated metaphor, the notion that the world is our footstool, a
mere illustration of our desires, waiting to corroborate our
notions of ourselves.[15] At the same time, as author he exploits
the very metaphors that he refuses to let Ivan Ilyich fall back
upon: the furniture may not lend itself to the protagonist's
purposes, but it certainly serves Tolstoi in an animated way,
first teaching his hero a pointed lesson, and then coming
back to mock and tease the funeral guests in a scene that

reminds one irresistibly of *Alice*. A low pouffe with broken springs keeps Piotr Ivanovich on edge throughout the interview with the widow, whose lace fichu has on the way to their tête-à-tête been snagged by the carved edge of the table. These may not be confirmations of the character's purposes, but they are surely confirmations of Tolstoi's authorial purposes, which happen to be in conflict with those of his characters.

What is more, Ivan Ilyich himself is condemned for not having learned to use metaphors, for borrowing the whole of his life, including his ideas of aesthetic decoration, from other bureaucrats who have gone before him. But his corpse, his redeemed body, for all its new-found dignity, seems to be the impresario of the furniture in the funeral scene, choreographing the dance of the pouffe, the table, the ashtray. This is the world of newly released metaphor, the freshly discovered, relaxed, humorous world of the imagination, where the tables can be turned on the people, the illustrations can come alive. "Alice-mutton: mutton-Alice." Ivan Ilyich has redeemed his world—metaphorized it—made it poetic; he has, at considerable cost, become an artist. This process perhaps began with his abandonment of others' language, in the merging of his words into a single sustained "oo," the note of pain. The virtuoso of the courtroom has already achieved a *sostenuto* beyond the reach of any trained vocalist.

But if we grant that Ivan Ilyich has finally gained entrance to the world of metaphor, does it follow that he is also free to follow fiction? And if metaphor is licit, but fiction is not, what is Tolstoi doing writing fiction? Does he envision one form of salvation for his character, another for himself? Or is Tolstoi perhaps not writing fiction? Certainly the homology between the structure of Ivan Ilyich's former life and narrative structure as such, both processes of postponement, forces itself on our attention. To repeat: in a number of ways,

Tolstoi seems to obscure the fact that he is writing fiction, almost as though it were something that made him uneasy. In fact, much of the strenuousness of the story derives from the attempt to suppress our awareness that we are dealing with fiction. Instead of moving through a series of changes that leads to an unforeseeable conclusion, Ivan Ilyich's biography is made of some homogeneous material that passes through a series of fixed roles or stations, as if carried on a conveyor belt. The life itself makes no progress, and at its end another life will take its place in the series, with nothing but a change of name. At the conclusion of the story the series goes into reverse, but it is the same series: "What had happened to him was what had sometimes happened to him in a railway-carriage, when you think you are going forwards, but you are really going backwards. . . . "

Nothing really happens, then. Even the event that kills Ivan Ilyich, the knock in the side while he is hanging curtains, is a nonevent; the organ that has been injured is a nonorgan, an appendix, or at most a floating kidney. Tolstoi would have us believe that he himself has not made anything go from A to B, that no fiction (as defined by temporality) has been generated. The not-writing of the story, then, has composed the story, has provided the pretext for producing sixty pages of prose. Has Ivan Ilyich been deprived of a substantial identity just so that Tolstoi should be able to make it seem that he is not producing fiction?

Ivan Ilyich's life is a lie, but so is every story a lie. There is always a danger that the story will recommence: it has already gone on too long. "Stimulate the action of one organ, check the activity of another—absorption ensues, and everything will come right." The words, the lies, will be absorbed, and life, and fiction, resume their pernicious course.

Still, there the story is, and it must proceed somehow. The story's force is generated from the suppression of exteriority by morality: the inside, the moral, is made more external than the action. But if Tolstoi has already found the inside, knows the interpretation, why keep on with the story? That is another source of its strenuousness: the morality and the life have to coexist. Under these conditions there can be no progress. Temporality has been almost completely suppressed, and with it fiction. But the suppression of fiction by morality creates an atmosphere of tension or violence that is itself a distillation of the fictional atmosphere, as though the central problem or contradiction of fiction had been addressed in this story: fiction exists in its own denial.

There is no need to follow the obvious extrapolations of this argument through Tolstoi's biography; clearly, like many another fiction writer, he lived this paradox, and there is no object in making belles-lettres out of his sufferings. What I would like to do is collect and summarize my observations to this point, to see where all of this is going, and then decide whether my conclusions can be brought into relation with the original pattern I had in mind, of the covertly moral, the explicitly moral, and the anti-moral story.

I began with one historical point (that there have been changes in didacticism during the past two centuries) and three structural ones. In terms of this story, what does each of the last three contribute? First, if there is a bad reader and a good reader, the story will presumably try to get rid of the bad reader. Second, if there is a good, or generous, writer and a bad, anxious, or possessive writer, it will try to get rid of the bad writer. Third, if allegory and fiction represent negative alternatives to science and metaphor (and the science-allegory combination does not enter into the question), it will try to get rid of fiction.

There is, in fact, a purging of fiction by both author and protagonist in the story, and an arrival at another plane, where they can frolic in the fields of metaphor. (The salva-

tion of Ivan Ilyich, I have said, is the curing of his dullness.)
There is also a purging of a first, bad writer; of the writer
who hangs on, who never lets go of his own words, so that he
is never sufficiently far from them to know whether they are
good or bad: and an achievement of the end-stopped form,
and the reversal I have spoken of, with the author showing
up at the beginning, before his story has started, to receive
his story. Finally, there is a purging of the bad reader by the
purging of the reader: that is, the reader is eliminated
altogether; he is made into the writer. This is quite a different achievement from that of, say, *King Lear,* where the good
reader in each of us is focused so relentlessly by Shakespeare's
castigation of characters with whom we identify that the bad
reader doesn't have a chance to get into motion. What follows
from the manipulation of the reader's role in "The Death of
Ivan Ilyich" is a principled violation of normal fictional and
dramatic practices, or of what might be called the Girardian
pattern, which gives the bad reader a chance to have his turn
in the end. There are, of course, other works that in their
own way do not permit this convenient outcome, that disap-
point the reader awaiting his victim: *Hamlet* ("The rest is
silence"), Dostoievski's *The Double* (the rest is babble).

In a deeper sense than the Derridean, all we are ever
doing is reading or writing.[16] When we are not contesting
death (writing), we are playing with it (reading). Chekhov's
"Ward 6" is about readers: implicitly, about writers. It is a
much more conventional story, in technique and structure,
than "The Death of Ivan Ilyich," inasmuch as it leaves it up
to the reader to specify the moral, and the author's relation
to that moral; in fact, there could conceivably be some controversy about what the moral is, and about the author's attitude
toward it, whatever it may be. To me it seems simple: don't
read. The implication of that moral also seems inescapable
to me: don't write. But the story has been written, and its

narrator even appears within it, in the first person. Its existence contradicts its message. At the very outset, in the vestibule to the asylum, there is a stinking heap of discarded clothing: the costumes or fictional trappings of the real body. And the building is surrounded by burdocks, nettles, spikes. Still, we are challenged to enter; we get past, climb over, and are in. But in where? In the real world, or in fiction?

The principal inmate of ward 6, Gromov, gave up reading when he finally assumed responsibility for his guilt about being a court bailiff, and went mad. Appropriately enough, his madness took the form of persecution mania. As an arm of the law, he had intruded injuriously into the lives of others. Reading, the most passive form of escape (we are informed that he read lying down whenever he could) had been his principal means of avoiding moral action: whether action for the necessary reform of an oppressive society, or simply the action of resigning his job. When Ragin, the kindly, ne'er-do-well hospital doctor, comes to visit him in the asylum, Gromov feels that he in turn is being intruded upon, as he had once intruded on others. Ragin, he feels, is nothing better than a spy. "A spy or a doctor who's been sent to test me — it's all the same." But espionage multiplies in the story. Soon Ragin in turn is being spied upon by his assistant (who covets Ragin's job) for spending hours conversing with a madman. Like Gromov, Ragin has preferred to avoid the necessities and difficulties of life, whether those involving action on behalf of others or those requiring self-defense; it is easier for him to read, or to hold long arguments with Gromov, contending that happiness and unhappiness are much alike. Unable to oppose the predatory characters who surround him, Ragin is eventually made to face an investigative commission, gradually loses his social and professional standing, and, after a single brief outburst of anger, is in turn committed to the institution that he had served. In the end, as reality forces its way up to his doorstep, Ragin too, like Gromov, abandons his cherished reading. Finally, when it dawns on him that he has become just one more defenseless inmate of the asylum, to be beaten and brutalized at will, he breaks down and suffers a stroke. The nighttime ambience of the asylum, dominated by the cold moon, surrounds his death, and in the last scene of the story his corpse lies with its eyes open to the light. Some sort of vision, at least, has been attained in the end.

Before that conclusion, there seems to be a constant reaching toward an unavailable clarity. One form taken by that reaching is espionage, or the suspicion of espionage. Gromov begins as an investigator, who later feels that he is being spied upon by Ragin; Ragin is spied upon by his assistant, Khobotov. But, one might fairly ask, why all this investigation? What is there, really, to spy upon? Though I may be accused of invoking an outmoded principle, I will say it is interpretation that is spying on interpretation: interpretation itself, that debilitating act, the negative energy of which gets fed back into and, indeed, generates the story. Tolstoi had blocked the possibility of interpretation by announcing his moral at the beginning. But here, Ragin and Gromov in their long philosophical conversations are whipping up an interpretation that is also a story. This story that they are composing aloud replaces the ones that they had been reading silently, as, in Chekhov's words, a song replaces a score. Yet, in the course of these very conversations, Gromov is teaching Ragin that even this story or song won't work; and that lesson is itself the content of the story called "Ward 6." With increasing malevolence, Gromov rejects Ragin's pseudo-stoical or Tolstoian philosophizing; a jail is not the same as a garden, even for the wisest man; these are cowardly fantasies. Gromov won't let that story rest as a story. He insists that life intrude upon it. In one sense it does, but in another, obviously, it can't. After all, what he gets in the end is not life, but Chekhov's story. He has summoned up a story to surround life, finally: life, which has been saying, "Tell us no stories."

But short of this final step—which may invalidate the whole procedure—"Ward 6" does reject reading and fictionalizing. Why? Because stories can permit an avoidance of the self and of self-recognition. They enable us to project oneself on a text without realizing that what one sees there is oneself. They enable one to remain blind while staring oneself in the face. They are a mirror that prevents us from seeing ourselves.

What is behind a work is ourselves. We should thank Tolstoi for preserving us, for all our frantic searching, from looking behind "The Death of Ivan Ilyich," because all we could find there would be our unrecognizable selves. Ivan Ilyich may find himself, but no reader of fiction can be expected to do the same. What looks like a truth ripped from behind a text turns out to be just one's own patch sewn on beside it. A text that allows us to interpret it, neither window nor mirror, rather like stained glass (to move toward the imagery of "St. Julian"), strikes us blind: it puts us in the idiot's position of being unable to recognize our own reflection, and at the same time effectively prevents us from looking into a real mirror.

A book, then, like an avuncular lover, or (for a man) like a woman, can be a diversion from oneself that enables one to see oneself without having to recognize oneself, for each of us is "Tourmenté de s'aimer, tourmenté de se voir" ("tormented by loving himself, tormented by seeing himself"—Alfred de Vigny, "La Maison du berger"). The animals work in this way for Flaubert's Julian: like the sadistic reader, the interpreter, he keeps "hunting" for something in them, refusing to recognize their pain as his own. When the animals cease to function as a text for Julian, when his unrecognized parents are dead, when all of Julian's diversionary selves (women or "uncles," so to speak) have been taken away from him, when even the inmost imaginary interlocutor, our questioner and audience, our deepest diversionary text of all, has died for lack of subject matter for dialogue, Julian must at last look straight at himself in the well; and his reflection is his father's image. There is no further point in blinding himself; he can now recognize both his father and himself.

One reason why "The Legend of St. Julian the Hospitaler" is a special story is that we are in fact spared the sense of inner dialogue: we do not have the feeling that we are eavesdropping on a conversation that we are really meant to overhear. Julian seems genuinely indifferent to the reader's presence. Ivan Ilyich, on the other hand, keeps up the audible argument with himself to the very end; so does Ragin, until the last scene, where his eyes are opened in the moonlight, for he has seen himself at last, as Julian had seen himself in the well; but by that point Ragin is dead.

To repeat: "Ward 6" rejects stories, negates the idea of a "content" to be discovered in a story, negates the preservability of an interpretation (which constitutes a kind of external soul for the reader). It turns one back on oneself, as Gromov turns Ragin pitilessly toward the "real." The real is not there in order to be interpreted—that is, as something in which to find, yet not find, ourselves. The real is not the content of any story. "Ward 6" extrudes, repudiates its own content. Ragin dies and the story is written. He knows himself. Like Ivan Ilyich in his own way, Ragin has been forced from false fantasy into true imagination, which was long since defined by Shelley as the ability to experience another person's suffering. His eyes are kept open even after death, to see what he had refused to see before. The moonlight illuminates his dead vision, and deprives us of the opacity that permits the interpretive delusion. Everything is clear, everything is in black and white at last; nothing is "colored."

Ragin has stopped talking. "I'm not going to answer. . . . It's all the same." Ivan Ilyich: "Let it go. . . . " A story can only be the undoing of a story.

But is "Ward 6" just the fulfillment of a Girardian pattern, in which the author and the protagonist simultaneously abandon fictional models and converge in death, while, at the same time, contradictorily enough, the author and the reader join in condemnation of the protagonist? In the silence with which the story ends there is something that goes beyond both the delusion produced by criticizing others and the self-comfort produced by criticizing oneself. The story steps into the clear: it does not pretend that it has anywhere farther to go. Although initially understood as "clarification," the moonlight in which Ragin's corpse is seen is finally no habitat for either real experiences or fiction. It is one step beyond the story, beyond psychology, especially beyond the psychology of clandestine treaties between readers and writers.

Where does "The Legend of St. Julian the Hospitaler" stand with respect to all of this? I have already written on this story, in which the bloodthirsty hunter of animals ends by killing his parents, does penance, and is taken to heaven by the leper Christ; and I shall not be able to avoid some repetition. Besides, there is the problem that the "Legend" is not exactly fiction. In any case, Julian has avoided confrontation with his father, because that would imply the immediate recognition of himself. He has instead searched the bodies of the animals for some interiority, for some secret that he is desperate not to find. As long as he can keep hunting, he can keep himself at arm's length, hidden behind the screen of animals. The animals are a baffle for Julian, as his job is for Ivan Ilyich, as philosophizing about stoicism is for Ragin. When Julian must stop hunting, when he no longer has a text behind which to hide himself, he must confront himself (his father) directly in the well. He has had Flaubert's cure—

stop interpreting. Don't look behind things, that is, hide behind things; face yourself, in the only dimension in which you exist. *"Nur in der Erfahrung ist Wahrheit."* ("Truth is found only in experience"—Kant, *Prolegomena to any Future Metaphysics,* Supplement.)

"St. Julian" is a kind of mirror of "Ivan Ilyich," of which "Ward 6" is in turn a kind of sidelong reflection. Both "St. Julian" and "Ivan Ilyich" try to suppress interiority, but by opposite means. It is the total explicitness of "Ivan Ilyich" that is such an offense. It bars interiority, by bringing everything to the surface, yet makes that interior—that is, morality, a "moral"—its whole explicit content. "St. Julian," on the contrary, is a story that labors to avoid its own moral, the revelation of its interiority. The demand that it enforces is not "be good," but "don't try to explain yourself." The stained glass is a signal, like Tolstoi's explicit moralizing at the beginning of his story, warning us that we are not to interpret. (In this sense, they both function, *mutatis mutandis,* like the "Notice" at the beginning of *Huckleberry Finn.*) Stained glass is not meant to be seen through; we should not expect the transparency that is offered, if only as an afterthought to life, in "Ward 6." The whole problem of Flaubert's tale is how the sweetness of a moral can struggle to the surface through the layer of silence that is imposed on the story by the speechless opacity of the stained glass. No image ever speaks for itself. Concepts code themselves spontaneously into images, but images do not factor themselves out into concepts. Energy is required to puncture the membrane between image and language. And in the case of "St. Julian," the moral ("Atone!") is such a cliché that one does not even think of articulating it: it can pass entirely unnoticed; Tolstoi's savage indignation would seem ridiculously out of place here. Instead of the surface of the story's being occupied by a moral, it is occupied by a refusal of expressiveness, by the repudiation not only of any possible stated moral but of all descriptions of subjectivity. To quote my own rather portentous commentary, "Julien has no one to talk to: neither the reader, the author, nor even anyone in the story, since he has been deprived of the purpose of speech, and therefore of the right to speak, first by his destiny's having been entirely preordained for him, and then by the events that fulfilled that destiny. Flaubert must say everything for him. He himself lives and dies in a place where speech is nothing; and because he does, because he has preserved the silent language, the story can radiate and glow when his life is finished, touching even the hallowed places where the mute saints hold vigil."[17]

"St. Julian" is, after all, a religious tale, even if it is so only in a purely moral sense; whereas the other two are not religious stories. The light that replaces death for Ivan Ilyich and the moonlight that falls on the eyes of Ragin illuminate another vision. They still need illumination, need to have things thrown open; Julian seeks no clarification. What happens to him, including his assumption, simply happens.

The refusal of interpretation that is criticism that is fiction, a refusal achieved by main force in "Ivan Ilyich" and by the deliberate cultivation of a kind of ignorance in "St. Julian," occurs more obliquely in "Ward 6," and does that through the action rather than by the author's announcing his editorial position. "Ivan Ilyich" makes the inside (the moral) the outside; "St. Julian" insists that there is no inside, only an outside; "Ward 6" carries its moral, its interior, off to one side, so to speak. Mainly we are aware of the fence surrounding the asylum, of the burdocks and the nettles, ending up with their spines in our heart. But Ragin is just as guilty of a failure of sympathy as Ivan Ilyich or Julian had been, is punished as decisively, and is illuminated as fully in the end. To contrast the two fictions (the legend has been dealt with): Tolstoi assumes the responsibility for the moral beforehand, whereas Chekhov leaves the moral embedded in the story: the author does not seize the nettle himself. Perhaps both are equally oblique: Tolstoi distracts us from his authorial maneuvering by trumpeting his moral; Chekhov blinds us by passing us on to the moonlight. What follows such moonlight? At best, someone else's dawn.[18]

Three knocks at the door of truth. Good thing that it never quite opens. These are, after all, just stories: moonlight, light, and Christ occupy the entrance and elide the confrontation. If we really met ourselves on the threshold, there would be no more to say. As for our redeemed selves, it is not literature that will reveal them to us. That is for life to do, at its best. We may, then, choose to read only in the right way; if we choose to read at all.

4

Yiddish Poetry of the Holocaust

(For Marvin)

MAY ONE, THEN, READ? AND SHOULD ONE WRITE? THIS question returns with an exponential increase in urgency when one moves from the problems of the individual to the public fact of political murder. If we admit that it was a reasonable question to ask about stories such as "Ivan Ilyich," "Ward 6," or "Saint Julian," what, then, are we to say, or ask, about the literature of the Holocaust? Here, that question, which was only one of the many one might pose concerning literature, immediately becomes the central question, almost the only one worth raising, and I shall necessarily recur to it more than once during the course of this chapter.

The subject I am going to deal with points toward ultimates, although it is undoubtedly made more ordinary by the limited kind of authority that I can bring to it. Having had no personal experience of the Holocaust, I cannot share the condition and the ideas of its victims, or of those who wrote of it at first hand. In an intermediate status, I share the

79

language of its events, which is a limited sharing: a symbol can refer to a number, an object, or an emotion (I am not sure where an idea fits into all of this), but one can depend on it only in the first two cases. In any event, the principal distinction of the following chapter, falling as it does amid an avalanche of publications on the Holocaust, lies in its specific topic, Yiddish poetry, which is still not well enough known:

I will allow myself only two general questions on the Holocaust, questions arising, perhaps, from an insufficient understanding of the subject. Both have occurred to me in connection with the reading of Viktor Shklovsky's memoirs, especially *A Sentimental Journey*. Why was it that the Russian civil wars, aggravated by the imperialist adventure in Persia during the Revolution, witnessed an immense outpouring of intellectual effort, not only in creative forms, but in the most abstruse scholarly modes?

To be sure, as Jean Améry has made clear,[1] there is a quantum leap from the conditions Shklovsky describes, to the boxcars packed with living people left to rot in the heat, or organized in death routines by the camps; but wholesale callousness and joy in others' suffering are surely not new under the sun. It is hard to see how the world of chaotic brutality described by Shklovsky, very little of it ordered by social idealism of any kind and all of it saturated in anti-Semitism, could have provided an environment so rich in nurturing qualities as to account for people's working feverishly at treatises on linguistic and literary theory while starving and freezing in cellars, with bombs bursting everywhere. Evidently some kinds of dehumanizing experience can intensify the significance of intellectual values instead of destroying them.

But second, a question that one scarcely dare ask: are the murderers redeemable?

That is to say — are *we* redeemable? And what would we be like if we were redeemed? The world has to get along with us as we are, and with itself as it is; and, the way it is, the worst and the best have much in common: their desire for survival, their sexual desires, their desire for power, their desire for novelty — and a thousand other desires that cannot be evaluated in terms of good and bad, but that simply are — these they share.

As for the impossibility of making substantial connections between ordinary experiences and the experiences of the Holocaust, that is undoubtedly true in most respects; still, there are some ordinary experiences that can also lead toward the "insight that discredits all illusions, including the illusion of hope. . . . "[2] The values of humanity, of the intellect, of creativity (which is itself largely just an understanding of death) cannot be abolished because they come along with human limitations. If we put too much hope in them, too much emphasis on them, then indeed we may feel them to be subject to abolition; but mankind is not so fragile as its values are. From the common soil of humanity something vital still grows. It is no accident that the artist in Tolstoy found this a congenial doctrine; for all his didacticism, he sees to it that the most substantial character to emerge from "Ivan Ilyich" will be, not the converted husband, but the unconvertible wife, who remains untouched by the categories of both sin and sainthood.

Perhaps for similar reasons some part of the worst villain shares in humanity, through his own need; indeed, the sheer abundance of villains guarantees this fact: torture and massacre have again become the very staple of the political process. Of course, in practice, who cares whether something human can be unearthed in all these people; it doesn't matter: let the victim make the law and impose the penalty. But at some other, transhistorical level, the level at which the need to think about humanity is either maintained or abandoned, dare we surmise, for a moment, that the worst still need the best? In a time when political torture is once more the universal rule rather than the exception, I venture to quote a gruesome anecdote from Shklovsky.

The man is being tortured. All around him is only the cold, hard wood of the rack; but the hands of the executioner or his assistant, though hard, are warm and human.

And the man on the rack rubs his cheek against those warm hands which hold him to inflict the torture.[3]

Maybe there is still some way to read that contact, together with the contract it implies, backward.

From what position can I take up a position to write about Jews, being a Jew? Only from a position of weakness, acknowledged weakness, in which all the arrogance of authorial posturing is sapped in advance. For once, the question of the stance of authorship (p. xii above), does not arise. I am not writing at anyone, from any vantage point. If I draw any strength, it must be from the ground of weakness, from the negation of strength. Perhaps there is no middle ground between the two positions. Perhaps we fool ourselves if we think there is some reasonable alternative to being either an Auschwitz guard or an inmate of Auschwitz; perhaps one has to be one or the other.

I have not been in, or near, Auschwitz or any part of the Holocaust. I do not say this in the challenging tone of a Leivick:

> I wasn't at Treblinka,
> Nor was I in Maidanek,
> But I stand on their doorstep,
> I wait on their porch.
> Doorstep—God's great world,
> With the other for a verandah. . . .
>   "A Treblinka-Candidate"

I present it as plain information. I haven't watched children being murdered. I have seen plenty of anti-Semitism; but experiences in my life that have nothing to do with anti-Semitism have taught me more about the Holocaust, and brought me closer to the state of mind of its survivors, than any of the brushes with the relatively innocuous forms of Jew-hatred that I have personally endured.

> In my lifetime I have had
> More than one invitation
> To drown in the inquisitor's delight. . . .
>   Ibid.

Being stoned in the streets of Quebec villages, being ready for "maudit juif" at every moment as a fresh shock, being afraid to walk back from school because the Gentile boys would attack me on my way home, reading signs in public places ranging from the polite "Gentiles only" to "No Jews or dogs allowed"—all this is trivial. It lines one up as a Jew, but so do much subtler and completely invisible hints. You can't compare it with facing the professional exterminators; I haven't even the capacity for self-projection to imagine what that would be like.

So much for the Holocaust and its recent revivals—I know nothing of it beyond what I read. But I suppose I know something of it in other ways. I know it through weaknesses in myself, Jewish weaknesses, pre-Holocaust weaknesses, that decreed limitations in my life and decided what I can and cannot do, where my impulses can and cannot lead me; and I know something of it through Yiddish literature, which talks a lot about it, because my mother, Ida Maze, was a Yiddish poet. She began to write about a year after she had lost a child.

It is hardly a novelty to say that the essential Jewish experience is the experience of loss, but it is a fact that is necessary to remember, in order to set Holocaust literature in the perspective of Jewish literature previous to that time. Jewish experience has always been a confrontation with loss, from Genesis on; it is only a question of when the feeling of loss will infiltrate one's life, get its grip on one; then one has had one's "churbn," one's Holocaust. The earthly Paradise, Canaan, the first Temple, the second Temple, Spain with its Golden Age, the Yiddish renaissance in Poland—a Jew is not ripe until the Holocaust has come home to him, until the historical experience has confirmed itself through contemporary political or personal trauma. Maybe that is why Freud was so preoccupied with the doubleness of trauma, with its submerging and reemerging before it takes hold: the colors don't show up in Jewish historical experience until watered with private tears.

It is also no news that Jews are preoccupied with children; if their own future is threatened, that of their child may surely be precarious. God may (God forbid!) even demand the sacrifice of Isaac. Bad enough that a sheep has to be sacrificed. The key to the Holocaust is the death of the child. Where do we go from there? For the arrest is complete—more than an arrest, a reversal of movement. Life turns back on itself, starts to run backward. Time, which is trauma, at last comes into its own; it no longer has to run away, or try to catch up with anything. It simply spreads over everything. Consider this poem:

> So today's your birthday, child;
>   And it's such a quiet day, my child
>   And it's such a pale day, my child!
> Over the quiet day

Over the pale day
Ravens hover round,
Sixteen sable ravens in a ring—
Sixteen of your years, my child,
Caught in a black wing.

So I am the mother
Of a sixteen-year-old son!
With whom can one share such a joy—
With the snow on your grave,
With the still day,
With the pale day?
—Such a joy!

                              Ida Maze
                         (Ida Massey)

The anxiety about children comes through in almost every Yiddish cradlesong:

Sleep my child,
For a little while,
In your little cradle
In your pretty cradle
I am beside you
And I will tell you
A pretty little tale.

What can the matter be?
Not yet asleep is she!
Midnight is nigh
If it were not late night
I would make a light
And say a spell against the evil eye.

No doubt have I:
It is the evil eye. . . .

                    Traditional

All that fear is fulfilled, more than fulfilled, in the Holocaust.

City without Children

Your playthings, my child, hold them dear
So much smaller than you though they be
And at night, when the fire goes out
Deck them with the stars of the tree.

Let the little golden horse nibble
The cloudy sweetness of grass
And put big boots on the boy
When the sea-eagle blows his blast.

Put her panama hat on your doll,
And in her hand a bell,
For not one of them has a mother,
And they cry out to God at the wall.

Love them, your little princesses—
I remember a day so mild;
Seven lanes full of dolls
But the streets without a child.

A. Sutzkever[4]

To the Child

Whether because of hunger
Or great love—
And your mother is my witness—
I wanted to swallow you, my child

When I felt your little body cool
Between my fingers
As if I were pressing
A warm glass of tea,
Feeling it go cold.

For you are no stranger, not a guest.
On our earth one doesn't give birth to
a second one—
One gives birth to oneself, to a ring,
And the rings join in a chain.
Child of mine,
Known in words as: love,
And not in words, as love itself,
Kernel of my dreams,
Hidden Third,
Who gathered, drove together
From the secret corners of the world.
Like an invisible storm
Two, to create, to warm—

Why have you darkened creation
By shutting your eyes,
Left me a beggar outside,
With the world of snow
You cast aside?

No cradle gave you joy;
(In every motion of a cradle
Hides the rhythm of the stars;)
The sun could shatter like glass
For you have never set eyes on it.
A drop of poison scalded out your faith;
You thought it
Warm, sweet milk.

I wanted to swallow you, my child,
In order to know the taste of my hoped-for future.
Perhaps you will blossom again
In my flowering
But I am not worthy to be your grave;
So I will make a gift of you
To the snow that calls,
To the snow—my first joy,
And you will sink
Like a sliver of sunset
Into its depths.
Carry my greetings
To the frozen grass.

A. Sutzkever (Vilna Ghetto, 18 January 1943.
The Nazis poisoned the child.)

What more natural than to go on from children to mothers
—Yiddish is, after all, Mame-Loshn ("Mother's language").
The first poem I quoted is a lament of a mother for her son;
this is a lament of a son for his mother. "My Mother," by
Sutzkever, presents the mother-son relationship in a harsher
light than usual. But for a child one must not cry; for a
mother one may. It has to be an easier sorrow.

It is a Friday night, and cooing can be heard from the attic.
The author's mother sits reading her Siddur by moonlight;
her prayers feed the doves like warm bread.

"In each of your wrinkles my life lies in hiding," says her
son, who sleeps nearby; "her hand dreams on my brow."

But the dream snaps. "Stop fooling me, mother: I know
you are dead." Three scarlet roses blaze in her heart: what,
or whom, do they stand for? The question remains unan-
swered; something else is happening:

Clash, you cymbals,
Rouse joyous laughter, drown out a scream;
In the fields they are hunting
My naked mother,
Her body in mirrors of snow like a beam.

She is hurrying somewhere—where, where? And she catches
sight of him just as the rifles ring out. But while they were
hunting his mother, where in fact was he?

With my carcass in a dog-kennel hid,
With dog-joy turned on myself in hate,
On lips a leech, a spider in ear,
I watched and spied through a crack over there
Where under the moon, that mirrored the night,
The wind played with the snow in flight,
And each pearl of snow with its shadow dark:
It gave me such joy, I wanted to bark.

(Cf. Piotr Rawicz, BLOOD FROM THE SKY: "How can you tell
Man?" "By the fact that he can bark.")
He searches for his mother's house, finds her room. A
glass of tea still stands on the table. He fills the guttering
lamp with his blood. In place of his mother, he finds a torn
nightshirt; in embarrassment, he presses it to his heart.

Like the shirt full of holes my days fall apart;
Its hem is a blade that saws through my heart.

Into your shirt I creep, out of my clothes,
As if into myself; it lies naked, exposed;

No longer your shirt, it's your shimmering
skin,
It's the shivering, leftover death you are in.

You speak to me
So plain, so true:
It's a sin, my child,
Don't act so wild:
To our parting bow
As what is due.
Where you are
There am I too
As the plum-tree's pit
Has all of it
And the leaves and the bird
And its nest and the rest.

The ease with which I have fallen into a kind of discursive
mode that would never occur to me if I were dealing with
another literature says something about Yiddish poetry. I am
stringing together poems on thematic lines, summarizing,
paraphrasing, surrendering to the mood—what sort of technique is this, after the days of critical "deconstruction?" I
hear nothing of this sort from the Tartu school, the Konstanz
school, the Frankfurt school, the Vincennes school. I myself
slip into the naiveté of the genre I am talking about. To put it
simply, there is not much sophisticated Yiddish poetry. That
doesn't mean that one can't talk about it in a sophisticated
way; but it takes the kind of effort one has to make to talk
about, say, Lermontov's poetry in that way. One must remember that there has never been, to my knowledge, a full-scale
university in which the principal language of instruction was
Yiddish; nor is there, to my knowledge, a major philosopher
who wrote in Yiddish. The literary practitioners of the lan-

guage were middle people; not fully educated (or they wouldn't be Yiddish writers, with very few exceptions—e.g., Dubnov) and yet not of the Folk; but self-educated people, aspirants to middlebrow sophistication, some of them immensely well read, but without models of complexity in their own language, without an elaborate stylistic tradition of their own to refine.

Typically, if they read English, they would know their Yeats but not their Pound; if French, their Verlaine but not their Mallarmé; if German, their early but not their late Rilke. Many of them were steeped in classical Russian literature, but were too young at the time they left eastern Europe to have experienced much of the impact of experimentalism from writers such as Biely, or to be aware of Russian formalism as a critical corpus; and it must be remembered that Russian poetry was, until quite recently, almost mechanically regular, especially in its meters, by Western standards. Pushkin was, after all, under the influence of pseudo-classicists such as Parny, and Pushkin set the standard for Russian poetry. So, on the whole, Yiddish poetry is written in rhyme, or in forms of free verse no more daring than its nineteenth-century models; and it tends to be explicit, thematically oriented, and readily paraphrased. Its depth, when it has it, is likely to be a depth of texture rather than of ideas; it does not frequently baffle one with the intricacy of its thought. Of course, I should not deliver myself of such generalizations; my knowledge of Yiddish literature is limited, and much that I am saying about it may well be wrong.

Certainly, there are perplexing passages in Sutzkever's "Green Aquarium," the pool of the past, where all that's made has been annihilated, becoming, with a sorrow that was not Marvell's, nothing but "a green thought in a green shade."

—I want to see the dead!
—What a request—Oh well. My word is
    more precious to me. . . . See!
A green knife cut open the earth.
It became green.
Green.
Green.
Green of dark fir trees through a mist;
Green of a cloud with burst bile;
Green of mossy stones in a rain;
Green appearing through a hoop rolled
    by a seven-year-old;

. . . .

And the solemn green of grass
    bordering a grave.
Greens flow into greens. Body into body.
And suddenly the earth has become
transformed into a green aquarium.
Closer, closer to the green whirlpool!

I look in: people are swimming around
like fish. Innumerable phosphorus faces.
Young. Old. And young-old in one. All
those I saw during my entire lifetime, and
death has anointed them with a green
existence; they all swim in the green
aquarium in a sort of silky, aery music.

Here live the dead!

Beneath them lakes, forests, cities—a
gigantic plastic map, and overhead floats
the sun in the shape of a fiery man.

I recognize acquaintances, friends, neigh-
bours, and doff my straw hat to them.

—Good morning.

They respond with green smiles, as a
well responds to a stone with broken circles.

My eyes splash with silver oars, scurry,

swim among the faces. Rummaging, they
see one face.

One would hardly call this a simple work. It reminds one
of Aloysius Bertrand's "Gaspard de la nuit," of Laforgue's
Moralités légendaires, in the tradition of the symbolist prose
poem, and of Bruno Schulz (for that matter, it also reminds
one of Der Nister, another Yiddish author who is far from
simple). Perhaps the strangest of the episodes in it is the one
entitled "The Box of Gopherwood," whereas one of the more
accessible is "Honey of a Wild Bee." Leyme, in the latter, is
not a persona for the poet, but simply a denizen of the Green
Aquarium.

The Night will stay this way: an old
maid, grey to the tip of her braid.
The moon, having left all her near ones
behind on the earth and seeing no one, is
saying her last confession on her marble
deathbed in the presence of the sole
creature in the city, the gravedigger Leyme,
who lies shrivelled down below, on Rud-
nitski Street, in a heap of sighing leaves.
Leyme, who has been a gravedigger since
he remembers his face, who sowed half
the graveyard with the children of men, will
never bury anyone again.
Children, old folks, all born here, have all
entered the kingdom of the stars. First—
they became flaming pyres. Bony winds, in
tattered shirts with stars of David, scattered and strewed their sparks around the
skull of the world in a bloody crown.

His graveyard has been shamed.
The tombstones shamed.
So they sink with lowered heads, like
insulted parents of the groom when the
bride has disappeared from under the canopy.
Leyme is shamed.

—Spade, where are you, we must bury
the moon . . .

Now he sees the moon with his glass
eye. The other is hung with a lock. Its
silver key is no longer in this world.
Once, half a century ago, a wild bee
stung out his left eye.
The story of the wild bee is inscribed
in a chronicle:
On a lovely summer day, when
Leyme was lowering a corpse into the
grave, the soul of the dead man flew
with him into the pit, disguised as a
wild bee. It had to tell him a secret
before parting with him forever.
Leyme, a simple soul, failed to understand the sporting of ghosts. He
didn't care for the whole hocus-pocus,
and he whacked the bee with his
muddy shovel.
The bee gave a childish cry. Its
polished, sunny little face took on the
look of the dead man. A second later a
screech was heard. Leyme clutched his
left eye, where the wild bee had entered, as into a beehive; and the eye
soon leaked out a red oozing wax under
the gravedigger's hairy paw.

The city buzzed round in circles. His
gravediggership was at stake. He
wasn't allowed near a prominent
corpse. But Leyme did not submit, and
the "circles" came to a stop. A doctor
named Barber inserted a glass eye, as
blue and almost as large as a chicken's
gizzard. And along with the lumps of
earth on the Zaretshe graveyard, Leyme
buried the story of the bee.

Winds, like cats mating, meow at his head.
    There is no redeemer. The dead are far
away. Let one of them bring him a beaker
of water . . .
    —Hey, spade, where are you, we must
bury the moon!
    But his spade, the graveyard wife of a
widower, is out of his reach.
    Hush. There is the spade roaming above
him. Roaming alone among the suspended
sparks. She is digging, his spade is digging
into resounding infinity.
    Leyme stretches out a long hand to the
moon. Puts a star to her nostrils.
    The silver feather does not stir . . .
    And then—I myself saw it happen—
the wild bee flew from his glass eye and in-
jected its last fiery honey into my heart.

                              Ruth Wisse's translation,
                              with minor variations

Speaking of difficult poetry, I must acknowledge that there
is at least one passage in Sutzkever's *Spiritual Soil* that is far
from self-explanatory. This is a moment in the Jerusalem

marketplace, just after the poet has stepped off a ship ironically named Patria, and is wandering about, half-demented,
in his new-found "home." It is a home prematurely discovered
and not yet discovered; it must be accepted as "home," though
it is hopelessly unfamiliar, and in a way his having found it
makes it necessary for him to go on looking for it all the
harder. So much at-home-not-at-home is he, that he begins
to feel he must be in some other world entirely, where such
words as *home* have a different meaning, if any meaning:
perhaps in his own green aquarium.

Here are those Indian turkeys, foolish
clowns,
And swarthy eagles fastened to their sticks,
Above, like human corpses hanging down,
Flayed carcasses of cattle sag
     from hooks.
A blinded camel makes his endless circle
Shackled, and the sesame he steps on
Gives oil, bricks show the yellow
     dribble:
The blind beast in the market is the last
     one;
His drooping lips are slavering
     and flopping—
Get me a pair of eyeballs, while
     you're shopping.

Where am I? Run for it, if your hutch
Of flesh you love. This market is pure lie.
And with some Jericho roses in a bunch
An Arab among goat-flocks bars my way.
"Hey, Jew, buy a rose, beyond compare,
A rose that lives forever, just add water,

With your eternal folk she'd make
   a pair. . . . "
Does he mean it, or is it a sneer?
The goats race on, guffawing, to
   their slaughter;
Around the customer, the shrouds
   of magic flutter.

Spiritual Soil,
2, xlv–xlvi

The humanized animal (camel, goat) necessarily carries us back to that other being sacrificed for man, Isaac's sheep. (Cf. Sholem Aleichem's story about the condemned poultry, "The Pair.") The passage from H. Leivick's *In the Days of Job,* translated by Leonard Wolf, gives one a strong sense of the necessities in the sacrificial theme. I must confess that the accusation of intellectual thinness I leveled earlier at Yiddish poetry begins to seem inappropriate in the face of the texts I have been using.

Job is summoned by his wife to curse God and die. Among the outcries of his friends and the hysterical demands of his wife, Job, calling in vain on the name of God, finally faints. At that point, instead of God, Satan enters.

Satan: Asleep, my lord? (Job does not
        reply. Satan withdraws to one side,
        musing.)

        At least until a real sleep overtakes him,
        A sleep with neither pain nor grief,
        Let him content himself with confused guilt.
        In the midst of his assertion of his
        innocence

He may begin to recognize his shame,
And stumble on disgust for his own
outcry.

On his departure, another visitor comes in. It is Isaac. Job
has awakened. Isaac, another sufferer, identifies himself and
describes part of his experience on Mount Moriah. When
Job falls asleep again, a huge sheep with a shaggy coat
emerges from the shadow thrown by the tent and makes its
way to his feet.

Sheep: And my throat. May it be cut? . . .
            what had I done to deserve the
            knife?
Isaac: Have I said that you deserved it?
Sheep: But weren't you glad when your
            father's blade
            Descended on me, instead of you?
Isaac: (Is silent.)
Sheep: I'm asking you to tell me: Weren't
you glad?
Isaac: Perhaps . . . yes.
Sheep: What do you mean — perhaps —
            Say, "Certainly."
            How frequently have I heard you
            Complaining of those moments
            when you lay
            And waited with your throat
            against the knife?
              See how deeply
            My throat has been carved. Was
            not
            Your father's knife your knife as
            well?

Or is the blood of a sheep not
really blood?
Perhaps I am an incarnation of
yourself,
A living prophecy regarding you;
The first inkling of the razor edge
That must inevitably cut your
throat . . .
If not now, then later . . . later.
What if the knife on Mount Morea
missed you?
Has not its sharpness revealed the
slaughter
Being readied for you generations
hence
By knives as long as the long
night? . . .

Why did you leap so lightly from
the altar
And thrust me on it with such
violence?
Why? One victim dragging the
other to
His death. Why are you dumb?
Speak.
Forget that I'm a sheep. Tonight's
The kind of night when even a
sheep
No less than man is privileged to
speak;
To murmur against death and call
For justice. Even a slaughtered
sheep.
And you. Consider yourself well.
Touch yourself with care—has not

Your father somehow slaughtered
you?
Touch your throat and every limb
with care. . . .
       Go, God can do
Without you both. He turns from
you.

He is with me and my carved,
drained throat.
With me and my seared flesh,
And you are Cains, both of you,
both.
Though you lament with the grief
Of Abel, to be the veritable Abel
Is beyond you, for Abel waits, like
me
Murdered and cast aside, for
someone
To make an outcry for his death.
But he waits in vain. He's been
forgotten — long ago. See where he
lies
Go and see.

(He goes off. Abel appears in his
place.)

The suggestion is strong that the guilt circles round to the
self, that we are our own and each other's murderers. If, like
Job or Isaac, one can, in the light of others' suffering, still be
so paltry as to complain of one's own suffering, one cannot be
without guilt. Any meditation on others' murder, or threatened
murder, of us merely confirms our identification with them,
through our own capacity for murder. Sheep we may be, but

lambs we shall never become. After all, we, the Jews, invented original sin. We, the Jews, are to blame for evil, even when, and especially when, victims. And we invented ethics because we aren't ethical enough. The guilt of others is only our own guilt.

The issue of guilt brings us around, I suppose, to the central problem of literature, which I have raised before: is literature itself not an inherently guilty kind of activity? Do Jews have any business being practitioners of literature?[5] Literature, if entirely honest to the individual, can choose to put the individual above the universal or ethical. This is not the individual in Kierkegaard's religious or creative sense, and certainly not in a selfish sense: but in the sense that whatever confrontation with experience one has had must enter into the writing, no matter how negative it may be. The individual can afford to put death ahead of life, to deny the value of life; the ethical or universal, having as its central principle a concern for others' survival, cannot afford to question the value of life. Honest literature, individual literature, may accept suicide, pure negation, may even embrace it as a necessary aspect of the creative act; all other literature may be accused of disguising that destructive negativity, may be accused of dishonesty.

There has been a gradual convergence of interest in these two themes, as was evidenced by the simultaneous publication of a number of books in the seventies on both subjects: literature and suicide, and literature and the Holocaust. Long ago, A. Alvarez, in *Beyond All This Fiddle* (London, 1968), pointed out that many suicides studied the literature of the camps before they took their lives. These are dangerous things to read about (p. 28): "They stir mud from the bottom, clouding the mind, rousing dormant self-destructiveness." He quotes Mailer: the crime against humanity becomes also a projection of one's own inner violence and misery. It becomes a kind of justification or realization of an unacknowledged wish, traumatic and obsessive because it is too true to something in oneself.

If the literature of the individual includes a record of confrontation with the absolute destructive and self-destructive force, if it holds hands with death, if it makes a joke of "making life work," it can hardly be accommodated in an ethical scheme. In its terms, to make life last longer, to have that as a purpose, is silly, as if the values of life could ever be exhausted by life or as if life could ever fulfill life. In its terms, for the self the ultimate justice is suicide. For us the ultimate justice is love, or self-sacrifice. Which is the greater justice? Asocial as it may be, the literature of suicide, whether as in Keats (e.g., "Ode to a Nightingale") or as in Sylvia Plath, touches general truths that are deeper than sociality; it unites us in the recognition of what is stronger for us than our most constructive impulses. "The blood-jet is poetry, / There is no stopping it." Not even with children. "You hand me two children, two roses." (Sylvia Plath, "Kindness.") The line, drenched in irony, emphasizes precisely the impossibility of compensating through children for the betrayals and the killing "kindness" of a certain quality in marriage. The injury of betrayal (the murder of the rabbit) has opened the blood-jet of poetry; children are subordinate to this awareness: the jet shoots beyond them.[6]

Jews cannot afford such luxuries. The individual may choose to confront absolutes; we have to be relative: for us, the ethical has to suffice. We, our history, our experiences, can provide the material for someone else's literature, for someone else's suicide. In a sense, the last place to look for literature about the Holocaust should be among Jews. Surely, in spite of everything that has been written to the contrary recently, there is something immoral in the idea of a "literature about the Holocaust." There should be no literature "of" the

Holocaust; and, above all, for Jews to produce it is wrong. It can only serve to disguise it or to justify it. Ruth Wisse says the antagonist in Sutzkever's poem "To the Child" is not the Nazi, but the father's suicidal despair. "He withstands the temptation of swallowing his dead future and transcribes his son into the ordered eternity of the universe."[7] But that's just the point: he does not dare to swallow his dead future, he cannot accept despair. Without that acceptance, we remain poised on the hither side of literature. If the poem is really an acceptance of despair, it is not quite Jewish. If it is not really an acceptance of despair, it is not quite literature. Is poetry a bulwark against despair, or must it reserve the right to join forces, somewhere, if it chooses to, even with "bestialization or madness" (Wisse, p. 15)?

But, to look at it another way, even if poetry were consoling, "All poetic relief has become . . . evidence of historical complicity."[8] Is it consolation that we seek? What is unendurable can be made endurable through images. Images are like lumps of mushrooms forced out of the soil when pressures cannot be contained. Have we a right to such consolation? To whom does it do justice?

Ours is a harder, and a tamer, fate. We must make do with life, such as it is—with its limitations, its compromises, its inadequacies, its ordinary love. No absolutes, and no transcendences, not even negative transcendences, for us. And our images must be images of the incomplete. If we are to read, or write, we will read, or make, parables, children's stories that leave the tailgate open to life, for the cows to wander in or out.[9]

The repudiation of the Gentile world is a repudiation of perfection, of absolutes, of the "big deal." Religious poetry we do have—even Plato allowed for poems in praise of the Gods—but our religious poetry is just a quarreling with the neighbor next door:

Reb Levi Yitzhok

Reb Levi Yitzhok in prayer shawl and tefillin
Is rooted where he stands
Before the altar, with prayer book open,
But will not utter a sound.

He sees the ghetto like so many pictures
Of agony, trouble and pain.
Silent and stubborn, the old man quarrels
With his old God again.

Itzik Manger
(trans. Leonard Wolf)

Even God had better be just a little God, a parochial God, of a measure to fit inside our tsores (troubles) rather than to embrace them. If he approaches us from the outside, a savior on a white horse, as in Mani Leib's "To Whom," he will find no one to greet him.

One poet challenges his God to start over.

The Beginning
I

Shall we perhaps go home now,
   you and I,
to begin again, small from the
   beginning?

Begin once more! Be the small God
   of a small people!

. . . .

Let us be provincial, you and I,
God and the poet,
Shall we perhaps go home, you and I?
Shall we perhaps, unconquering,
go home?

II

Us did you choose.
You have chosen us.
A small God. A small people.
They have acclaimed us both as great,
in order to scatter us as dust
and undo us completely.
With you they have bestarred a
    whole universe.
It is too much for your strength!
Are such multitudinous nations for
    such as you
who have but recently
left the workbench of Abraham?
. . . .
Why did you abandon your tabernacle
and your small tent,
faring forth to become the God of
    the universe?
Therefore, we became your disobedient
    children,
shakers of pillars, starters of
    world fires.
It was you who first became the Jewish
    International,
and into the world we followed you
and were nauseated with your world.

Save yourself! Together with the
  pilgrims, return,
return to a small land.
Become once more the small God
  of a small people.

Jacob Glatstein
(trans. Etta Blum)

Yet somehow we never lose our relationship to this parochial, unreasonable, expansible or contractible, accordionlike kind of God: he

lets no one be
so utterly
a paradigm in fire.
There is no one He will equally desire
to find, to lose.

Aaron Zeitlin, "I Believe"
(trans. Robert Friend)

The refusal to acknowledge other gods is the refusal to acknowledge the reality of evil, of that "other," the foreign thing, from which coldness and murder come. As long as the Jewish God is alive, mankind, in spite of itself, has a refuge from itself. Still, in the end, what seems to make most sense is to give up our attempt to come to any kind of terms with the outside world, take our God's hand under our arm, drag him into the house, and slam the door. Nor is there any danger that we will then simply find ourselves confronting, after all, the god of Otherness, the enemy within, if for no better reason than that the enemy without will always keep us fully occupied dealing with him.

Good Night, Wide World

Good night, wide world
Big stinking world!
Not you but I slam shut the door.
With my long gabardine,
My fiery, yellow patch,
With head erect,
And at my sole command,
I go back into the ghetto.

Wipe off all markings of apostasy!
I roll my body in your grime;
Glory, glory, glory to you,
Crippled Jewish life!
I cast out all your unclean cultures, world!
Though all has been laid waste,
I burrow in your dust,
Sorrowing Jewish life.

Swinish German, hostile Polack,
Thievish Amalekite — land of swill and
guzzle,
Slobbering democracy,
With your cold compress of sympathy,
Good night, brash world with your electric
glare.

Back to my kerosene, my shadowed tallow
candles,
Endless October and faint stars,
To my twisting streets and crooked lantern,
To my sacred scrolls and holy books,
To tough Talmudic riddles and lucid
    Yiddish speech,
To law, to duty, and to justice,
To what is deeply mine.

World, joyously I stride
Toward the quiet ghetto lights.
Good night. I give you in good measure
All my redeemers;
Take your Jesus Marxes; choke on their
daring
Burst with each drop of our baptized blood.
And still I trust that though He tarry,
My waiting will spring newly day by day.
Green leaves again will rustle
On our withered tree.
I need no comforting.
I walk again my straight and narrow way:
From Wagner's heathen blare to Hebrew
chant
And the hummed melody.

I kiss you, cankered Jewish life,
The joy of homecoming weeps in me.

Jacob Glatstein
(trans. Marie Syrkin)

Quite irrelevantly, I would like to finish with a song writ-ten nearly a century ago by David Edelstadt.[10] It is the melody that, perhaps with Shlomo Shmulevitch's "Die Mezinke," comes up most frequently in my mind. The text, intended to be in the manner of the sentimental Russian poet Nadson, is a strange medley of themes, moods, and styles, a compendium of literary and political clichés; its gong tone is not even Jewish: clearly, the vesper bell—or is it the Angelus?—is not sounding from a synagogue. Yet it unites all these things—sense of loss, inescapable relation to an "outside" world, naïve social idealism, poetry, death, sentimentalism—in a final statement that is at the same time,

anachronistically, one of the earliest statements of Yiddish
poetry. The knell is heard in advance, and it is good for the
future; it has not stopped ringing in my ears. None of us, in
fact, will forget it. It has nothing to do with the Holocaust;
but its healing melancholy foresees and gently sets behind it
what all of us will have to know.

> No longer call me, Muse; and with
>   your magic fingers
> The strings of my sick heart no
> longer touch:

The poet is condemned to death: his song is over. As he
looks back on his career (Edelstadt died at 26; his model,
Nadson, at 24) he recalls nothing but merciless exposure; he
has known no shelter, moral or physical: "Above his head, to
greet him as he wandered, / The piling heavens' stormiest
clouds unfurled." But there is no time even for retrospect:

> For death is knocking at his life's
>   closed chamber,
> And says: "Know that your day's
>   work now is done.
> Put out your fire, lay down your hammer;
> Come, do you hear? The evening
>   bell's begun."

> The evening bell has tolled—yes,
>   I can hear its clanging,
> My knell sounds clear in each
>   relentless stroke.

He wishes that he could live on, to dream, to sing, to struggle against the oppressors of his folk, to match its scarlet standard with his blood. "But what avail now the most sacred longings—"? The storm of his brief life is over; his tears, his dreams, his poetry have no further voice. "Death calls; the evening bell tolls on."

The awkward ballad-pathos is difficult to render in translation, and the original is never thought of without the enhancement of its melody. I give the musical notation here, first in the version that I remember from my mother, then in the standard version, transmitted to me by the Yiddish poet M. Shaffir.

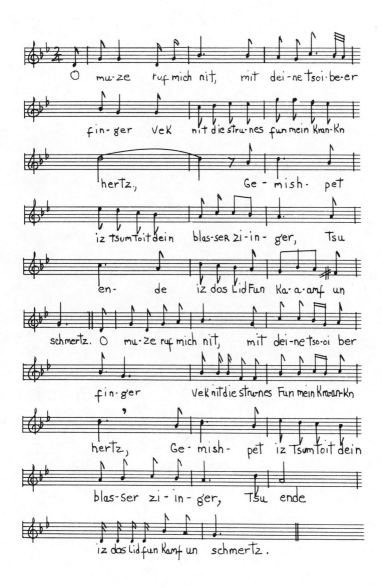

5

The Effortless in Art and Ethics

(A) Meditations on "The Frog King, or Iron Henry"

> "The beautiful lines insisted
>   on being traced —
> without weariness. . . . I saw that
> they 'composed' themselves by
> finer laws than any known to men."
>
> Ruskin

> "Self-taught am I, and God has
>   planted all kinds of songs in my
>   heart."
>
> Phemius, in *Odyssey* 22

EASE, OR EFFORT? TWO CHAPTERS (3, 4 AFTER N. 3) HAVE begun with that question: the strain of writing, of getting into a posture to write. In this one I want to talk about that part of thinking, of writing, which isn't a strain, which we can

113

trust to be right precisely because we have no control over it.

It is night—I am sleeping in a small hotel on the island of Cyprus. I wake up, and write down a melody that has come to me in my dream: a procession of young people, dressed in beautifully colored robes, has gone by, singing:

In the morning, I tell my companion the dream. (There is barbed wire separating the Greek and Turkish sectors of Nicosia, but the worst of the war is still to come).

I am at my summer home in Roman Valley. In my dream I am watching an opera with an acquaintance, who says—or I say—while the music is in progress, "I've no idea what it is." A very thin, slight, swarthy singer with a beautiful, melting bass voice begins a simple melody, in which he is joined at the end of the second bar by the choir, all of dark complexion, and dressed in informal clothes. I retain only the first few notes of the aria, not really enough to be worth repeating.

But frequently, I am so discouraged by the complexity of the music that I am hearing, or am about to hear, in my sleep, that I deliberately stop the dream, in despair that I do not possess sufficient musical knowledge to write down what is coming. More often, I simply sleep on, reluctant to lose my rest for the sake of capturing a few notes the principal merit of which lies in the fact that they have come to me during a dream. Sometimes even Mozart's melodies, though, have the effortless, unpremeditated movement of musical somnambulism, as if they had come to him already completely made up, and all he did, in the most rigidly literal sense, was transcribe them (e.g., "Dove son i bei momenti" from *The Marriage of Figaro*).

In any case, this music that comes to me, or to others, ready-made, in dreams—where does it come from?

Strictly speaking, the question is neither easier nor harder to answer than the same question would be if asked about a melody that one thinks of when awake. But there is one important difference: the dream music has come without effort. It has not gone through stages, or emerged by a struggle, through layers of resistance; it is simply there, with no prior notice. (Coleridge, we are told, heard "Kubla Khan" all at once, as Mozart heard his symphonies).[1] Nothing prepares for it. It does not have to be invented, or even allowed to unfold. All that has been taken care of for one, or has happened beforehand.

It is a thesis of this chapter that there are processes in the mind that are effortless. In fact (to leap ahead of myself) the mystery is how effort can creep into the mind, rather than how the mind can function without effort. Desire may involve effort; but why thought? By the principle of sufficient reason (i.e., why shouldn't consciousness simply be there, doing its job and being as conscious as it can be?) or by a cautious application of Occam's Razor (i.e., why complicate the idea of consciousness with effort when it is a viable concept or entity without it?) we arrive at a consciousness of which effort is no necessary attribute, what John Clare might have called "An easy thoughtlessness of thought" ("Pastoral Poesy"). Surely the mind doesn't have to exert itself to think:[2] after all, what would it be doing if it weren't thinking? It can't help thinking any more than it can help perceiving. The music in my dreams reveals what I might otherwise never have known: the existence of a nonlaborious space in the mind. It may be said of consciousness itself, pure consciousness as such, in contrast to act, that it is effortless.[3] What I am suggesting is that there is a pure substrate of act that is as effortless as that pure substrate of consciousness. (Marcus Aurelius says that a good man no more expects a reward for doing a good deed than the eye does for seeing: both acts occur entirely without effort. To stretch a connection: perhaps there is even some relation between good deeds and the grace of a melody's coming to one in dream.)

Who is to tell whether there is not a chamber in our minds, a musical kitchen, so to speak, where the melody that later appears in our dream is prepared *before* it is served up in the dining-room of the dream; or possibly it has even been prepared elsewhere, without our knowledge. (Cf. Saint Bernard: God does three things in us: *thinking, willing, acting:* the first without us, the second with us, and the third through us).[4]

In neither case (i.e., whether that kitchen is in us or is somewhere else) is there trace of effort; and the only evidence of self we have under any circumstances is work.[5] If "we" have made up the melody, there is at least no indication that that making-up has required the "com-posing" process that even the most inspired conscious musician engages in when he produces new music. With these melodies, the effortless space has erupted into the realm of effort: like Athene, such melodies spring forth full-grown and fully armed.

There is an analogy to this "kitchen patrol without tears"

in the stories or plot lines that sometimes occur in our dreams, revealing their intention at the end, without the prior expectation of the dreamer, as if the dream actually had more foresight than the dreamer.[6] It is as though, in these cases, the incoherent emotional material of our everyday lives had been summarized and organized spatially on a microchip, etching it with the stress lines of certain abstract possibilities, the atemporal chip's then unpacking itself in the dream as a series of images, with the potentiality for surprise that all temporality entails.

But what seems to us to have happened is that somewhere we have (or someone has) gone through the labor of organizing a plot line, whereas all we have received in the dream is the plot line itself. We have no record of work, of expenditure of energy, on the part of the plotter. Hubert Aquin's *Neige noire* seems to be an attempt to locate that foyer, workshop, or antechamber of creation, and to place the auditor, or, in this case, the spectator of film, in it himself, so that he will himself have to go on "ceaselessly transforming the unforeseeable into the unforeseen."[7] Lyotard produces an even more involuted wording in trying to deal with the problem of the preconscious in the Freudian system:[8] it is up to repression "to unfold into a visible temporality that which is not and never has been a future that descends into the past as it emerges into the present."[9]

To repeat my earlier question: in principle, why should simply being a mind require work? What is the job in consciousness? Surely consciousness has no limits to its energy. Why should the mind limp when it can leap?

One thing that makes us believe that the mind is entirely committed to the work ethic is our assumption that it is entirely committed to language. When we catch our mind in operation, it is usually full of words, and words, for the most part, have to be thought up. At the same time, though, we have glimpses of a mental backstage where there is no labor of articulation in progress. The proportion of the thoughts we actually articulate in language to those that we have is no greater than the proportion of percepts we recognize to those which go through us.[10] If we tried to spell out in words all the thoughts we have in a lifetime, we would never get done. We think our mind labors because language labors. But behind the labor of language there is the unlaboring mind.

It is not so much that the mind can move faster than it seems to when we know it only through language; it is that that inner level does not know the meaning of effort, much less the constraints of clock time.

Of course, it is not only language that works. Our bodies work too, and desire works, or has to; all too seldom can it coincide with the effortless inner process, and just be itself. Still, musical dreams do represent such moments: they reveal that desire too can be fulfilled with the same absence of effort with which thought is generated. The workless atelier is available to consciousness, to thought, and to desire alike.

Other kinds of aesthetic events besides music can present themselves to us ready-made, without our having contributed to their production.

I have always had after-images at night when I have gone picking berries during the day.[11] No matter what I might have been doing in the intervening time between being out in the fields and going to bed, the berries would spring into my vision, quite unexpectedly and without preparation, the moment I closed my eyes, not even necessarily in sleep. In fact, on a dark night, it would sometimes suffice for me to step out on the porch, and, with my eyes wide open, I would suddenly be seeing blueberries, or blackberries, at times highlighted with an intensity that approached the painful.

Last summer I had the same experience, but with an

important difference. Sometimes I would find myself presented, not merely with patches of blue or black berries in
random distribution, but with purposefully organized, aes-
thetically satisfying arrangements of berries, as in a picture.
These were no mere after-images; when those little blue
lamps would begin to glow in my inner visual theater, they
had already been transformed into a work of art. Without my
having given a single thought to the berries for as long as
eight or ten hours, I would abruptly encounter them again;
but, at *these* times, not merely as pleasing or as obsessive
images, but as well-planned configurations of visual materials that I myself was forced to admire. These blue lights that
would come on instantly when I closed my eyelids were
patterned, better spaced, more intense, more jewellike than
the original blueberries. They represented effortless acts,
after-images that had improved and organized themselves in
me to the greatest advantage for beauty. Neither dreams nor
fantasies, they presented themselves without my having made
any effort or contribution to them, self-organized by my
inner spacing equipment. They also, incidentally, contributed to the undermining of one of my deepest assumptions:
namely, that genuine acts of the imagination are necessarily
carried out in conjunction with the conscious will.[12]

In arguing that we have something in us that of its own
accord forms not merely patterns, such as psychologists have
long known about, but works of art, I believe I go beyond
Gombrich in *The Sense of Order.* There does seem to be
automatic equipment that works "in us without us"[13] to order
things for aesthetic advantage; we are not limited to automatic equipment for practical functions such as orientation
or balance. This is something more than the "subjectless
information-processing" of the Artificial Intelligence people.
This other equipment can make melodies without our com-
posing, and patterns of blueberries without our painting.[14]

What else emanates from this space, besides music, pictures?
Perhaps metaphors. I should like to explore this possibility
once again in terms of Tolstoi's "The Death of Ivan Ilyich."
After a strenuous life that has been pure fiction, artificial and
sedulously imitated from others, totally lacking in spontaneity or originality, Ivan Ilyich, as corpse, is discovered at his
ease, poking fun at the funeral guests. Once denizen of a
fiction, he is now an occupant of the space of poetic images,
which, as it turns out, is also an ethical space. The dull,
imaginationless Ivan Ilyich is now an artist, who can play
with the images that once played with him. He can encour-
age pouffe, ashtray, and coffee table to bump and catch at the
mourners, as the window-sash had caught at him. From this
pure space,[15] after death, the imagination can emerge, and
laughter is possible at last. The seriousness of fiction and of
mimesis has been given up. Ivan Ilyich's previous life can be
written off as it is written down.

During the story, as Ivan Ilyich's illness advances, he
begins to move inadvertently toward effortlessness. He finds
that he feels better when he can rest his feet on his servant
Gerassim's shoulders. He is starting to take a load off his feet,
to accept ease; after his death, his ally, the broken sofa,
similarly celebrates a release from fictional pressures with a
snap of the springs. We shall encounter that springing snap
again in the story of Iron Henry.[16]

The king's youngest daughter is playing with her golden
ball beside a well. The ball falls into the well and vanishes. A
frog appears in response to the girl's lamentations and offers
to retrieve the ball in exchange for the right to share the
princess's board and bed. She agrees to the bargain, but
without the slightest intention of keeping her part of it. The
next day the frog arrives at dinner-time and demands that
she fulfill her promise. It is only at her father's insistence
that she complies, but when the frog actually demands that

she let him get into bed with her, she throws him against the wall. He falls back in the form of a handsome prince and she promptly accepts him as her husband. A wicked witch had enchanted him, and she alone could save him. The next day, as he is taking her back to his kingdom in his coach, they hear a snapping noise behind them. The prince thinks that the coach is breaking, but his servant, Henry, tells him that what he has heard is the snapping of one of the iron bands that Henry had fastened around his heart to prevent it from breaking with sorrow after his master's enchantment. This episode is repeated twice more, and each time the prince assumes the coach is breaking, whereas "it was just the sound of the bands bursting from the heart of faithful Henry, because his master was free once more, and was now happy."

There has been, then, a story prior to the story: it actually began with the enchanting of the prince and the subsequent binding of Iron Henry's heart, before any of the action around the well or in the palace took place. The snapping of the bonds around Iron Henry's heart, the relief from pressure, is the relief from the suspense we have been feeling in the framed story, which, despite the ostensibly happy ending, can have no adequate outlet within that story. In fact, the tension we have been enduring in the story simply because it *is* a story is relieved by our being thrown back into a space before *any* stories, a space out of which the labor of stories comes, "the nothingness from which the germination of meaning has taken place" (Goux, *Les Iconoclastes,* p. 98). The snapping of the bonds is a reminder that story can be effortless, even more effortless than the wish-fulfillment that the story first tells us was possible at the time of its action; finally, that the ethical, too, can be effortless. The myth of the frog, and the fiction of his metamorphosis into a king, both involve strain; the pure space in which the bonds snap has not had to be labored through.

What happens to the reader (listener) when Iron Henry's bonds snap? He/she experiences a feeling of syncope, *Wonne:* swoon, fainting.[17] That feeling is a liberation from the condition of myth that bound him (Iron Henry); but it is also a freedom in love, and pleasure, for the service that can now be carried out (Iron Henry is a *servant*); this is not fiction, with its inescapable overhanging anxiety, unresolvable suspense. (The only relief from fiction is, of course, to start another fiction). The prince, in fact, is more anxious and unsure of himself when he emerges into his fictionality as king than he had been while a frog, in myth. A proper frog-king would have taken his Proserpine back to the underworld with him, not merely have allowed himself to be turned into a meek and dutiful husband.

The only sign we have of Henry's iron steadfastness, as well as of his liberation, is a sound; but that sound has a disturbing force. It is with a sense of consternation that we realize the strength of what has snapped, as its energy is transferred to our feeling of relief. As in the crossing of the Simplon Pass (Wordsworth, *Prelude* 6), the goal has been reached before we were even aware that we were approaching it. And the beauty (what Wordsworth calls "Imagination") lies in the recoil that follows the realization: in the "flooding" of awareness by the imagination. As strong as the bonds were, so weak do we feel when they break. The space around the sound is uncluttered by action, anticipation, or explanation; it is a *new* sound; and, as pure sound, it escapes from between the blind violence of myth and the pusillanimous imagings of fiction. The beauty of these sounds lies in their lack of explanation, in their clarity. They are as empty of background as the smell of cut grass and linden-flowers after rain; they flood the sense with free beauty ("The sense faints picturing them." "West Wind,"1.36).

The free space that surrounds the snapping of the bonds

is, perhaps, a part of universal generative space revealed. But let me draw back from this boundary of ultimates to a more governable area of inquiry. It is instructive to read another of the Grimm stories, "The Elves and the Shoemaker," for the sake of the light it throws on the subject of effort from other positions in the perspective. As in the case of "The Frog King," the ethical issue is by no means clear; why do the elves work cheerfully at their shoemaking as long as they get nothing in return, but reject their task as soon as they are rewarded? One might say that the shoemaker and his wife have refused the free gift of the elves' assistance, and placed the elves under an obligation, by insisting on paying them, substituting a contractual for a voluntary arrangement. But in the terms of my argument, the shoemaker and his wife have subverted a deeper principle. They have attempted to defeat the representatives of the effortless and to invalidate their achievements. The naked elves live in Paradise; work is not work for them. The elves inhabit a nighttime space where things take place; they are not *done*. The elvish work-shop is the workless workshop of the mind.

As soon as the elves are dressed up, as soon as they have to take on the self-conscious forms that clothes represent, they experience work as work. After the Fall, we must dress; after the Fall, we must labor; after the Fall, we are in the world; after the Fall, we shall die.

The elves are not acceptable as naked truth, so they have to be de-realized, and, being now unreal, vanish, having been declared mere dreams. They are demoted from their mythic status by the assistance they receive. The shoemaker and his wife impose the status of fictional beings on the elves, tricking them out in the trappings of fiction. And, like the Frog King, as merely fictional beings they are not viable.

When the shoemaker and his wife show that they no longer need the elves by giving a gift in return (clothing, especially *shoes:* walking-oriented, labor-oriented symbols), they violate the phase of naked ease in which the strenuous "clothing" or "dressing up" of actual dreams potentiates. (In this way they reverse the sequence of events in "The Death of Ivan Ilyich"). The beginning of that symbol-assuming process in dreams may also be what we catch a glimpse of when, in the space provided by the beginning of Alice's dream, the White Rabbit hurtles by on his mysterious errand, muttering to himself, as the fallow land of the preconscious releases itself into articulated shapes.

(B) Myth, Fiction, and Ethics (A Response to Girard and Lyotard)

In order to find our way back to that space from which the elves have come, before they assumed clothing and melted offstage like a dream, we must escape the implicit violence of transactions such as that by which they were waylaid. They were denied their freedom; or, rather, freedom as such was denied — the freedom to do, as well as the freedom to give. They were trapped within the human condition with a pair of shoes (or an apple), and permanently denied access to the paradise of their source, a paradise of which the shoemaker and his wife had also been granted a glimpse, but which they had not understood, and which they had quickly translated into the conditions of their own world — that is, repudiated and destroyed. They could not understand freedom; therefore they had to deny it. Their act has something in common with the gesture by which Lyotard, for all his good will, attributes a "figure" that implies a "violence initiale" to the very inception of a dream-thought (*Discours, Figure,* p. 270); I would rather say that behind thought and "figure" or image alike there is a "nonviolence initiale," in which even the image itself may partake, or which it may express.

The space of freedom, then, that pure space from which the well-formed musical dreams of my beginning come, the pure space that surrounds the cracking of Iron Henry's bonds, is a space in which there is no violence. The story "The Frog King," including the story of Iron Henry's own life, is the dream that has come from this space, although the space itself does not become manifest until the story is past (as the space in "Ivan Ilyich" is not seen until the protagonist's life is over).

But up to the manifestation of the space, the story, or dream, of the Frog King contains plenty of violence. In the beginning, despite his apparent sympathy with her ("you're screaming so that a stone would feel sorry for you"), the frog imposes a contract on the girl that she cannot reasonably fulfill, and exacts a literal compliance with its conditions. He doesn't flinch from tale-bearing, and enlists the paternal influence to extort a love that he cannot win. The girl, for her part, is no better: she begins by addressing the frog as "old water-slapper," shifts to "dear frog" when she thinks he may serve her purpose, and makes him promises without the faintest intention of fulfilling them. The frog, in turn, complacently ignores her distress as he eats his fill from her plate, and orders her to carry him to her bed as though she too were enjoying every moment in the sequence. The reciprocal, barely suppressed violence in the ill-tempered girl inevitably erupts again, and she smashes the frog into the wall.

Then, quite abruptly, the violence ends. The frog is a prince and all is well. Whatever the ethical economy of the story may have been, and it is hard to tally up the account so that it balances, everyone seems satisfied by the outcome. The myth, in which violence had a natural place, and is accepted as part of the necessary order of thought and feeling, gives way to fiction, which is the attempt to drive out violence: only good may remain in the fictional domain. Myth has a home for violence; it legitimizes fear and externalizes it; fiction is the denial of the naturalness and necessity of violence. That is why it always seems to be didactic: it seeks an idyllic state. But it does not go on to the ethical choice; it remains nostalgic for its mythic energy. It substitutes fear and insecurity for violence. Fiction is the weakness of an incomplete ethical order.

But the doubtful "pax ficta" or "facta" of fiction is not the only, or the last, word of the story. Iron Henry does remain to pick up the pieces, and to show that there is a security behind, or beyond, the fiction, to depend on. He guarantees the action; his fresh-forged iron bands, symbols of steadfast love and duty, hold the events together, hoop them around, from a point before the narration of the story begins. The solid mythic-metamorphic conditions that obtain at the opening of the action are revoked as the importunate frog, with the assistance of his ally, the king, requires the princess to quell all her instincts in favor of ethical principles: don't be ungrateful; never go back on a promise. But we cannot approve of the frog, who will use any means, including blackmail, to achieve his purpose; nor can we admire the princess, who is rewarded for no ethical act: not for insight into the good qualities beneath a loathsome exterior; not even for self-control. The move to the world of ethics cannot be made smoothly, though the father does try to ease the transition. He attempts to lend humanity and give meaning to an arbitrary contract assumed under the conditions of myth. But finally the institution of the ethical must also occur arbitrarily, after the culmination of the violence that has accumulated in the action, when the girl breaks the frog against the wall. The ethical, then, is established as abruptly, in the end, as it is in Aeschylus's *Eumenides,* though frog and girl cling to their selfishness as though it were going out of style.

When the crisis is past, the metamorphosis has occurred, and the mythical world has been left behind, a strange new doubt befalls the newlyweds, casting a pall on their happiness. The frog king (or is he merely a prince? the wording goes uneasily back and forth) is less sure of himself now than he had been when he was a frog. Clearly, he misses his frog form.[1] He had acted with complete assurance as long as he was a frog — or, if we prefer, a phallus. It is only when he has to become an amiable husband that he begins to falter. The naked frog has no hesitations, no anxieties, no compunctions, no sense of guilt.[2] He seems to represent pure unself-conscious libido. But now he himself does not believe in his new condition (nor should he: men are closer to the condition of frogs than to that of kings, especially of kings created *ex machina*). He fears that he is just a character in fiction; that he has no right to his chariot, and that it may break down at any moment. Three times he interprets the snapping of the bonds, which signifies the victory of Iron Henry over the bondage to myth, as the collapse of his own fairy-tale. We have no right to resort to fiction just because myth is over.[3] This is why Iron Henry is needed, to remind us that not the master's career, but the humble servant's, is what matters. In the end the prince lapses into an almost pathetic dependence on his servant, Iron Henry. His, Henry's, is the pure poetry of good, little though his master, or the girl, may illustrate or deserve it. The ethical bonds need and brook no fiction. The sound of the snapping bonds stands by itself, incomparable and unrelated to anything else.[4] And what seems the end of the new dispensation to the fiction-dwelling frog-turned-king is the beginning of perfection for Iron Henry.

In the bands around Iron Henry's heart is also invested the suspense of the plot. As I have suggested before, the tension that has been building up during the development of the story appears to have been relieved by the girl's act of violence, which is rewarded by the transformation of the frog. But, in fact, the suspense is not really over, because it has been resolved only at the level of the action, and it soon revives, revealing the permanent anxiety beneath all fiction that drives it to resume even before it is finished. The prince, as we have seen, soon shows that he does not believe in the story the protagonist of which he is supposed to have become. The persistence of tension *beyond* the transformation is betrayed by the relief we feel when Iron Henry's bonds snap, in a supererogatory expression of the ease that was supposed to have been achieved within the fiction, but that we realize had never been reached at all. Myth works with violence; fiction denies violence; ethics subtends violence. The force of anxiety in the story has been transferred to the strength of the iron bonds, and it is only in the power of their voluntary breaking that the witch's spell is truly broken. They absorb the full force of the mythic sword, forged into the bonds of peace, bonds that can themselves in the end be dispensed with. Fiction, which pretends to turn its back on the power in myth, remains forever its slave and its anxious sycophant.

Fiction is bound to violence not only through its dependence on myth, but through its reliance on interpretation, the retrospective view. Dream is oriented toward the future. It is always pre-aware, as our understanding of a read sentence is, as the king is when his daughter answers the knock at the door, as the story itself reveals itself to be when Iron Henry's bonds snap. But the Frog King is a retrospective reasoner, incapable of accepting the unforeseeable, unable, once transformed, to keep his grip on the forward motion of any vehicle, whether carriage, metaphor, sentence, or story. He himself has been made king by an act of retrospective interpretation—that is, by an act of violence, applied to the frog image, in order to transform him into a king—and he bears the marks of his origin. What his career seems to prove is that if one tries to interpret, that is, translate, an image, one drops into fiction.[5] If one tries to deal with a sound (the sound of the cracking), one discovers oneself in the domain of a pure Kantian ethics, an ethics free of specific content or limitation.

In pointing out that Iron Henry provides the security beyond fiction for the story to depend on, as the weakness of the "king" becomes manifest, I am thinking of "The Frog King" as permitting a critique of the Girardian theory of fiction, which makes literature primarily a deconstruction of myth. Girard leaves us with nothing but transcendence as a way of avoiding the implications of that deconstruction and of the recurrent mythic violence that it reveals: a cycle of crises that only another act of violence — scapegoating — can interrupt. And if I am accused of simplifying Girard's position, or of failing to take into account the evolution of his thought, I can only point to the *Eumenides* chapter (20) of his forthcoming work on *Job* in reply. There Girard emphasizes once more the collective violence that lies at the root of the supposedly modern and civilized Greek legal system introduced with the Areopagus: it is after all *only* the old furies who guarantee the integrity of the new state. In fact, from Girard's point of view, the *Eumenides* would seem to be one of the few literary works that reiterates the old mythic truths in an entirely unambiguous way. In any case, my own interest is not so much in the conflict of the fictional with the mythical: I see "The Frog King" rather as a story about the conflict of the mythical with the ethical. Fiction is only a minor by-product thrown off by the victory of the ethical, a substitute for myth that remains beset by uncertainties, weaknesses, and distinctly unethical implications. It represents the futile claim that one can eat one's cake and have it: that one can describe things as they are and at the same time claim that they are better than they are.

The pattern I find in "The Frog King," then, would oppose a kind of ethical apocalypse to Girard's pattern of recurring violence. This ethical apocalypse, expressed in both the strength of the embracing iron and the freedom that surrounds the snapping of Iron Henry's bonds, is something that takes place now; like the nonviolent, effortless space from which our dreams come to us, it has been, and it is, *in* our lives; it is not, as in Girard's system (where what we know in this world is only violence), referred, and deferred, to a future transcendence, after the human nightmare of mutual imitation and destruction has run its course.

6

Toward the Rehabilitation of the Image

THE QUESTIONS RAISED IN THIS CHAPTER GROW OUT OF THE previous ones, even though they are in some respects distinct from them. These questions are: (a) is there such a thing as an easeful language? and (b) is there such a thing as an easeful image? In part, the last question has been answered in the affirmative in the section on "Ivan Ilyich," where I argue that metaphors rise from an effortless space. But, speaking in broader terms, I suggested that language is usually associated with labor; and that images are generally a "dressing up," with all the strenuousness that that activity connotes, of something that in its purest form (as in the space surrounding the snapping of Iron Henry's bonds) is purged of all visualized content. By the time the image has formed, we are, by and large, in the world of work, of clothing. Still, it may not be without value to explore the at least relatively easeful elements in the domain of language and of the linguistic image.

"Easeful" is, of course, a word of Keats's. The grasshopper, poet of earth, rests "at ease." He indulges in the laziness of the poet, celebrated by Friedrich Schlegel in the "Idleness" chapter of *Lucinde* that Schubert admired.

On the Grasshopper and Cricket

The poetry of earth is never dead:
　When all the birds are faint with the hot sun,
　And hide in cooling trees, a voice will run
From hedge to hedge about the new-mown mead;
That is the Grasshopper's—he takes the lead
　In summer luxury,—he has never done
　With his delights; for when tired out with fun
He rests at ease beneath some pleasant weed.
The poetry of earth is ceasing never;
　On a lone winter evening, when the frost
　　Has wrought a silence, from the stove there shrills
The Cricket's song, in warmth increasing ever,
　And seems to one in drowsiness half lost,
　　The Grasshopper's among some grassy hills.

Reversing the moral of Aesop's fable on the ants and the grasshopper, Keats favors the grasshopper. The undertone of nature, the voice behind the voice, heard summer and winter, is the grasshopper's; whether in life or in dream, "The poetry of earth is ceasing never." It is the natural poetry, the poetry of the effortless. The grasshoppers are poets; Plato tells us that they were once people: but "when the Muses came and song appeared they were ravished with delight; and singing always, never thought of eating and drinking, until at last in their forgetfulness they died."[1]

We need not be reminded of Keats's pleas for negative capability, nor even of his concern with the antechambers of thought (cf. chapter 5), of "What the Thrush said," the "Ode on Indolence," and so forth. But in the sonnet on "The Floure and the Lefe," quoted in chapter 3 above, Keats describes another kind of effortlessness: it is the way we respond to what we read, at a level that remains inaccessible to any deliberate act of mind; we know things, as we read, that can never be reconstituted by any form of effort.[2] Everything that happens in that poem happens by surprises ("And oftentimes he feels the dewy drops / Come cool and suddenly against his face"). In the end, the effortlessness with which the message, or melody, of the Chaucerian poem has been communicated is reflected in the condition of the reader, prostrated, overwhelmed in a self-surrender that is the white shadow of the poem's own ease.

> Oh! what a power hath white simplicity!
>   What mighty power has this gentle story!
>   I that forever feel athirst for glory
>   Could at this moment be content to lie
>   Meekly upon the grass, as one whose sobbings
>   Were heard of none beside the mournful robins.

In dreams, as in Keats's description of reading poetry, one can sometimes feel the bit drop from the mouth of language. In dream, language can be laid down with as little effort as the pavement of a moonlit sky. In fact, far from being produced with effort, language in dreams is a sediment that actually lightens, or relieves the mind-fluid from which it has silted out. And all our conscious attempts to articulate are just an effort to reach back to that effortlessness, to allow that unconscious process to resume.

Catachresis may be understood as another of the areas in which language can move without effort. In his discussion of the Simplon Pass episode in Wordsworth's *Prelude*, David Haney describes the implosion of the mind, flooded by the imagination, as analogous and parallel to the entering of catachresis into a semantic gap.[3] There is a usurpation, without resistance, of a space in both language and narrative. Wordsworth resorts to the word *Imagination* "through sad incompetence of human speech" (6.593), simply because there is no proper word to describe the experience. "Just as the catachresis-figure extends itself into a semantic gap, the imagination does not replace something that is already there (as a metaphor would), but enters a gap in the poem's narrative. . . . The poet, 'halted, without a struggle to break through' [1850: 'without an effort'], paradoxically encounters no resistance from the force that comes 'athwart' him; conversely the Imagination's . . . usurpation of the poet's text encounters no resistance because it enters a gap in the narrative." " . . . the initial kinetic energy of usurpation is effortlessly translated into the potentiality of a 'home' in the 'evermore about to be.' " As Haney would have it, "a transition from 'figure' to 'catachresis' . . . occurs when the failure of a figural act becomes the vacuum which necessitates a catachresis." In any case, there is a space, an unprepared space, created by the poet's having crossed the Alps before he is aware that he has done so, into which the Imagination must flood, as into a pocket of lost time, an unoccupied space in memory. That space is empty, and what moves into it goes without resistance.

To proceed from the possibilities of an effortless language to the same issue in the domain of the image; is there image unmarked by effort? Or, on the contrary, does the "figure," to repeat Lyotard's comment, always carry the stamp of a "violence initiale," that same force of the Fall that Lyotard continues to discover in language as well as image many years after the writing of *Discours, Figure?* "Perhaps every sentence, even a 'familiar' one, an easily recognized sentence, contains the force of something that is falling on you, of something that is charging upon you."[4] Certainly the image has had an even worse press than the word as a vector of violence. In the dominant traditions of modern thought, the image is the source of error and blindness; the arena of the mind must be purged of idols before thought can be safe from distortion. What might be called the Jewish tendency in modern philosophy (though most of its representatives are not Jewish) has produced a widespread hostility to images, a new iconoclasm (see above, chapter 1). Images represent idolatry and superstition, dreams and metaphors are escapism and delusion, et cetera. But a misapprehension lies beneath this version of the Jewish tradition; or, rather, it is a shallow interpretation of that tradition. "Thou shalt make no graven image" means anything but "thou shalt stick to abstractions."

True, the injunction to love the Lord one's God with all one's heart, and with all one's soul, and with all one's might (Deut. 6:5) may seem to leave little room or time for other feelings. But the love of God is itself partly rendered in images, and the Old Testament (at least beyond the Pentateuch), God knows, skips like a lamb with illustrations, stories, metaphors. They may be employed only in the service of God; but, with that proviso, why may they not be used again? Surely Philo proved that it is possible to be a Jew and still to live in images.[5] The élan that carries us into a metaphor is not something that we should withhold ourselves from, any more than we should withhold ourselves from sexual love (certainly not a Jewish decree). Metaphor is the universal language, the truly international element in every language, as sex is the international and transtemporal form of communication at the physical level. The image is in some ways the midwife and in others the wife of the idea, not its casket: the image enables the idea to take shape and to be born. "Imagery is sometimes not the mere apparelling of a thought, and of a nature to *be* detached from the thought, but is the coefficient that, being superadded to something else, absolutely *makes* the thought as a *third* and separate existence."[6] Even the widowed image of modern literature (Gogol, Hopkins, Kafka, Robbe-Grillet) continues to seek its lost completion (see below, chapter 8). If metaphor is an act of naming that accompanies the experience of love, what should Jews, or their tradition, have against it? Metaphors are just the content of the experienced world under a different name, under a good name. If images are all a variety of metaphor, they are all rooted in some good. They offer resting-places, islands of pleasure, sensory expressions of right feeling, alternatives to both fixed abstractions and endless commentary, to both the Platonic and the rabbinical or Derridean traditions. Images are not only records of painful memories, psychological debris, things to hide behind, or, as Sartre would say, sunken, degenerate ideas. As in my experience of after-images' having turned into pictures, images can represent an improvement rather than a deterioration of the events they record: as in the Song of Songs, they can function as a reinforcement rather than a diminution or an evasion of feeling.

Images as the expression of love do not militate against the love of God any more than other expressions of love do. Images may be symptomatic of dislocations in the affective system; but not because they are images: lots of other things can serve that purpose too. I suspect the notion that images necessarily have something wrong about them stems from an association of images with schematization on the part of people who do not, to begin with, have the experience of vivid images and therefore do not know it exists. They think of vivid seeing as the derivation of a schema from something seen, like making a postcard out of a spruce tree. They are photographers in thinking rather than artists, and their notion of seeing is that it is a reduction to something that can be repeated or reproduced. The intense involvement with the thing seen, so that it glows and trembles, is something of which they have no notion. They are, to put it simply, not in love with trees; they are people who are not visually alive, whose eyes have no appetite. "Ubi amor, ibi oculus," Lyotard quotes Hugh of St. Victor as saying.[7] And what's so wrong with that? As Sir Andrew MacPhail once retorted, in justification of his odd little book, *The Master's Wife:* "And if I have merely created an image, the ancient defense remains: An image makes us know, love, remember."[8]

The other, more substantial objection to images comes from those who find in them the threat of idolatry or superstition. They fear the potential of savagery in all literal belief, in the conviction of presence, in the expectation of seeing God in the flesh. To be in church on Easter morning, I gather, may be to feel the rising of the man-God as a thrilling and terrifying possibility, as actually happening. A panic, a madness, an ecstasy, a breathtaking thing-about-to-be that has already taken place. But also attended by a possibility of violence. To question is to be turned into Pentheus, crazed to witness by one's own disbelief, negative testimony to what can be described only through that which it is not: finally, to be destroyed by the believers.

This is a kind of seeing, and feeling, that makes the pleasures of metaphor pale. The choice, at least in the simple options of Western religion, becomes God-man or man-God, and all other choices, whether of schools of philosophy, modes of expression, or life-styles, cluster around this choice: witness to the Resurrection, or Jew. One who watches the rising of God, voyeur par excellence, eyes fixed upon the grave-clothes' stirring, or impatient auditor and disputant in arguments with God.

Let there be a mediate seeing that is not the first small step on the plunge to violence, the murderous intolerance of the eye. After all, the eye has some claim to authority. Appearances may be deceptive, but what we see, we see: we do not deny what we see; it would make no sense to reject it. We can rest in certainty when we see something, even an optical illusion. There is no such thing as a visual experience that doesn't make sense. Every picture is as real as what it seems to be: "The image cannot lie."[9]

But at this point I must go back to some of the hard questions about images that have been raised recently, particularly by J.-J. Goux, though the inquiry necessitate a digression from the effortless. Is the image, in fact, always the image of the mother, and are we stuck with the option of exiling images (mothers) or surrendering to the blind fury of *Blut und Boden,* to the orgiastic seasonal cycle of lust and murder? (Even Shelley's "Adonais" asks that same question; Bernard-Henri Lévy's *Le Testament de Dieu* answers it with an emphatic affirmative.) Is the image's silence, its refusal to speak, the silence of the rejecting woman-mother, who forces language, as a *pis aller,* upon eternally suppliant man? Only to a poor juggler (i.e., to someone who has no pretentions to potency—"Our Lady's Juggler"—) is she prepared to speak. (The Orpheus and Eurydice myth and the story "Rumpel-stiltskin" can be read as variants on this theme.) Will the image, already widowed, be entirely without a future if woman repudiates all her former roles? If she does, is there any way for the sexual energy that resides in metaphors to be rescued? Or is that sexual energy, after all, only a voyeuristic energy, invested in image rather than woman so that man can *image* woman as mating with someone else, and so confirm her inaccessibility to himself? (see the *Othello* section of chapter 2 above).

These are questions that may be better suited to musing than to reply, but they are not quite rhetorical questions either. There may be ways of preserving the independence of the image, rather than relegating it to the role of patsy in sexual politics. I have already pointed out (n. 6, above) that images are not only images: they contain ideas inaccessible in any other form—ideas that would not have occurred if they had not occurred in metaphor. What is less obvious is that part of every image, even of a naturalistic image, is not an image of something external to itself, but is cast forward from the self. This part of it is not representational, whether of woman, mother, or anything else. (Nonrepresentation in images is not to be confused with abstraction, which always, even through its etymology, implies representation).[10] Even if woman be required for the fulfillment of the image, that fulfillment is other than woman alone. That added element, what one might call the extra, nonrepresentational part of image, can be seen as an element of holiness in the very midst of an iconoclastic system. It is one thing to abstain, quite properly, from representing the irrepresentible,[11] another to withhold the measure of grace that can be contributed to the creaturely through the artist's vision.

Again, a distinction no doubt needs to be made between, on the one hand, "abstraction" as male form imposed upon a female nature, in the dualistic pattern attacked by Lévy and Handelman,[12] and, on the other hand, a style of thought in which corpus and commentary grow continuous, in "the purity of a writing that goes from man to man, over the ruins of all allegory" (Lévy, p. 163; and does the ruin of allegory imply the end of image?). But the repudiation of dualism in favor of a continuous textuality need not entail a rejection of the senses: this may be an appropriate extrapolation from invidious Greek or Christian divisions between intelligence and matter, but not from a style of thinking that accepts the physical world on common terms, without repudiating it and without requiring its redemption. It is a good place, if we can live in it, full of sap and pleasure. It also helps us think; its experiences and images supply the materials and the means for thinking; they do not drown, overwhelm, or overbody thought, they do not enwomb or entomb it so that it ceases to be it. They help to incubate thought, but they also ensure that thought will not be only the repetition of something already written. And if "they" be (for man) female, so much the better.

It is too soon for me to adopt a fixed position on this difficult question, but let me say provisionally that through such considerations it may be possible to revise modern iconoclasm so that it can accept some images, some metaphors, some symbols, perhaps even some emblems. In a symbol, Creuzer says, reason can get "totally and in one moment an alliance with the senses"; and an impresa reveals "an aspect of the structure of the world which would seem to elude the ordered progress of dialectic argument."[13]

Besides, words, our principal alternative to images, have their disadvantages too. Words always have some "business"; images may be disinterested. Words belong to the world of ulterior purposes, where nothing can ever be left as it is. As I listen to the brook in the valley, I think of what I am going to say: "As I listen to the brook in the valley." As I look at the stars, I can think of nothing to say that would not seem ludicrous. A landscape can impose silence as effectively as a slap on the mouth.

Words are tied up with our private emotional purposes to a degree to which images, which have one foot in the objective world, cannot be. Images are objective to the extent to which they have their roots in the real world; words are objective to the extent to which they have their roots in other people's minds. These are different kinds of objectivity.

For all these reasons I should like to make a plea for images; and I should further like to divorce their enjoyment from whatever intensification of the specular may occur in the experience of revealed religion. Images are what makes language worth using. They leave silent traces of motion and empathy, and they ask for no payment. They do not even ask to be remembered. As I have mentioned several times before, where Lyotard (p. 270) says that in the inception of dream-thought there is already a "figure" that implies a "violence initiale," I would rather say that behind thought and image alike there is a "nonviolence initiale" in which the image may partake, or which it may express.

So, to return to "The Frog King": in stressing the absence of any image connected with the sound that has accompanied the snapping of Iron Henry's heartbands (*not* the breaking of his heart, which they were intended to prevent; illogically, they snap because his heart is *no longer* breaking), I necessarily overemphasize and simplify. The advantage in having the sound at this point, rather than any possible visual effect, is more technical than moral: it is that sight would have involved an explanation: as I have said, sight always already makes sense. The sound can be free of interpretation. It can even be detached from the ethical theme, rather than understood as merely an expression of that theme. After all, the sites for an ethical bond between Iron Henry and the Prince are weak. The retainer's love is almost self-enclosed, or perhaps self-sufficient: one hardly expects or wants an object worthy of it. The justification given for the sound that we hear is sufficiently detached from that sound, not only in time, but also in substance, for the sound to retain its independence. The explanation follows at a psychological distance more remote than its distance in time.

The cracking of the bonds can also be thought of as a summons to justice: a calling of the prince to account. Clearly, the new prince feels guilty, or he wouldn't be worried about the carriage's breaking down, and he wouldn't have so much difficulty recognizing the sound each time it occurs. This reconstructed princeling hardly seems continuous with the man, whoever he was, to whom Henry had once, in his preexistence, found it appropriate to offer his fealty; we wonder what it is Henry sees in this timorous being to warrant such intense loyalty. Is the sound a recall of that other prince, from the preconceptual space before the narrative began? For Iron Henry has clearly committed himself to a higher obligation than his merely uxorious master.

In any case, the sound is free from the assemblage required by the visual, and even, paradoxically, free of language. A crack, and freedom is declared. As I have said, the noise does not only signal the freedom; it also develops a space around it, which we can then experience, retroactively, as the freedom itself. This is an area through which the wave liberated by the shock of sound can propagate at will, unbroken by reefs of thought or by visual impediments.

A whole additional branch of iconoclastic theory could be developed from Lacoue-Labarthe's fine essay on rhythm, "L'Écho du sujet," at the end of *Le Sujet de la philosophie.* For Lacoue-Labarthe, aural rhythm is repetition, and, as such, imitation; the expression of obsessive recurrent desire. Without it, the visual field remains unorganized, and perception becomes impossible. Rhythm, therefore, founds perception, and, in its absence, nothing can be seen: we touch on "l'irrévélable," and the image disintegrates. Only sound makes vision, and, with it, mimesis, possible.[14] But, even without this additional avenue of inquiry's being explored, one more major objection to images still remains to be dealt with. This is the standard iconoclastic criticism; it is produced even more regularly than the caveat that vision may create impediments to reason or become an agent of violence. The conventional complaint about images is that they paralyze the mind: they have a stunning force. I quote a passage from Hartman in which the "festering" paralysis produced by vision in Tennyson's poetry is described. "The trouble with Tennyson is that his poetic dream-work seems at first no work at all. It is so easy, so unlabored—deceptively 'idle,' to use a charged word of his own. . . . Such impassibility is perhaps part of the infection, an unresolved narcissism of festering lily, or psyche. Yet this liaison between specular and poetic is precisely what fosters the illusion of completeness and so the attractive fetish we call a poem. For a moment the et cetera of language is absorbed into that fetish. . . . "[15] I would counter with Keats's line, "The poetry of earth is never dead." Poetry develops its own et cetera.

In an essay on Proust, John Erwin reviews the basic iconoclastic position from a theological as well as a literary point of view. The usual approach to iconoclasm in Proust is through the aesthetic: it is the area in which Proust becomes entangled with Ruskin. In the essay "John Ruskin" Proust accuses Ruskin of idolatry, of failing to heed his own injunctions: of following pleasing images for their own sake rather than for the sake of the truth that they may bear. This is the sort of error that Proust imputes to his novelist, Bergotte, who has a tendency to become infatuated with the sound of his own words. Yet, of course, Proust himself remains unsure of his position, for he concludes the Ruskin essay with the contradictory remark that aesthetic pleasure is precisely that which accompanies the discovery of a truth.

In any case, John Erwin's approach is different. (It has affinities with Carol Jacob's, for which see below, n. 18). As he understands it, iconoclasm is patriarchal tyranny, the forbidding of metaphor, of the right to see: an Oedipal decree.[16] (For Goux too, to repeat, iconoclasm is the refusal to let the son see the mother; forbidden images are always implicitly female.)[17] Erwin reads Proust's dependence on the involuntary memory, effortless though it be, as an acknowledgment of the image's seductive power. It takes over the writer's thinking process and leaves him passive. Similarly,

Charlus "exaggerates the pose as passive receiver of impressions with which Proust celebrates the *mémoire involontaire* and so not only transgresses the Father's command to be fruitful and multiply but also—supposedly—abdicates his own authorial privilege." The involuntary memory is a pretext for pretending that one can do no more; that one wasn't doing one's own writing in the first place, and that it is not possible for one to take things in hand now. Stunned by the image, one will never go on to become a father oneself. "The genuine logos is always a dia-logos; and the guardian spirit of the symbolic and differential realm is a Father barring the image's closure of dialogue, of stilling prematurely. . . . "[18]

If all this were true, the injunction against the use of images would be well justified. But Erwin's real point is that all this only *seems* to be so, and that, in the distributed textures of *A la recherche,* in its discursive, nonmetaphoric prose, creative power is actually reclaimed and recovered. Or, as I would put it, the rejection of idolatry is not ipso facto iconoclasm; there is still a use for images in the roll of discourse, and, although they may at times threaten to arrest our thought, they can, again, become the very bearings on which the "et cetera" of thought moves forward. As Novalis says, poetry does not do, but makes it possible for others to do.[19]

What we need to remember is that an image, or indeed a word, is always generated in expectation of a reply. I say reply rather than response, because we tend to forget that language is basically dialogue.[20] Oral language is privileged not only because there is something more direct, or more immediate, about it than there is about writing, but also because it is essentially dialogue. And in dialogue, images have something more fluid or tentative about them than they do in writing. An image launched toward another speaker is undogmatic; it is not meant to freeze the auditor into a position of assent or denial, but keeps the provisional nature of truth—something riding on an image—evident.[21] The question becomes rather, "What prompts us to more ideas of our own," than "What is the truth?" As Emerson puts it, "it is not instruction, but provocation, that I can receive from another soul."[22]

In this function and condition the image has nothing objectionable about it—not even in terms of the Biblical injunction against images. Outside dialogue, on the other hand, we always seem obliged to say yes or no, because we can stop long enough to let ourselves set in an attitude of submission or rejection: we let an image tell us what is truth, or what denies it. (In fact, perhaps the image is what, in Cardinal Newman's terms, makes the difference between inference and assent.) But, for the speaker himself, what he says can never be true; he is not blinded by his own images; and in dialogue, the provisional character of images is clear to both speakers. In dialogue we do not fool one another with the pretense that we are speaking truth. The wheels of one's interlocutor's mind may spin when he is confronted with an image, but he will recognize its merely human quality as something that has only provisional status in the discourse of its speaker. And the image is in turn a kind of flywheel that balances and sustains the motion of thought between two minds; in its absence, one cannot even really tell what one is thinking, or what to think next.

This frustration with a mind that works too literally, without propelling images, in dialogue, is deftly captured in the well-known anecdote about the two Jews who meet in a railroad station. (I give it in brutally abridged form.) "Where are you going?" says one of them. "To Pinsk," says the other. "Don't try to fool me," retorts the first; "you say you're going to Pinsk to make me think that you're really going to Minsk, when I know perfectly well you're going to Pinsk!"

In the alternation between abstraction and imagery that is

our mental process, and that seems to have as its object the creation of the paradoxes that we then call thought (as Merleau-Ponty calls contradiction the very condition of consciousness),[23] Minsk is the image that gives Pinsk its reality. An image makes something wrong, right. But why was Pinsk wrong the first time around? It lacked the provisionality of the image, Minsk, and so did not really give a clue to the direction being taken by the speech or, indeed, by the speaker. Dialogue must be unstable in order to proceed; the image helps provide the instability that gives dialogue its momentum. Once we have started an image, or been started on one, we can no more control the direction of our movements than we can if we have stepped on a banana peel. To be sure, we no longer have to exert effort; but, by the same token, we have surrendered to the thing that is carrying us along.

The A on either side of B, the Pinsk on either side of Minsk (especially the first A), is needed as a kind of flange or lever to depress, to start the dialogue; it is a provocation,[24] or an occasion, rather than itself an integral part of the dialogue. It makes the image (Minsk) pop up, and then the ball starts passing back and forth, the ball of meaning, or of thought, or of provisional truth, of whatever it is that goes between people in dialogue. Minsk is needed to create the imbalance that will set off the oscillation; from that moment, something must constantly be retrieved. As Wittgenstein says, "Ich philosophiere jetzt, wie eine alte Frau, die fortwährend etwas verlegt und es wieder suchen muss; einmal die Brille, einmal den Schlüsselbund." ("Now I philosophize like an old woman who is constantly mislaying something and has to look for it again; first it's her glasses, then it's her bunch of keys" [*On Certainty*, #532].) And, to the extent to which the image has initiated a process that has something of the pendulum or at least the seesaw about it, it helps maintain a motion over a fulcrum, or is it on a bearing, with a minimum of effort, other than the effort of balancing, itself. Viewed as fluid contradiction, then, metaphor has no prohibited essence for Judaism.

Claudette Kemper Columbus has spoken of an "extrafused" image, which (to simplify) is there but unspecifiable. Perhaps the object, center, or focus of dialogue is in some sense such an "extrafused" image, one that hovers over the images that roll back and forth from mind to mind, without necessarily coinciding with any one of them.

In dialogue, then, the figurative founds the literal in a special way: by guaranteeing the provisionality of truth, revealing it as just a swirl in the stream of thought, and so ensuring the continued possibility of dialogue itself.[25] Within the individual mind, the constant torque exerted through images to produce corrective contradictions of the given prepares us for dialogue, and attempts to provide the raw material for it. But the goal of even the most telling insight, the most daring reversal, is to set us free on the oscillating waters of an intermental sea, where the easy roll of minds surrenders its own effort to some latent wisdom greater than any of its certainties.[26] "Du musst bedenken, dass das Sprachspiel sozusagen etwas Unvorsehbares ist. Ich meine: es ist nicht begründet. Nicht vernüftig (oder unvernünftig).

"Es steht da—wie unser Leben."

("You must consider that the play of language is, so to speak, something unforeseeable. I mean, it has no foundation. It isn't reasonable [or unreasonable].

"It's just there—like our lives" [*On Certainty*, #559].)

In order for people to trust one another, they must sometimes be able to abandon the strenuous search for truth and allow their language to make a detour through God.

7

Orpheus and Eurydice

AND YET—AND YET....

It must be evident by now that this book has been written in two different, not to say sharply conflicting, states of mind. (At times I have felt as though I had been composing another *Rousseau juge de Jean-Jacques*). Rather than attempt a specious reconciliation between them, I have thought best to let each one seek its extremest formulation, in the hope that whatever insights each provided into the subject of my inquiry would yield more understanding than some intermediate approach. Which perspective provides the more comprehensive view, whether one could eventually be extended to include the other, or whether different moods produce ideas that are genuinely and necessarily irreconcilable, remains to be determined.[1] But the fact is that one can reconsider the Minsk-Pinsk story and come out in a quite different place, despite the apparent conclusiveness of the interpretation I had reached at the end of my previous chapter. The present chapter is a postscript, then, but it is also something more: a review of the same material from a radically different point of view.

Why are the two men in the anecdote in conflict to begin
with? What accounts for the atmosphere of arbitrary antago-
nism with which it opens? Why is it presumed that one man
is trying to keep his destination from the other? What is
he trying to conceal? What are these cities, anyway?

Perhaps only part of our problem has been solved, and
another part merely suppressed.

One possibility is that the men are trying to best each
other in a business deal. But, even if this be so, the cities
remain in memory as though they were the true objects of
contention. To revert to a Freudian reading, let us say that
"city" = "woman," and that the men are quarreling over
a woman. If Pinsk is the true destination, then it—city,
woman—must be concealed. And to conceal it, what better
than a metaphor, "Minsk": that is, an image; that is, again,
a woman?

Image may make possible the "easy roll" of discourse—
between two men—but it takes place over a woman's body:
suppressed, tacit, but giving rise to hostility nevertheless.
Concealed in image, it will breed conflict between the men, a
conflict the source of which remains occluded. It may make
discourse possible—or even necessary—but at the price of
turning it into a quarrel. And the discourse has to come back
to a woman, or a woman/place—Pinsk—anyway.

Biodun Iginla says of the bewitchment in one play that
does settle many quarrels, *A Midsummer Night's Dream,* that
the "lived dream" in it is "the absence of metaphor."[2] Its
"little desiring-mechanisms . . . are nonsignifying" (p. 36), that
is, nonmetaphoric: they do not stand for something else.
They are individual, specific erotic experiences. They express
woman in revolt, refusing the status of metaphor. The liberation of woman, then, would presumably mean the end of
metaphor and the end of the image.

Must we start all over with *The Bacchae* then, after all? Has the Arcadian myth of blueberries, of the effortless, of a secret nonviolence in us, to yield to some rougher truth? Has the painfully fabricated intertexture between ethics and aesthetics to show a rent so soon? What rehabilitation of the image can there be, if the image is always suppressed female erotic desire, silenced, forbidden to speak, reduced to an "image"? We are no better off than we were with an iconoclasm that banned the image-woman entirely: "rehabilitated" images, half-domesticated images, will always remain subversive. The spontaneous disappearance of images would seem to be the only answer. From the male consciousness? That implies a reform (if it be a reform) that seems almost beyond attainment. From the female consciousness? Were they ever there to begin with? Have women ever needed images?

I have said that the eradication of images from male consciousness seems beyond attainment. For the male, the very first awareness of femaleness seems already to be symbolic: woman comes into being, for man, as symbol of herself rather than as herself. In the bewilderment that follows the impulse to transgression, man gives birth to woman: but to woman as image.

In *The Prelude* 12, 1. 225ff., Wordsworth describes a frightening childhood experience: coming across a memorial to a murderer in a mountain valley. As he flees uphill, he sees

> A naked pool that lies beneath the hills,
> The beacon on the summit, and, more near,
> A girl, who bore a pitcher on her head,
> And seemed with difficult steps to force her way
> Against the blowing wind.

She is mentioned again:

> The female and her garments vexed and tossed
> By the strong wind.

Like anyone subject to trauma, Wordsworth in this scene clearly identifies as much with the transgressor as with the victim, and, as I have said, in the moment that follows transgression, the vision of woman is born to him. But it is the vision of woman *as image,* carrying the burden of her metaphoricity right on her head: the pitcher, the very *symbol* of her sexuality. She is already clothed, but something still tears at her clothes, as though trying to strip off the signs of her investiture; her role as bearer of the symbolic is a difficult one, strenuous to carry out. Yet she is not seen as hostile or resentful; she seems to accept the necessity of her image-bearing role; but, like an Undine, she has clearly just come from some place where different conditions prevailed. What was that place? In part, it may be thought of as the space before the "clothing" or "dressing up" of ideas that I tried to identify in my last chapters—the prestrenuous, naked place from which thought and dreams arise (cf. the "naked pool.") But the wind that moves with her seems to express something else. It is an elemental force that speaks of her, without clothes, with herself as the only pitcher, undisguised, not yet dressed, asymbolic. It harks back to a stage, already irrecoverable yet also impossible to leave behind, when she was everything herself, not yet an image of herself, or "The female."

Nevertheless, although I have been saying that the disappearance of images from the mind seems an improbable eventuality, the image may in fact have weakened; it may no longer occupy a secure position in our mental processes.

There is a class of images, half-disqualified images, that I am inclined to call "widowed images." The modern image: the meaningless object (as it is encountered in Gogol, Hopkins, Dostoievski, Roussel, Camus, Sartre, Robbe-Grillet) is the widowed image, that is, the image as widower. But since the widowed image can't be both male (i.e., tenor) and image (i.e., vehicle, female, "nature") simultaneously, it must express itself as sterilized, that is, meaningless, or tenorless, female "vehicle." Such images are meaningless or "nonsignifying" because they lack their erotic counterparts, their completion, and not because they express an individual, unrepeatable erotic event.[3]

Kafka is caught between a solid, classical-Jewish iconoclasm and a modern widowed iconoclasm, in which there are no substantial images to break.

One can also think of Hegel's dislocation of content from form at a certain stage in the history of art as illustrating the "widowing" of images. Objects are left to go their own more and more independent, less and less "beautiful" way, as abstract form prevails.[4]

A clear instance of the widowed image can be found in Hopkins's *Journals.* Hopkins describes a piece of wood that he has seen in a daydream; he realizes that it is part of an outhouse. "I had seen it longer together and had that day been wondering what it was: in reality it is used to hold a little heap of cinders against the wall which keep from the frost a piece of earthenware pipe which there comes out and goes in again making a projection in the wall. It is just the things which produce dead impressions, which the mind, either because you cannot make them out or because they were perceived across other more engrossing thoughts, has made nothing of and brought into no scaping, that force themselves up in this way afterwards."[5] These are things, as Hopkins would say, of which he has not "found the law"

(p. 146); things in which one does not hear "the *form* speaking" (p. 163); for "ugliness even [would be] better than meaning-lessness" (p. 195). They are objects in search of a vitalizing love, but condemned to wander forever through the mind, always seeming about to capture, or recapture, meaning, but remaining unfulfilled: eternally stuck, so to speak, in the outhouse of the mind, adjacent to love.

They are, one might say, Orpheus-objects. Orpheus too was a kind of widower. But Eurydice, not Orpheus, is at fault for her second decline into the underworld. She did nothing to help. Her detachment forces him to look back: he is overwhelmed by a mad, uncontrollable desire to look (Vergil, *Georgics* 4.1.488). Why? because he is jealous. He knows that she wants her bottom-world, her underworld, world of dark eros, hidden from his sight. There is no indication that she had ever struggled to rejoin him. And so not only the possi-bility of their being united, but eventually the very structure of civilization (Daedalian harmony, Daedalian carpentry, product of redirected sexuality) must collapse. No matter how roundabout the sublimated sexuality and what it con-structs, there is nothing and nobody to see in the end; at the moment of coalescence, there is nobody there: the House of Usher falls; Feathertop (Hawthorne) is broom again. The female truth, the crack, appears, to break apart the building or the work of art.[6] Myth and social relations both collapse, as, for example, at the end of "The Miller's Tale," where Alysoun alone emerges unscathed from among her various men, with all their plans and ideas—and not only unscathed, but sexually fulfilled (having had her "solas") to boot.[7]

Eurydice gets rid of Orpheus, so he can go on being a poet, messing around with language; and she, of course, will be the content of his poetry, but she will not have to tag along with him. She is safely away from him and his words. Who needs his language and his odes, anyway? His odes to absence?

Stones and animals may be impressed by them, but certainly not women. He is a little like Rumpelstiltskin, a figure of fun, fit only to be torn to pieces by other women as sensible as Eurydice, who care no more for his efforts to confine love in language than she does. (In one version of the folktale, Rumpelstiltskin does tear himself—together with his long-winded name—apart in his fury and despair.)[8] Rumpelstiltskin (German: Rumpelstilzchen), too, gets what he deserves, from the miller's daughter turned queen. He is the child's father; what other claim could he have had on her baby? After all, it is he who has been locked up with her night after night, spinning straw into gold (surely an excellent metaphor for love-making). But the queen simply can't associate Rumpelstiltskin (i.e., "What's-his-name?") with her baby.[9] Basically autoerotic, she simply accepts sexual experience as feeding into her, as for her use; its product, a fortiori, is hers alone. The man is not connected with the child for her, whatever his role in its conception might have been. It is simply her child; she has a child; the man, alone in the story, has a name—nothing but a name, though. He pities her, foolishly, and gives her the chance she is looking for: to send him packing, vested with nothing but language, that is, with nonsense: "Rum-pel-stilz-chen." She shows no trace of pity for him; he gets one portion of Pandora's single delusive blessing, Hope, and after that, nothing but mockery. If he wants to pride himself on his name, let him content himself with a name. And so he remains, or what is left of him. Let us pray for him (as, in one version, we are asked to do).[10]

This variant of the age-old custody-dispute theme, then, recurrent from *The Eumenides* through *A Midsummer Night's Dream* to *The Magic Flute,* once more raises the whole question of woman's relation to language. This question was answered, flatly, by the medieval philosopher Alain de Lille in *The Complaint of Nature:* the vagina is substantive, the penis only adjectival.[11] What room does this leave for metaphor, with its doubling, its secret or unconscious element? All is plain and open. Woman as silent and mysterious picture may be the source of metaphor, of our struggle to combine image and meaning. But woman herself, as substantive, as the noun itself, will tolerate no such instrumental role.

All these problems, as I have mentioned several times, are taken up in Goux's *Les Iconoclastes,* and some of them have already been discussed in chapter 4. Are the sexual and the intellectual aspects of iconoclasm necessarily related? Is iconoclasm a respectable philosophical position, from which images are rejected simply because they are inadequate to express ideas, or is it merely an attempt at suppression of the specific (female erotic) event in favor of a generalizing, unlivable (male) abstraction?

One should perhaps observe, at this point, that, except in the Platonic variety of iconoclasm, images need not be considered identical with objects; one may value objects (things in this world) without consequently approving of images. The question is further complicated by the fact that, even in the plastic arts, abstraction and nonrepresentation are not the same thing.[12] Nor, for that matter, are mimesis and representation identical.[13] Mimesis is associated with images in their disapproved sense because it is a dependent function; it hangs on the object; it is derivative: in Goux's terms, an attempt to gain access to the mother or woman one can't possess, in an attenuated form. But representation, as we have it in, for instance, primitive Mesoamerican sculpture, starts off from a position of power with respect to its object. It dominates the object; it does something *to* it rather than deriving *from* it. One might say that the object is actually sacrificed in the act of representation; here, artistic representation is just an aspect of a sacrificial culture. The kind of abstraction this art produces, in which the violence of the form constricts and crushes the individual variation into, for instance, a beak-face, bears little resemblance to most modern abstraction, in which the artist waits for the object itself to assert its formal possibilities. No individual face can resist or delay the abstracting force of myth; indeed, no individuality had as yet been conceived of to resist it.

From among these various complications of the problems surrounding image and representation, the one I would like to pluck for consideration is, once more, the difference between a Platonic and a Jewish iconoclasm. As I have suggested above, it is one thing, in the Platonic style, to reject the things of this world as inadequate embodiments of ideas, quite another, in a Jewish mode, simply to reject embodiments of divinity. To divinize a body or an object is not to glorify it, or raise it to a higher power: it is, on the contrary, to rob it of its specific virtue, to reduce it, and subordinate it to an ulterior purpose. A fetish or an icon is an object betrayed. The things of this world are the things of this world; and there is no other world. Therefore we approve these things, and accept them.[14]

Together with them, to the best of our limited ability, we accept woman as herself rather than as symbol of herself, "sur les ruines de toute allégorie" ("over the ruins of all allegory"):[15] woman who has a special power and, in Jewish tradition, a direct relationship to God. But none of this requires images to be either denied or adored. In a Platonic situation, much as we may try to evade images, we cannot get away from them, for they are all we have, whether in the form of objects, or as imitations of objects; and one remains in a chronic state of frustrated desire, yearning for originals to which one can never have access. It is hardly surprising that Plato had to resort to the analogy of sexual love to describe our desire for the Forms. His theoretical model imposes a schema that requires a sexual analogue; and images are bad because they are always inadequate imitations of ideal love. It was a short step from Plato's homosexual comparisons to the cult of eroticism among the later Neoplatonists and the school of Chartres.

I seem to be coming around once more to the opinion that the image need not be rejected by Jewish thought (despite all that pointed to the opposite conclusion at the beginning of this chapter). Certainly, to the extent to which image is simply object, thing of this world, it need not be rejected. The strange cup at the beginning of *Portrait of a Lady* is an object. It may have some symbolic dimension, but it is, also, an object. For something to be nonmetaphoric, it need not be abstract. Here I think that Goux, for all his brilliance, misses an important point.[16] For Jews, he says, "The Eternal becomes a place that cannot be metaphorized. . . . " Judaism "subtracts a non-figurable site (the Eternal) from all the variegated richness of imagination's productions."[17] Perfectly true: but that doesn't make the Eternal an abstraction: and when he tries to show Marx and Freud forcing specificity to crumble under the impact of Law, Goux is discovering in Marx and Freud a non-Jewish strain, if indeed it be there at all. The disappearance of the fetish (pp. 102–3) in economics is not identical with the instauration of abstraction. It is not the castrating rule of abstraction, as Goux would have it (p. 134), to which a Jewish Law would force all particulars to yield; under Jewish law there is nothing but particulars. There is no Mandate. What we have is what we are.

But, as we have seen, Jewish dialogue (Minsk and Pinsk) is not immune to the infiltration of suppressed sexuality, with the nattering that accompanies it. Something more open is needed. Not the crabbed tradition of Kafka, oblique, always bringing one up short against some possible refusal. Not disputatious quibbling or even coruscating subtlety: that is not all the literature that Jews have to offer. The plain, open speech of Deuteronomy 6 and the equally plain and open words of the Song of Solomon, full of the pressure of immediate and present experience, may help us toward an appreciation of what an adequate love of God, the sexes, and language should be. In the Song of Songs we have the realization of love right here and now, not at some uncertain time and in some indefinite place. For, as it can be said that "separation from the loved one is the most painful foretaste of death,"[18] so it can be said that the best thing in life is to wake up and find one's beloved here, in this world of things.

Here is an image. "Thou art beautiful, O my love, as Tirzah, comely as Jerusalem, terrible as an army with banners. Turn away thine eyes from me, for they have overcome me" (Song of Songs 6:4–5). And here is the same thing without any images: "And thou shalt love the Lord thy God with all thine heart, and with all thy soul, and with all thy might" (Deuteronomy 6:5). What is the difference? They mean the same. And were those really metaphors, or similes? These are real things: Tirzah, Jerusalem, the army. These cities are not Minsk or Pinsk. They are not subterfuges. They exist in solid form, in the true world. Metaphors of this degree, at least, some men cannot do without. They are open; they are not machines for the evasion or the repression of desire. One can talk openly, even in images. And (to hark back to my previous chapters and the songs that come in sleep) effortlessly, too:

> And the roof of thy mouth like the best wine for my beloved, that goeth down sweetly, causing the lips of those that are asleep to speak.[19]

For all that this was intended to be a disqualifying postscript, I cannot quite yet bring myself to say: love is past; the double vision of metaphor is gone; good riddance.

8

Brahms's Deconstruction of a Text by Goethe: Of Honesty in Music

IN 1774, AT THE AGE OF TWENTY-FIVE, GOETHE PUBLISHED *Werther*.[1] This story of an unhappy love affair that leads to suicide brought Goethe a flood of letters from young men who found in the novel a reflection of their own mood. One of these youths, by the name of Plessing, was singled out by Goethe for a direct response. In the fall of 1777 Goethe left behind his beloved Charlotte von Stein and, subsequently, a group of friends whom he had accompanied on a boar-hunt, in order to undertake the double mission of visiting Plessing and of climbing the Brocken in winter.

The stanzas of the poem that refer to Plessing were set to music by Goethe's contemporary, Reichardt. This setting was seen by Brahms, who chose the same text for his "Alto Rhapsody," op. 53, in 1869. Evidently troubled by confused feelings about sex ever since his adolescent days as a pianist in sleazy taverns, Brahms appeared unable to propose to his adored Clara Schumann after her husband's death, but did eventually fall in love with her daughter Julie and possibly even made an offer of marriage. The first *Liebeslieder Waltzes* (op.

52) are often understood as a declaration of love; the "Rhapsody" as an expression of despair, written after his proposal was rejected, or perhaps merely ignored. (Whether Brahms's hesitations in his dealings with women are attributable to latent homosexuality must remain a matter of conjecture).

These are the bare facts surrounding the composition of the poem and the musical work. They allow us to review in a musical context the problems of accommodating eros to art.

Winter Trip in the Harz Mountains (Goethe)

Hawk on a heavy cloud,
My song,
Rest on soft plume,
Watch morning prey,
My song.

A God
Has marked a path
For each,
That races
The fortunate
Straight to their happy goal.

But whose heart
Is pressed by anguish,
He fights, in vain;
The limits
Of the brazen thread will open
Only to the bitter shear.

Into the quaking thicket
Drives the rough beast;

And long since have the spires
Sunk into the swamps
With the sparrows.

It's easy to follow the coach
Driven by Fortune,
Like the ordered train
Over improved roads
Behind an entering Prince.

But who is that there?
His path gone in the undergrowth,
Branches clash behind him;
The grass stands up;
Absence has swallowed him.

Who can heal his pain
For whom balm has turned poison?
Who from fullness of love
Has drunk up hate?
Despised turned despiser
He gnaws himself
In secret; in self-depriving self-seeking.

Is there on your harp, Love's Father,
One tone
One he can hear, then quicken
His heart! Free clouded gaze
To look over the thousand springs
That well beneath him
Unseen by his thirsting,
From the waste.

You who of joy much make,
Too much for each,
Bless brothers' hunt

On wild beast track,
Bold youths'
Exultant murder;
Late avengers of ruin
Heaped on stick-wielding, helpless
Hill hands.

But pour gold cloud
Around me only;
Surround with winter's green,
Until rose re-ripen,
Damp hair of your singer,
O Love.

With darkening torch, him
You light
Over fords at night,
Over hanging roads
Over empty spaces;
Into his heart you laugh
Thousand-colored Dawn;
Up, high, you carry him
With biting storms;
Winter-streams topple from crags
Into his psalms,
And
The spirit-rows
That crowned that pate
Laureled by observant peoples
Snow-hung
Turn on his altar of most loving thanks,
That dread top.

You with unexplored bosom,
Open secret, tower
Over the astonished world
And look down from the clouds

Down upon its kingdoms and its splendors
Watered from the veins of your brothers
By you
Through those
Who stand about you.[2]

The "Alto Rhapsody" of Brahms is about sexual tragedy. What is that tragedy? It is, presumably, the tragedy of Brahms's own life, his inability to reach sexual conclusions with either Clara Schumann or her daughter—or perhaps, for that matter, with any other woman. To a lesser extent it may also be about Goethe's sexual tragedy with Charlotte von Stein. But it is also about everyone's sexual tragedy: that men cannot quite give women what women want; nor build, through their relations with women, even through empathy with women, something that they want themselves. Either there is too much sex—the female "sed non satiata," or too little—the male; no equation seems to produce a mutually satisfying, lasting match between the two.

Mary Wollstonecraft ridiculed Rousseau for such assertions,[3] but they have been at the core of male myths about sexuality ever since Teiresias suffered. I said that men cannot provide women with what they want even if they attempt, through an act of empathy, to identify with women and so, in a sense, to live through them. Teiresias tried just that. He became a woman for seven years, and so learned all about sex; but his knowledge did not help him when he became a man again; he was promptly struck blind by Hera for telling the truth, namely, that sex resides primarily with women, and cannot be transferred to men. In other words, he was struck blind by a woman, that is, castrated, that is, returned to his condition of sexual inadequacy as soon as he became a man again. (Philo, incidentally, maintains that men are basically asexual;

women may become candidates for beatitude only after becoming as sexless as men.)[4]

What kind of music would Brahms have wanted to compose, or would he have wanted to compose at all, if he had been in Teiresias's state of mind while Teiresias was a successful harlot? What poetry, if any, would Goethe have wanted to write if he had had a genuine, that is, female, awareness of the primacy of sex? In the latter case, at least, we may have a clue. After the beautiful Christiane Vulpius, of lower class and less genteel than Frau von Stein, had instructed him in a different attitude toward life, Goethe scoffed at the melancholy poet: "Do not sing in mournful numbers / Lonely, lonely is the night." ("Singet nicht in Trauertönen / Von der Einsamkeit der Nacht".) "Let a poor dog take his lust / Mixed with sorrow, if he must." ("Sei ein armer Hund erfrischt / Von der Lust, mit Pein gemischt!")[5] It is possible, on the other hand, that unlike poetry, music, even melancholy music, has no shortfall in the composing, though it may fall short of sexual experience for the listener. It seems to have body, wholeness, integrity, that is, "organic form," without suppressing or denying sex; the libidinal thrill is simply dissolved into it, not separate or separable. Or maybe this is true of only some music, not of Brahms's "Alto Rhapsody."

What sort of peculiar poem is the "Harzreise im Winter?" It has a macho aggressiveness about it, forced and excessive, from the outset. Goethe tells us that he deliberately put mysterious tones into the poem in order to make it sound more poetic, but at the same time he made it sound like a complicated deception. It starts out with a gratuitous gesture of hostility: like a hawk, we are told, looking for prey. But who will this prey be that the poet and the hawk, the lonely hunters, will be tracing through the underbrush? None other than the fleeing misanthrope whom Goethe has presumably come here to help, deliberately abandoning his companions and their pursuit of the wild boar. There is a confusion of objectives in the poem, a mixture of aggression, sympathy, tenderness, triumph, and self-exaltation, that makes one feel it must be concealing something. Why should the poem assault the unhappy hermit like a stooping hawk? And who in fact is this lurking outsider, "abseits"—doubly "ab"—("ab-er ab"—away, he, away) disappearing through the bushes, more like a wild animal than a human being; he is surely not recognizable as the reasonably civil youth with whom Goethe held a long conversation at Wernigerode. Why the orgiastic bloodthirstiness in a poem of healing and reconciliation? And why stop to award himself, the poet, laurels of love in the midst of his mission of mercy? The majestic phallo-centricity of the conclusion, with the streaming mountain towering over both the astonished world and its subordinate brothers, adds to the sense of incongruity. One can only fall back on a phrase from the poem itself to describe it: "open but secret" ("geheimnisvoll offenbar.")

I have no reading of its secret, only a questioning of the stabilizing force that the poem was supposedly meant to exert on Plessing, and that Brahms's setting too calls into question. The stated themes are sharply discordant. Is Goethe's success, or anticipated success, in love, supposed to consti-tute an object-lesson for the disconsolate Plessing? Are the hunters closing in for the kill just expressing a harsher aspect of the same lust that is implied in the mountain-climbing scene? Or is that scene, finally, ambiguous too? I find myself forced back on some naive Freudian questions: is the Brocken a phallus, or is it a breast, to be gazed at, admired, but never completely penetrated? "You stand with unexplored bosom / Open but secret / Above the astonished world." ("Du stehst mit unerforschtem Busen / Geheimnisvoll offenbar / Über der erstaunten Welt.")

If the encounter with the melancholic Plessing seems peculiar in the midst of this poem devoted to several forms of assault, all at least implicitly sexual, it is, if anything, still more unnatural in a later prose version of the episode.[6] The interview with Plessing is marked by the same ambiguities as Goethe's response to Plessing's letter: "he was just like his letter, interesting but not attractive" (p. 219). Goethe himself is incognito: he has assumed the identity of a voyaging artist who is somehow supposed to be familiar with the famous author, Goethe. Though he still finds the young man's presence "without charm" ("ohne Anmuth"), he offers him a surefire cure for his unhappiness: "one can save and free oneself from a painful, self-tormenting, gloomy state only by the observation of nature and by hearty participation in the external world" (pp. 223–24). Not surprisingly, "My young friend seemed very restless and impatient, as one begins to get irritated with a foreign or confused language the meaning of which one cannot grasp." Goethe's renewed attempts at "undertaking a cure" are dismissed "with the assurance that nothing in this world could or would satisfy him"; "the result is "that my inner being closed up and I held myself in good conscience to be completely free and absolved of any further obligation toward him" (p. 225). A reference in Goethe's correspondence with Charlotte von Stein for early December 1777, "walking with Plessing in the mountains" ("mit Plessing spazieren auf die Berge") finds no equivalent in the *Campagne in Frankreich* passage, and Goethe's subsequent relations with the young man (pp. 227–29) end on the same unsatisfactory note. At no point is there any reference to the woman whose rejection presumably threw Plessing into despair.

One may choose to attribute the stiff and somewhat condescending—or, more accurately, unconvincing—tone of Goethe's prose account to the fact that Goethe was an old man by the time he set the story down, no longer likely to sympathize with sentimental idealism. Nevertheless, he seems haunted by the event; as Brahms was unable to get rid of his "Alto Rhapsody," whatever it meant to him at the time he composed it, so Goethe was followed by the memory of this confrontation for thirty-five years, and felt compelled to write about it twice toward the end of his life.

From the beginning of Goethe studies, it was apparent to critics that Goethe identified himself with the mysterious figure in the "Harzreise." His repudiation not only of the man but also of the mood is suspect, that mood of the time which he later described as pure egocentricity: "separate individualized natures became dominant, without concern for universal Reason, which should after all rule over all Nature." ("Die besondere individuelle Natur allein, ohne Rücksicht auf die allgemeine Vernunft, die doch alle Natur beherrschen soll, zur Sprache kam" [p. 210].)

"Die allgemeine Vernunft, die doch alle Natur beherrschen soll. . . . " Perhaps. Let us abandon the detached and prosaic tone that didn't work for Plessing: it will not work for us. The thing to be "beherrscht" isn't there; it slips away. It isn't subject to reason because, in this very text, it has chosen to disappear. Not only can Nature not be subjected to reason, but neither can reason itself be subjected to reason; as it extends itself, it withdraws from itself: "reason alienates itself from itself in the very act of taking control of unreason."[7] It collapses upon itself, disappears from itself, as Goethe has turned into Plessing. It goes no one knows where; and the grass stands up again. Its trace? even its trace is gone, no longer available for interrogation. Nor, for that matter, is its bearer available for sympathy, much less for domination ("beherrschen"). Let the "Vater der Liebe" go in quest of him, hunt him down if he can. But even the Father of Love may find himself at a loss to apply his standards of reasonable love in the space without standards from which reason comes and to which it must return, but into which love, unreasonable love, plunges us at a stroke. Could the old Goethe have forgotten, or did he only pretend to forget, when he described his attempts to cure this young man of his transreasonable condition, what he himself had once written to Charlotte von Stein? "No, my love for you is no longer a passion, it's a disease, a disease that is dearer to me than the most perfect health; a disease of which I do not wish to be cured." ("Non mon amour pour toi n'est plus une passion c'est une maladie, une maladie qui m'est plus chère que la santé la plus parfaite, et dont je ne veux pas guérir.")[8] As Shelley says, "What would cure, that would kill me" ("The Magnetic Lady to her Patient"). This is a language so formulaic that we don't usually take it seriously, but it needs to be researched more carefully to establish its referents. What exactly is, for instance, the space into which this potential client of Goethe (turned psychiatrist) has made his escape? Let me take an oblique approach to an answer.

We are told that he was in love, and was rejected. He remains, then, in an in-between state, in which the experience of love remains with him, but without an object. But what, again, is the experience of love? As I have said in the previous chapter, first and foremost, it is the experience of disproportion. The effect is greater than any possible cause. Love breaks down the wall between the unlimited within us and the limited without, or the limited that we embody. Brahms's music, say in some of the *Liebeslieder Waltzes,* is that wall: it illuminates the limitations of the text (one side of the wall) by the limitlessness of the music (the other) and conversely. I have said that love is the experience of disproportion; in fact, it throws causality itself into question, not merely because the characteristics of the beloved are never adequate to the feelings that they arouse, but because the feelings that love makes available are, like some internal reservoir, out of measure with anything we can think of as being induced by any measurable cause whatsoever.

Yet the phrase "internal reservoir," although it does convey part of the truth, is also misleading: that "reservoir" is internal only in the sense that it is not part of the outside world; but it is too great to be thought of as being contained in any individual being. On the other hand, it is not something that can be crystallized in a concept like a "God." (To repeat: "Dionysos" makes it sound far too specific). But it does make one feel that one is in contact with something larger than one's own, or anyone's, experience as contained in the rational, describable conditions of human life. As Hawthorne puts it, it is something more "than human power . . . can make manifest in deeds."[9] Being in love teaches one that if life were destroyed, Life would live on. To the lover, as normal experience pales to the point of unreality, it seems that those who are not in love are only marginally, or verbally, alive, sharing only in the vocabulary of life.

Another discrepancy that love teaches is the total disproportion between life and the body. When Goethe says to Cupid,

> Du lärmst so ungeschickt; ich fürchte, das Seelchen
> Entflieht, um dir zu entfliehn, und räumet die Hütte.

> (You're carrying on so violently, I'm afraid the little soul
> Will run away, just to get away from you, and vacate the house.)

he must be taken seriously. Only in love does the separateness of life from its embodiment become obvious; and, as a corollary, its separability.

This space outside form that the fugitive Plessing has escaped into, is the space we move in in the Rhapsody. Some features of the work often remarked upon—such as the laboring of the word *Menschenhass* in part 1, or the shift to C major in the second, more optimistic part of the Rhapsody—follow the conventions of imitative form; but much of the time the music reveals its disproportionate character through arbitrary movements—in many places there seems to be no reason for it to be going in one direction rather than in another.[10] One cannot predict the movement of the voice in relation to the words, as one cannot predict the actions or the movements of the hidden protagonist; they are both working in the matrix, that is pre- or extra-form. That matrix outside form is hard for us to inhabit. It is the place where, as Gustav Mahler said, "space and time no longer separate anything."[11] "But the living / all make the mistake / of distinguishing too clearly." ("Aber Lebendige machen / alle den Fehler, dass sie zu stark unterscheiden" [Elegy 1, ll. 80–81]. Rilke loved the Goethe poem, by the way, but disclaimed any understanding of the music.)

> Between sleep and waking,
>   dreams persist but I am quickly
> victim to the world's precision—
>   (John Lane, from "Waking in the Blue Ridge")

What every lover knows without fanfare, about life and death, from his vantage point within life, Rilke asserts with some grandiloquence: "The eternal streaming / carries all ages with it through both kingdoms / and sounds above them in both." ("Die ewige Strömung / reisst durch beide Bereiche alle Alter / immer mit sich und übertönt sie in beiden.") But

praise the anonymous lovers, the heroes, he says: "Begin /
always again / the ever inadequate praise." ("Beginn /
immer von neuem die nie zu erreichende Preisung"; 11.39–40);
they, the lover-heroes, are sucked back into Nature, content
in their experience and knowledge, carrying no name; the
other heroes, the official ones, can safely be left to their own
devices; even their death is just a kind of advertisement: "the
hero will hold himself high: even his death was only / a
chance, to help him become what he is" ("es erhält sich der
Held, selbst der Untergang war ihm / nur ein Vorwand, zu
sein"; 11.41–42).

I have said repeatedly that life is not the measure of life.
Music, Nietzsche tells us, conveys this very fact: it "gives the
inmost kernel which precedes all forms. . . . "[12] Once again,
we are outside form, or before it.

But does music always and necessarily function within the
realm of love? Is it really the food of love, rather than just
more evidence of the schism between desire and expression?
Literature and music both, presumably, work by the achievement of a unity in which all the forces that entered into the
creation of the work are amalgamated and something is
produced that goes beyond any of them. The success of this
effort at least with respect to poetry has been questioned, for
instance, by Neil Hertz in his fine essay on Longinus: Hertz
points out that the reintegration of scattered materials in
literature (in this case, the parts of Sappho's body, which has
disintegrated under the force of an erotic experience) creates
a deceptive effect, the effect of the sublime, which renders the
audience susceptible to the ulterior purposes of the author.
But under careful scrutiny the trick, or, if we prefer, the crack,
in the organic unity, shows up.[13] (Cf. Nietzsche on the illusory
reconstitution of the individual, nearly shattered by the Diony-
sian musical experience, through Apollonian [imagistic] inter-
vention.)[14] This argument, by the way, has been recently

extended from the sublime to the beautiful by Frances Ferguson in her essay on Burke.[15]

In poetry, then, one may say that there is not so much an integrating as a recuperative force at work; organic form is not applied to previously inert materials, but rather reverses the momentum of some force that has shattered the poet and his/her world, employing its energy in a boomerang movement for an attempt at restoration, at binding together. To shift images, one could say that every metaphor, as a momentary expression of the organic impulse, takes a stitch in a rent reality; "allegoresis," or the continual application of metaphors, is a zipper that joins the two parts of the riven world together again. In either view, the key is repair or recuperation.

Music, or at least some music, may be different. I venture to say that music welds the future, literature primarily the past;[16] therefore the integrity of music may be greater, and the possibility of its achieving a genuine integration, despite the Fugues (cracks) that traverse it from time to time, more instant. It need not suppress eros, which always shows through in literature, revealing literature's substitutive or sublimational nature, but can incorporate erotic energies in an indivisible whole, not subject to being teased apart again. There is no thread to pull on, no hairline crack to force apart, no hint of a deficiency to worry.

I am prepared to make this assertion, with the appropriate hesitations, about much music in the classical style, even about patches in Brahms where he lapses into familiar forms (though whatever Liszt, or even he himself, might have thought, Brahms was not at heart a classicist).[17] Music uses eros, uses the thrust of rhythm, to produce something that need not, or at least does not, acknowledge a derivative nature, a sublimational character, an insufficiency by comparison with the erotic itself. But what to do with the "Alto

Rhapsody," which is a declaration of its own inadequacy vis-à-vis the erotic? Apparently at first Brahms didn't even want the work to be printed or performed, and for many years avoided performances of it.[18] From the vantage point of that part of one that simply has nothing to do with time, in later life "he, who so often said, 'Life steals more from one than death does,' used to refer to himself as the 'outsider,' with a glancing reference to the 'Alto Rhapsody.'" "In various self-ironising ways Brahms tried, self-tormenting, to free himself from the overwhelming impression of this work. Years later he took up the melody of the prayer again ... and, again addressing himself, added the words from Goethe, 'Enough, at last, you Muses! ... / You cannot heal the wounds dealt by love; / But lessen the pain only you, you kind ones, can." ("Nun, ihr Musen, genug! ... / Heilen könnet die Wunden ihr nicht, die Amor geschlagen; / Aber Linderung kommt einzig, ihr Guten, von euch!") This is the end of "Alexis und Dora," a poem that begins as an idyll, but moves toward loss and bitter jealousy, as the love-gift (the girl Dora) is understood to be potentially anyone's prize.[19]

In neither the "Harzreise im Winter" nor the "Alto Rhapsody" does the woman who is presumably at the root of all the trouble appear. To follow through on Frances Ferguson's suggestions: beauty, the female attribute of literature, acts to *conceal* the superior power of woman over man, even though that power is itself the content of literature. It is only appropriate, then, that the woman herself, the source of the controlling power, should be concealed (the sane woman in the cellar, so to speak). Goethe turns Plessing over to the "Vater der Liebe." (The fullest commentary before Garlington's on the Rhapsody, by the way, was written by a woman with the name of Liebe).[20] It is at the point at which the father is invoked that Brahms brings in the male choir, presumably to assist its brother in distress: or, possibly, as a male support group with which the composer himself can identify, to ease his own sense of isolation. He becomes, briefly, father over himself, creating brothers for himself. It would hardly seem appropriate, in this piece, to assign the traditionally feminine musical functions of healing and consolation to a woman. Nevertheless, the female voice remains dominant; the males are only an accompaniment; Hugo Riemann points out "the fullness and dullness of the male choir, with its limitation in point of range. . . . "[21] In a bold but painful ironic stroke, Brahms has given this music voice through a woman, the woman who fails to appear in the text, but who nevertheless has the whole thing in her mouth.[22] The hidden source, enveloped in the poem, has become in the music the patent envelope itself.

It is by devices such as this that the music accomplishes certain things that the text doesn't, or can't, or doesn't dare to do. As Nietzsche puts it, "what the poet *qua* poet was unable to achieve . . . might be achieved by him at any moment in his character as musician."[23] "For the listener certain things are suggestively linked by the music, which would have been impossible without destroying the poetic form of the language." (Kross, *Die Chorwerke von Johannes Brahms,* p. 302 and nn.). What further connections, or connectedness, beyond language does the music convey? It reveals the basement membrane of the world, not only the collagen holding mere words together. When Brahms says "life steals more from one than death does" ("das Leben raubt einem mehr als der Tod"), he means that, within life, he has become acquainted with something greater than anything that is circumscribed by the conditions of life: he has experienced the disproportion between unavailable eros and life. Even in the apparently sweet, casual *Liebeslieder Waltzes* that precede the Rhapsody, this disproportion can be sensed. Though they supposedly represent a Hymeneal dance, a Prothalamion, there already lurks in them a confrontation between the limited experiences of life and the absolute condition behind it. The straining, lamenting tone at the point where the male voices join the female for the first time in no. 5, "How happy were the maiden, if her beloved came" ("Wie wäre die Dirne fröhlich, wenn ihr der Liebste weit [sic]"), strikes axe-blows at the words that try to contain the feeling. Seldom has the word "fröhlich" sounded so agonized. In no. 4, an innocent, lilting tune is played off against limitless desire — "Einem, einem zu gefallen sonder Ende Wonne sprühn" — "Let me *spray* limitless rapture to please one, one man" (in no. 3, women "drip rapture" ["Wonne tauen"]). Even the first line of no. 4: "Would that I, poor girl, could glow like the red beauty of sunset" ("Wie des Abends schöne Röte möcht' ich arme Dirne glühn") — conveys quite an expectation. Schopenhauer warns against giving too much prominence to the role of words in songs, for fear of disturbing the stasis of music.[24] In such songs, Brahms has chosen to do just that — to destroy the balance that music was meant to maintain.

In what does the act of honesty and even more, the heroism, of Brahms, and of the protagonist in the "Alto Rhapsody," consist? Brahms has unmasked, or, to use a later word, deconstructed, the "Harzreise im Winter," turned Goethe's lie into the truth, moved what was "abseits" into focus. Brahms had the courage to face the condition that the poem only alludes to, and to lay it bare in music, itself usually the most life-masking of all the arts. Heroism is here the ability to confront the unconditioned, unaestheticized fact of sexuality: the courage to enter a musical space where, for once, the Apollonian spirit does not rescue us from the Dionysiac universal.[25] "For it can indeed happen, in Dionysiac art, that despite everything, except under conditions of extremest vigilance, nature may speak out in her true voice, in her voice without pretenses. . . ."[26] To put it simply, Brahms is

the man who let the truth about sex into music. Brahms's heroism is the willingness to acknowledge that for himself, for Goethe, for Plessing, female desire is uncontainable: that love is just as certainly unavoidable as it is impossible; and that, after the failure of love, one still has not escaped that negative immensity, the erotic, though turned to poison—"Oh, who can heal the pangs / of him, for whom salve has turned to poison?" ("Ach, wer heilet die Schmerzen / dess, dem Balsam zu Gift ward?") Who could say of the "Alto Rhapsody" what Schopenhauer said of the music he knew: "it restores to us all the emotions of our inmost nature, but entirely without reality and far removed from their pain"?[27] The heroism of Brahms was to risk the move from the contained sexuality of classical music, in which erotic energies are absorbed into the energies of the musical work, to another, less comforting kind of achievement. His was the heroism to face the uncontainability of eros — even by music, the medium of his own genius — while going on living in the universe that eros has revealed.

9

Conclusion

As I think back over my subject, the relation of ethics and image to literature, beside which I have now dwelt for some time, a few observations seem sufficient to sum up what I have been saying. With a topic so complex, a simple recapitulation will probably accomplish as much as an elaborate review.

First, I seem to share the suspicions of fiction that have always accompanied the genre, if not, perhaps, for exactly the same reasons as other critics. I have described fiction as the weakness of an incomplete ethical order (chapter 5). But fiction, guilt-ridden, ends up undoing itself, withdrawing its own mandate; it is its own worst enemy, and it tries to make sure that we will not take it seriously (chapters 3 and 5). Although it temporizes, in the end it points beyond itself.

Poetry raises a different set of problems. I have said that poetry is not unethical, but anti-ethical, because it accepts the primacy of asocial forces, despair, death, desire. It goes beyond the need for survival to face the effects of these forces (chapters 4 and 7).

As for the image, I have had to deal with it in several

stages. First, I pointed out that the image can function out-side poetry, as an expression of erotic vision (chapter 1), or as a propelling force in dialogue (chapter 6). In these contexts, it does not share in the generally life-denying character of poetry. Second, I tried to show that a place can be found for the image even within the generally iconoclastic tradition of Judaism (chapter 6), despite some major obstacles (chapter 7). In chapters 1 and 2 I offered some ideas about the activity of images in dreams.

Having said these things, which only invite to a discussion of the basic issues all over again, I am unavoidably drawn toward another familiar topos: "Why write?"

So far, for me, this question has always led to a defense of writing, and the result has fallen, more or less comfortably, into the "Defense of Poetry" genre, familiar from Horace and Boccaccio through Sidney and Shelley. But apart from the effects, moral or immoral, on others, of writing (and its effects on others is what these authors are mainly concerned with), is writing itself, for the author himself or herself, a cowardly activity? Once having seen through the contract of classical music, why did Brahms go on writing music? Should he have stopped?[1] *Is* there any defense?

This time I can barely persuade myself that Yes would be an honest answer. After asking, with some seriousness, whether a Tolstoi or a Chekhov should have written, I now find myself faced with the necessity of confronting the same question for my self. What is our business? What are we all about?

Old Kant said that "the more a cultivated reason concerns itself with the aim of enjoying life and happiness, the farther does man get away from true contentment. This is why there arises in many, and that too in those who have made most trial of this use of reason, if they are only candid enough to admit it, a certain degree of misology—that is, a hatred of reason; for when they balance all the advantages they draw, I will not say from thinking out all the arts of ordinary indulgence, but even from science (which in the last resort seems to them to be also an indulgence of the mind), they discover that they have in fact only brought more trouble on their heads than they have gained in the way of happiness. On this account they come to envy, rather than to despise, the more common run of men, who are closer to the guidance of mere natural instinct. . . . "[2]

Whether it be possible to use the mind, "a cultivated reason," entirely in such a way as to exclude self-indulgence or, what for Kant is equally reprehensible, the pursuit of happiness, remains a question for committed Kantians to argue. But Kant does put it on the line: think, or enjoy; don't mess around with both at once as though the two were interchangeable. Thinking—that is, writing—is legitimate only to the extent that it does not seek pleasure; as the pursuit of pleasure, it is the merest substitution, "an indulgence of the mind," for all its apparent detachment from selfish goals. Here Kant could be Chekhov, chiding Gromov and Ragin for their escapism. As a form of the search for happiness, writing is nothing more than sublimation (as Shakespeare had Berowne tell us in *Love's Labour's Lost*), and is therefore best abandoned. Yet can it be anything *but* that?

Perhaps something more, even in a Kantian sense; but, for the moment, it may be better for me simply to repeat, about writing, what I said previously with reference to Ashbery's "Self-Portrait": " 'Something like living'; both more and less."[3] Literature is always too much and too little; for desire, too little; but (to recur for the last time to the topic of several previous chapters), for Judaism, possibly too much. Writing is largely a display of human weakness, which Jews cannot afford; yet it is also less than the whole truth of desire. It is not by contrast with so-called "real" things that literature is inadequate; that is just the usual comparison of apples with oranges. It is not even by contrast with what Wordsworth calls "the freedom and power of real and substantial action and suffering" (1802 Preface) that art is insufficient. It is in comparison with our own inner desire, an experience as inward as that of art itself, that art reveals its shortcomings. The fact that desire is bigger than literature, and bigger than music, means that literature and music choose to be incomplete. To that extent, and in that sense, which is, to be sure, a limited, but nevertheless a significant sense, they are immoral.

The basic structures in life are imposed on a nonstructure;[4] they're anchored in sand. To attempt to make the work, or the argument, better rounded, more complete, only makes it more of a lie, that is, increases the tension between it and the reality of desire that surrounds it. And desire itself cannot be grounded.

In an earlier version of this conclusion I had thought of using Kate Greenaway's picture poem on the averted woman, "Margery Brown, on the Top of the Hill," to illustrate the impossibility of grounding desire in any structure; as truth is provisional, sexual love remains provisional too. "Oh, a knight is there, but I can't go down, / For the bells ring strangely in London town." The question to which that poem led me was: if love itself cannot be grounded, where can ethics be grounded?

Perhaps a palliative approach to this problem might be considered through what might be called an ungrounded ethics.

At least since Coleridge, it has been assumed that we live in an ethical context to begin with—that every one of our acts has an ethical dimension; that even perception is either ethical or unethical. This presumption implies that we are already conscious at every instant that something may be wrong, that we are making a choice that might or should be different. Nietzsche warns us against indignation, but the ethical man is always indignant. Yet underneath moral awareness, things simply are as they are, and happen as they do. If one can sink to that level, one may realize that ethics is something that may be called upon when it is necessary, rather than a condition of perpetual militant vigilance, waiting for the satisfaction of justice done or indignation assuaged. (This is a fact hard to remember in the face of both personal outrage and the repeated outbreaks of political ruthlessness that mark our social order). The surge of pleasure that comes with the impulse to an ethical response is only the other side of anxiety and its attendant hostility. Ethics is not heroic, but, when it must be invoked, a sad necessity; and it can work or fail as the powers that act on one support or undermine it. It isn't something in itself; it is nothing to pride oneself on, for it always reflects a loss. (Something of the nature of such a tentative ethics, not necessarily incompatible with Judaism, is adumbrated in Philippe Boyer's "Le Point de la question."[5]) Only when wrong is done is wrong created, that is, only when wrong is done does ethics arise—each time; it does not exist in advance. It is not to be hypostatized; one may not even wish to think of it as resting on fixed principles, or on any body of doctrine.

Yet such a fluid conception of ethics is difficult to maintain. It requires a greater ethical effort, so to speak, to sustain than a positive ethical doctrine does. We crave a stable ethics, even a robust ethics. Still, there has perhaps been only one enclave in life where such an ethics has ever existed. If it is desire that helps to undermine the categories of the ethical, any moment of harmony in the relations between the sexes will tend to the restoration of those categories and of the social order. (I would prefer to think of society as being in a state of imbalance, with interludes of possible peace, rather than, as in Girard's model, in an equilibrium that breaks down in

spasms of repeated violence). The area in which sexual conflict may be temporarily suspended is simply parenthood.
Perhaps, in fact, there is no other situation in which a stable
ethics has ever worked, however imperfectly. For whatever
other purposes men and women come together, they have
children; and these children create, or recreate, the ethical
imperative, together with the relief from violence that men
and women by themselves might never have known. Ethics
and desire find themselves, willy-nilly, at least briefly and
provisionally reconciled. The "hidden third" may make possible the first mutual openness, before ulterior purposes
claim us again.[6] And even if the parents do not love each
other, they may still both love the child. After all, both
Rumpelstiltskin and the Queen wanted the baby; and only
Ivan Ilyich's son was really able to love his unappealing
father.

It might be hoped, then, that in the writing that is done
for children some rapprochement between the ethical and
the literary would be possible. Interestingly enough, De
Quincey identifies the function of children in society with
the function of literature itself ("The Literature of Knowledge and the Literature of Power"). Of course, children's
literature also turns readily enough back toward myth, with
all its violence. Yet in a poem such as, for instance, A. A.
Milne's "The King's Breakfast," it is the child for whom the
poem was written who mediates the reconciliation between
the female forces in the poem and the king; it is the child
who makes available a "King's Breakfast" for us all.

        The King asked
        The Queen, and
        The Queen asked
        The Dairymaid:

"Could we have some butter for
The Royal slice of bread?"

After many painful delays, the butter is eventually produced,
and all—the cow, the dairymaid, the queen, and the king—
are reconciled, in this poem written for an unnamed child.

I end this aside with a speculative afterthought, which
harks back to my chapter on Yiddish literature and its preoccupation with children. The explosion of interest in children's
literature during the last fifteen years may signify nothing
more than a new Romantic sentimentality. But, as a rule,
ideology attempts to compensate for something we fear we
have lost, or feel may be lacking, and this case is no exception.
If it is not our hitherto inviolate memories of childhood that
are threatened, could the endangered value be the contract
with children that gave us adults, until recently, the illusion
of relief from the instability of all other relationships? I ask
this question not as an aside. Hitherto, the context produced
by the child has been the most comprehensive of the alternatives to private desire. It is not impossible that *A High Wind
in Jamaica* and *Lord of the Flies* were really harbingers of a
change in the texture of human relations. Only recently has
it been acknowledged that the sudden demands we make on
children for emotional maturation may not be entirely
salutary. Do children now cast a cooler eye on the filial bond;
is every child now necessarily an "ironical child"?[7] It has
long been acknowledged that adults are like children; perhaps we have to begin to face the possibility that children are
not unlike adults: less different from us, and consequently
less lovable, than we once thought they were; "no child, / But
a dwarf man", as Wordsworth warned they might become
(*Prelude* 1805, 5,11.294–95). One wonders whether this securest
enclave of ethics in Western culture, parenthood, the sponta-

neous and uncalculated love of adults for children, has been breached at last. Has a time come when we must actually begin to ask ourselves whether Lear's reconciliation with even one of his daughters could only have been a fantasy, invested with the special poignancy appropriate only to a fantasy?

If so, perhaps a new *King Lear* will need to be written. Let us hope there will still be a Cordelia in the cast.[8]

To return to the matter of our craving for a substantial ethics in a more general sense, and setting aside the question of parenthood as a possible exception to the tyranny of desire, I would argue that even the worst of us have a need for such a stable ethics, otherwise we (they) would never read literature. Saints and villains both read books; often, they read the same books, and they take pleasure in the same books. Can it be that a book (let us say, for instance, the novel by John Coetzee called *Waiting for the Barbarians*) affects a villain in a different way from the way in which it affects a saint, or at least a reasonably decent person? I find that hard to believe. In a sense, neither saint nor villain really even has a choice: we have the experience that the author directs us toward.

To take a more difficult example: did the Beethoven works played by the inmates of Auschwitz affect the audience of mass murderers differently from the way in which they affected the musicians? Even in that extreme case, I would be inclined to say No. It seems that we all take pleasure to some degree in the idea of the good when we read, or when we listen to music. It must be that a shutter in the villain sets aside his basking in virtue too easily when interest intervenes—as if there were some lost paradise there that there is no point trying to linger in. I can think of no better reason why art should be attractive to markedly unethical people (especially if we grant Kant's premise that art always embodies a kind of fluid, unspecifiable ethics). Perhaps virtue is, after all, what everybody lusts after in books.

But, in literature, kindly readers and villainous ones may both be only the dupes of virtue, both receiving merely the kind of inexpensive ethical thrill that comes buffered by sadism and sublimation. An aesthetic ethics at its best may not be good enough, if indeed the good is what we are after. (As I suggested in chapter 3, the hypothetical reader who has left anxiety and violence entirely behind may choose not to read at all). On the other hand, as I have said previously, one may hold that literature is morally inadequate not primarily because it contains elements of sadism (chapter 3), nor even because the good cannot be represented at all (introduction), but because it avoids confrontation with the full reality of desire. If desire is a larger and more inclusive category than ethics, "the good" may in fact be understood as little more than an aesthetic hypostasis that is, appropriately, elaborated only in artistic fantasy. In this case the work of art may be rejected by those of developed or Nietzschean insight as being, not insufficiently good, but too "good" — even immoral in its acceptance of the delusion that a supporting structure of morality sustains our lives.

In the event, though, most of us still turn toward literature: perhaps, after all, for the sake of an ethics that, whether because we are too wise, too weak, or too bad, we cannot find fulfilled in life itself. Even in this postliterate, postaesthetic, and possibly postethical age, we all continue to seek out art, with its unnameable ethical satisfactions, ambiguous as the very status of ethics itself may be. If ethics be a delusion, it is at least a delusion shared by saints and sinners alike.

Appendix

The Frog King, or Iron Henry
(Translated from the 1857 Edition
of the Brothers Grimm)

IN OLDEN DAYS, WHEN WISHING WAS STILL OF SOME USE, there was a King who had three daughters. All were beautiful, but the youngest was so beautiful that the sun itself, which has, after all, seen a great deal, was astonished every time it shone on her face. Near the King's palace there was a great, dark forest, and in the midst of that forest, under an old linden tree, there was a deep, cool well. When the day was very hot the princess went out into the forest, and sat down on the edge of the cool well; and when she was bored, she would take a golden ball, which was her favorite toy, throw it in the air, and take pleasure in her game. Now it happened once that the princess's golden ball didn't fall back into the hand that she had reached out to catch it, but on the ground nearby, and it rolled straight into the water. The princess followed it with her eyes, but the ball disappeared, and the well was so deep that one could not see the bottom. Then she began to weep bitterly; she wept ever louder, unconsolably.

As she was lamenting, someone called out to her: "What is the matter, Princess? You're screaming so that a stone would feel sorry for you."

She looked around to see where the voice came from, and caught sight of a frog that had stuck its fat ugly head out of the water. "Oh, so it's you, old water-slapper!" she said; "I'm crying about my golden ball that has fallen into the well." "Put your mind at rest," answered the frog. "I can take care of that; but what will you give me if I bring your toy back up?"

"Anything you want, dear frog," she said. "My clothes, my pearls and jewels, even the golden crown that I wear."

The frog answered: "Your clothes, your pearls and jewels, even your golden crown I have no desire for; but if you will love me, and I can be your comrade and playmate, sit beside you at your little table, eat with you from your little golden plate, drink with you from your little goblet, and sleep in your little bed—if you promise me that, I'll get you your golden ball back from the well."

"Oh, sure," she said: "I'll promise you everything, if only you'll get my ball back!" But she thought to herself: "What nonsense that silly frog talks; he sits and croaks in the water with others like himself; he can't be a companion for a person."

When the frog had obtained the promise, he dipped his head beneath the water and sank down; after a bit he came kicking himself back up with the ball in his mouth, and threw it on the grass. The princess was very happy when she laid eyes on her lovely toy again; she picked it up and raced off with it. "Wait, wait," called the frog; "I can't run like you!" But what good did it do him to shout his "Quack! Quack!" after her as loud as he could? She paid no attention to him, hurried home, and had soon forgotten the poor frog, who had to go back into the deep well.

Next day, when she was sitting with the King and all the courtiers at the table and eating from her little golden plate, something came splash, slap, splash, slap, crawling up the marble staircase; and when it had got to the top, it banged on the door and called: "Youngest princess, open for me!" She ran over and looked to see who it was; but when she opened the door, there sat the frog! She quickly slammed the door and sat down again, terrified, at the table. The King could see that her heart was beating violently, and he spoke: "Oh, my child, what has frightened you? Is there a giant before the door who wants to take you away?" "Oh, no," said his daughter: "it's no giant, but a hideous frog." "What does the frog want of you?" "Oh, dear father, when I was sitting in the forest yesterday beside the well and playing, my golden ball fell into the water, and because I cried so, the frog brought it back out again; and because he insisted, I promised that he would be my companion, but I certainly didn't believe that he would leave the water; now he's outside and wants to come in to me." Meanwhile the knocking began again, and a voice called:

> "Princess, youngest daughter,
>   open for me;
> don't you know what yesterday
>   you said to me
> by the cool well-water?
> Princess, youngest daughter,
>   open for me!"

Then the King spoke: "If you've promised, you must keep your promise. Go and open up for him." She went and opened the door. The frog hopped in, following right behind her, to her chair. There he sat and called out: "Lift me up beside you!" She didn't want to, till the King ordered her to.

When the frog was up on the chair, he wanted to get onto the table; and when he was sitting there, he said: "Push your little golden dish closer, so we can eat from it together." She did so, but it was easy to see that she wasn't acting willingly. The frog had a good time with his food, but almost every little bite stuck in her throat. Finally he said: "Now I've eaten my fill, and I'm tired; carry me up into your little silken bed, and we'll lie down to sleep." Then the princess began to weep; she was afraid of the cold frog, which she didn't even trust herself to touch, and which was now supposed to sleep in her pretty, clean little bed. But the King looked at her angrily and said: "Whoever helped you when you were in trouble, him you must not later scorn; what you have promised, that you must abide by, and the frog is your companion." There was nothing for it; whether she liked it or not, she had to take the frog with her. Bitterly angry, she picked him up with two fingers, carried him up, and set him down in a corner. But when she was in bed, he came crawling up and said: "I'm tired; I want to sleep just as much as you do; pick me up, or I'll tell your father." Then she grew furious, grabbed him, and flung him with all her might against the wall, saying: "Now you'll get some rest, you hideous frog!" But what fell down was not a dead frog, but a living young prince with beautiful, friendly eyes. Both by right and by her father's will this was now her dear companion and husband. Then he told her that he had been enchanted by an evil witch, and that no one but the princess could have released him from the well. The next day they were to ride to his country. They fell asleep.

The next morning, when the sun woke them, a coach came driving up with eight white horses; they had white ostrich feathers on their heads and were harnessed with golden chains. Behind them stood the young King's servant, faithful Henry. Faithful Henry had felt such sorrow when his master had been turned into a frog that he had had to fasten three iron bands around his heart so that it would not burst with pain and sadness. But now the coach was to take the young King to his own country. Henry lifted both of them into the coach and got up again behind; he was full of joy at his master's liberation. When they had gone a certain distance, the prince heard a cracking noise behind him, as though something had broken. He turned around and called:

> "Henry, did something break in back?"
> "No, Lord, it's not the coach that cracked;
> A band I'd fastened on my heart
> For sorrow's sake, just came apart—
> For sorrow when in cold and wet,
> In that deep well, a frog you sat."

Again, and yet again, there was a cracking on the way, and the prince assumed each time that the coach was breaking; but it was just the sound of the bands bursting from the heart of faithful Henry, because his master was free once more and was now happy.

Notes

Notes to Introduction

1. Jean-Paul Sartre, *L'Imaginaire* (Paris: Gallimard, 1940), p. 245. Cf. Arthur Schopenhauer, *Sämmtliche Werke,* (Grossherzog Wilhelm Ernst Ausgabe, 5 vols. Leipzig: Insel Verlag, n.d.), 2:1136: "Das Leben ist *nie* schön . . . " ("Life is *never* beautiful . . . "). Schelling says that art "actually excludes relation with everything pertaining to morality" ("selbst die Verwandtschaft mit allem, was zur Moralität gehört, ausschlägt"). *System des transzendentalen Idealismus* (Hamburg: Felix Meiner Verlag, 1957), pp. 291–92.

Friedrich Nietzsche, in *The Birth of Tragedy,* repeatedly opposes the true aesthetic to the merely moralistic; moralistic literature, unthinkable at the time of *The Bacchae,* really begins for Nietzsche with the novel, which in turn has its seeds in the Platonic dialogue. (As for music, Nietzsche remarks that Wagner thought the category of beauty was entirely inapplicable to it [chapter 16]). But cf. Immanuel Kant, *Kritik der Urteilskraft* #59, where the beautiful is taken as the symbol of the morally good, or Ludwig Wittgenstein, *Tractatus* 6:421: "Ethik und Ästhetik sind Eins." ("Ethics and aesthetics are one and the same thing.")

Whether Sartre is or is not right in general, the moral and the aesthetic do seem to meet, whether symbiotically or antagonistically, on the ground of the sexual.

2. See the collection of essays by this title under the editorship of H. R. Jauss (Munich: Wilhelm Frank Verlag, 1968).

3. Cf. *Utilitarianism,* in *Essential Works of John Stuart Mill* (New York, Toronto, London: Bantam Books, 1965), pp. 183–248; see pp. 215–16. A recent work on ethics by Alasdair MacIntyre, *After Virtue* (Notre Dame, Ind.: Notre Dame University Press, 1981) advocates a return to Aristotle (and, of course, repudiates Nietzsche).

On the sterility of an ethics derived from general principles, see Jean-François Lyotard and Jean-Loup Thébaud, *Au Juste* (Paris: Christian Bourgois, 1979), especially pp. 88–90. (My thanks to Herman Rapaport for this and numerous other references.) Stuart Hampshire argues in a similar vein in *Morality and Conflict* (Oxford: Basil Blackwell, 1983).

4. Walter Benjamin, in *Ursprung des deutschen Trauerspiels,* says that the sphere in which the moral essence of man is perceptible cannot be reproduced. See *Gesammelte Schriften,* 5 vols. (Frankfurt am Main: Suhrkamp Verlag, 1974), 1:1, 284. On the inadequacy of language for the representation of desire (complementary to its inadequacy for representing the good), see chapter 8 on Brahms below.

A more comforting, if perhaps less philosophical, opinion than Benjamin's is offered by Irving Howe: "One reason his [Shalamov's] work achieves high literary distinction is precisely the moral quality of his testimony. The act of representation yokes the two." *New York Review of Books,* August 14, 1980, p. 37). Morality, in other words, is for Howe the informing force of literary value (cf. Chapter 3, below, re Tolstoi).

5. The question, "Can one imitate virtue? And should one write about vice?" does not seem idle after one has read, say, the description of Heraclide's rape and suicide in Nashe's *Unfortunate Traveller,* or Isaac Babel's "Crossing into Poland."

6. "Über Sprache überhaupt und über die Sprache des Mens-

chen," in *Gesammelte Schriften,* 5 vols, (Frankfurt am Main, Suhrkamp Verlag, 1977), 2:1, 153.

7. See Merle Brown, "Poetic Listening," *New Literary History* 10 (Autumn 1978): 125–39, esp. p. 126.

8. Cf. Laurent Jenny, "Il n'y a pas de récit cathartique," *Poétique* 41 (February 1980): 1–21.

9. Aristotle, *De Anima* 431a: "The soul never thinks without an image." Cf. 432a.

10. F. W. J. Schelling, *System des transzendentalen Idealismus,* p. 297 ("die Kunst das einzige wahre und ewige Organon zugleich und Dokument der Philosophie sei"). See the whole of pt. 6, "Hauptsätze...," sec. 3; also Kant, *Kritik der Urteilskraft,* secs. 49 and 53. It is obvious from these chapters that Kant did not believe thought either could or should be purged of its imagistic elements, despite his iconoclasm in other passages.

Elizabeth Bruss's *Beautiful Theories* (Baltimore: The Johns Hopkins University Press, 1982), which traces the process by which criticism has attempted to infiltrate the domain of creative writing, may be seen as an extension of this discussion in Schelling and the other German Romantics.

11. Epigraph to Nathaniel Mackey, *Gassire's Lute: Robert Duncan's War Poems* (MS).

12. Wallace Stevens, *The Necessary Angel* (New York: Random House, 1965), p. 36.

13. Jean-Joseph Goux, *Les Iconoclastes* (Paris: Seuil, 1978), pp. 58–59; and p. xii, above (there is no image for the good).

It is interesting to recall that there is a Nietzschean form of iconoclasm as well: in *The Birth of Tragedy,* of course, the visual is always illusionary. Freud may be regarded as the inheritor of this tradition from Schopenhauer and Nietzsche. See chap. 1, n. 36 below.

14. Sartre, *L'Imaginaire,* pp. 45, 151.

15. *Les Iconoclastes,* p. 24. Cf. Heinz Werner's *Die Ursprünge der Metapher* (Leipzig: W. Engelman, 1919), which derives metaphor from taboo. A typical remark in Lyotard on image as violence may

be found on p. 270 in the Paris, 1978, Klincksieck edition of *Discours, Figure.*

One interesting way of coping with the guilt aroused by the iconic impulse was the theological doctrine, sometimes associated with Gregory the Great, that distinguished between central and peripheral images; irreverent or unorthodox material could then be relegated to the periphery.

16.   See n. 12 above. Cf. Viktor Shklovsky, *A Sentimental Journey* (Ithaca and London: Cornell University Press, 1970), p. 232: "Art is fundamentally ironic and destructive." It is hard not to feel that Hazlitt's famous essay on *Coriolanus,* in which the imagination is identified with violence and sadism, has more than a germ of truth to it.

17.   (Paris: Gallimard, 1980), p. 80; see also pp. 90, 97, 131.

18.   Frances Ferguson, "The Sublime of Edmund Burke," *Glyph* 8 (1981): 62–78, 75–77.

19.   *Abstraktion und Einfühlung* (Munich: R. Piper & Co. Verlag, 1959), p. 84.

20.   Mill argues that the basic human need is security; a violation of our sense of security, then, would be a threat to "the very groundwork of our existence." *Utilitarianism,* p. 239.

21.   Cf. the distinction that Marilyn French finds in Shakespeare between action (masculine, irreversible) and language (feminine, reversible): *Shakespeare's Division of Experience* (New York: Summit Books, 1981).

22.   On the word as threat or judgment, see Benjamin, "Über Sprache überhaupt . . . ," *Gesammelte Schriften,* 2:153–54.

23.   Cf. Maurice Blanchot, "L'Écriture du désastre," *Nouvelle revue française,* no. 330–31, (July–August 1980), 1–33.

24.   See chap. 3 on fable.

25.   Benjamin, *Reflections,* p. 211 (on Brecht). For the German, see *Versuche über Brecht* (Frankfurt am Main: Suhrkamp, 1966), p. 126.

26.   Cf. Robert Alter, "Sacred History and the Beginnings of Prose Fiction," *Poetics Today* 1 (Spring 1980): 143–62, esp. refs. to S. Talmon, pp. 144–45.

27.   "Pourquoi tous les malheurs, finis, infinis, personnels,

impersonnels, de maintenant, de toujours, avaient-ils pour sous-entendu, le rappelant sans cesse, le malheur historiquement daté, pourtant sans date, d'un pays déjà si réduit qu'il semblait presque effacé de la carte et dont l'histoire cependant débordait l'histoire du monde? Pourquoi?" Blanchot, "L'Écriture du désastre," p. 4.

28. Cf. Edward Alexander, *The Resonance of Dust* (Columbus, Ohio: Ohio State Press, 1979), p. 243, quoting Chaim Grade.

29. Jeremiah 8:5: "Why then is this people of Jerusalem slidden back by a perpetual backsliding?"

30. Cf. Henri Meschonnic, "Il n'y a pas de judéo-chrétien," *Nouvelle revue française*, no. 326 (March 1980), pp. 80–89.

31. My references are to the manuscript of Bucher's dissertation, *De la vision et de l'énigme* (University of Paris, forthcoming).

Notes to Chapter 1: Words and Images: Harmony and Dissonance

1. "L'image, dit Husserl, est un 'remplissement' (Erfüllung) de la signification. L'étude de l'imitation nous a plutôt donné à croire que l'image est une signification dégradée, descendue sur le plan de l'intuition" (Jean-Paul Sartre, *L'Imaginaire*, p. 46). I have empha-sized the physical level in "intuition" by translating it as "perception," in keeping with what I take to be the spirit of the passage.

I should like to thank Laurence Michel for numerous sugges-tions about *Hamlet*. For other references and ideas in this chapter, I am indebted to Richard Abrams, Charles Altieri, James Bunn, Noam Chomsky, Mili Clark, Stephen Freygood, Joseph Graham, Susan Handelman, Melez Massey, and Jerry McGuire.

2. The ease with which written language slips into falsification is well conveyed in this passage from an unpublished paper by David Waasdorp. "Language attempts to communicate truth, but it. . . . denies the passage of time. The words remain fixed at one moment, in one place, and no action occurs, no process is completed, and no condition exists or continues. 'I wrote this paper today and I

will type it tomorrow,' all occurs within the space of a second or however long it takes to visualize the words. The second action has not happened, may not ever happen, or takes a day or more to happen. The first action too is a lie. It is necessary to employ imagination to determine the purpose of the words exactly. The writer remains a magician because he has destroyed time, and he has destroyed the space that truth occupies in humanity."

3. M. Zavarzadeh believes that even literary criticism can be rescued from the condition of metalanguage. See his unpublished essay on Ihab Hassan, "The Critic as Conservator": "*Criticism as Writing.* . . . is a criticism that demolishes *metalanguage* and becomes a language." On the relation of poetry to metalanguage see Wendy Steiner, *The Colors of Rhetoric* (Chicago: University of Chicago Press, 1982), p. 125.

4. The demand for a purification of the poetic idiom (what might be called the anti-Wordsworthian tradition, as in Dante or Shelley) is also a way to reassert the responsibility of language to itself, and to a truth "above the heights attainable in learned discourse, philosophic disquisition, the exposition of religious feelings and ideas, the narration of real events or imagined life-experiences for meeting varieties of mentally dignified human interest." Laura Riding Jackson, *The Poems of Laura Riding* (Manchester: Carcanet New Press, 1980), p. 1. I am obliged to Jerry McGuire for the reference. Cf. Philip Church, "Editorial," *Kenyon Review*, n.s., 5 (Fall 1983): 119–21.

5. "Drängt zum Bilde." *Ursprung des deutschen Trauerspiels*, p. 351. See below, chap. 6, n. 20, on the impossibility of transferring certain semantic elements in speech to writing.

6. Robert Musil, *Gesammelte Werke*, 9 vols. (Reinbek bei Hamburg: Rowohlt, 1978), vol. 6, 120–21.

7. "Die Organisation überhaupt ist die in ihrem Lauf gehemmte, und gleichsam erstarrte Sukzession." Schelling, *System des Transzendentalen Idealismus*, p. 161. Cf. Ilya Prigogine, *From Being to Becoming* (San Francisco: W. H. Freeman, 1980), chap. 5.

8. Shklovsky, *A Sentimental Journey*, p. 188.

9. Cf. the attempt to construct a purely auditory, nonspatial

world in P. F. Strawson, *Individuals* (London: Methuen & Co., 1959), pt. 1, chap. 2. Two recent works on spatial form in literature are Joseph A. Kestner's *The Spatiality of the Novel* (Detroit: Wayne State University Press, 1978), and Jeffrey R. Smitten and Ann Daghistany's *Spatial Form in Narrative* (Ithaca and London: Cornell University Press, 1981). On the spatiality of music see Kestner, *The Spatiality of the Novel*, p. 138. A thorough analysis of formulae such as "spatial form" and "Ut pictura poesis" is to be found in Wendy Steiner's *The Colors of Rhetoric* (Chicago: University of Chicago Press, 1982). Arthur Efron has also pointed out to me the important essay by David Gross, "Space, Time, and Modern Culture," *Telos* 50 (Winter 1981–82); and see D. Barton Johnson, "Spatial Modeling and Deixis," *Poetics Today* 3 (Winter 1982): 81–98.

10. Cf. Sartre, *L'Imaginaire*, pp. 107–10.

11. Re Wittgenstein, see, e.g., Jean-Maurice Monnoyer, "Ludwig Wittgenstein," *Nouvelle revue française*, 330–31 (Juillet-Août 1980): 218–23: "toute perception est immédiatement proposition" (p. 222). On the deficiencies of visual images, see M. R. Mayanowa, "Verbal Texts and Iconic-Visual Texts," pp. 133–37 in Wendy Steiner, ed., *Image and Code* (Ann Arbor: Michigan Studies in Humanities, 1981), as well as John D. Lyons, "Speaking in Pictures, Speaking of Pictures," pp. 166–87 in *Mimesis*, ed. John D. Lyons and Stephen G. Nichols, Jr. (Hanover and London: University Press of New England, 1982), pp. 175, 180–82, and passim.

12. See Ian Begg, Douglas Upfold, Terrance D. Wilton, "Imagery in Verbal Communication," *Journal of Mental Imagery* 2 (Fall 1972): 165–86. On the unity of particular instance and generalization see E. H. Gombrich, *Symbolic Images* (London and New York: Phaidon, 1972), pp. 183, 158, 233, 167, 187; and, for the same in Descartes, Bernard Williams, *Descartes* (Harmondsworth, Middlesex: Penguin, 1978), p. 92. Yet one must remember Leibniz's caveat, "Nempe nihil est in intellectu, quod non fuerit in sensu, nisi ipse intellectus." *Die Hauptwerke* (Stuttgart: Alfred Kröner, 1958), p. 117. ("To be sure, there is nothing in the mind that was not first in the senses—except the mind itself").

204 *Irving Massey*

13. For a powerful argument on the other side of this issue see Sartre, *L'Imaginaire,* passim, but especially pp. 136–39.

14. The first reference is from Samuel Taylor Coleridge, *Collected Letters,* 4 vols. (Oxford: Clarendon Press, 1956), 1:646; the second from *Notebooks,* 3 vols. (Princeton: Princeton University Press, 1973), vol. 3, entry 4181.

15. See also Claud DuVerlie, "Beyond the Image: An Interview with Alain Robbe-Grillet," *New Literary History* 11 (Spring 1980): 527–34.

16. "Two Types of Visual Metaphor," *Criticism* 19 (Fall 1977): 286.

17. Cf. Coleridge, *Notebooks* (New York: Pantheon, 1961), vol. 2, entry 2441. For a capable attack on the essentialist theory of metaphor, see Fred G. See, "The Kinship of Metaphor," *Structuralist Review* 1, no. 2 (Winter 1978): 55–81.

18. Jerry McGuire reminds me that much of this argument is in Shakespeare, *Love's Labour's Lost,* 3.4.289–365.

19. See chapter 3, below, on "St. Julian." Cf. St. Thomas, as quoted in Gombrich, *Symbolic Images,* p. 14: "It is impossible to proceed from any thing mentioned in the Scriptures to an unambiguous meaning."

20. See Israel Scheffler, *Beyond the Letter* (London: Routledge and Kegan Paul, 1979), pp. 128–30, on "Metaphor as Exploration"; also C. S. Peirce on the nature of the symbol, as quoted in Roman Jakobson, "Quest for the Essence of Language," *Diogenes* 51 (Fall 1965): 37: in contrast to the icon, which "belongs to past experience," and the index, which "has the being of present experience," the symbol is oriented toward the future: "it serves to make thought and conduct rational and enables us to predict the future." Whether images function in this way in folktale, which often denies direction and motivation, or in myth, remains an open question.

21. The role of images in scientific thought is a subject of continuing debate. Quite apart from the question whether images contribute to creative theorizing, there is dispute over the role of visualization in the very act of scientific thinking as such. See Arthur I. Miller, "Visualization Lost and Regained: The Genesis of

the Quantum Theory in the Period 1913–27," in Judith Wechsler, ed., *On Aesthetics in Science* (Cambridge: M.I.T. Press, 1978), pp. 73–102; Martin Gardner, "The Charms of Catastrophe," *New York Review of Books,* 15 June 1978, p. 33; J. Molino, "Métaphores, modèles et analogie dans les sciences," *Langages* 54 (June 1979): 100; and several of the articles in David S. Miall, ed., *Metaphor: Problems and Perspectives* (Sussex and New Jersey: Harvester Press and Humanities Press, 1982). See also Paul M. Churchland and Clifford A. Hooker, edd., *Images of Science: Essays on Realism and Empiricism* (Chicago and London: University of Chicago Press, 1985).

22. See n. 1 above. Alastair Hanay's *Mental Images: A Defence* (London: Humanities Press, 1971) took issue with the prevailing doctrine before it was fashionable to do so. Ned Block's *Imagery* (Cambridge: M.I.T. Press, 1981) illustrates the later reversal of opinion. And, of course, Gaston Bachelard had always been a defender of images.

23. *Glyph* 2: 37–63. The passages cited are on pp. 48–50 of the essay.

24. See, for instance, Burke's *Rhetoric of Religion* (Boston: Beacon Press, 1961) p. 27, with reference to Augustine. For a similar appeal to Platonic simultaneity in the image, by a seventeenth-century writer, see the quotation from Père le Moine in E. H. Gombrich, *Symbolic Images,* p. 161.

25. Valéry, *Oeuvres,* 2 vols. (Paris: Gallimard, 1957), 1:1318. On the indivisibility of sentences cf. Michael Dummett, *Frege* (London: Duckworth, 1973), pp. 3–7.

26. Henri Bergson, *Matière et mémoire* (Paris: Presses Universitaires de France, 1965), p. 139. Sartre says that the more engrossed one is in reading (fiction), the fewer mental images one will have (*L'Imaginaire,* p. 86). When I wrote this chapter I had forgotten how persuasive Edmund Burke is on the dissociation of words from images (see "Of Words," in *A Philosophical Enquiry*).

27. Bergson, *Matière et mémoire,* p. 130.

28. Cf. Ibid., p. 207 and passim, on the indivisible and unconscious nature of lived experience in time. Bergson tries to avoid the

opposition between space and time by arguing that movement creates space instead of occupying it (p. 244).

29. A view of poetry imputed to John Ashbery and accepted by him. See William Packard, ed., *The Craft of Poetry* (New York: Doubleday, 1974), p. 118. Cf. the "Forward Animation" of *Shadow Train.*

30. In Karl Kroeber and William Walling, *Images of Romanticism* (New Haven: Yale University Press, 1978), pp. 1–12.

31. *Cornell Review* 4 (Fall 1978): 115–26.

32. George L. Dillon's *Language Processing and the Reading of Literature* (Bloomington: Indiana University Press, 1978) also engages many of the problems that I raise in this section of my essay, but to somewhat different effect. Dillon is primarily interested in the ways in which we deal with various kinds of sentence structures.

33. Here I depart from Valéry, who in many other respects anticipates my model (*Oeuvres,* 1:1331). See my earlier book, *The Gaping Pig* (Berkeley: University of California Press, 1976), pp. 5–6.

34. Cf. J.-F. Lyotard, *Discours, Figure* (Paris: Klincksieck, 1978), p. 178: "It is through letting itself be invested by the sensory as that which cannot be 'read,' through putting itself to school to the immediately figurate, that it (the mind) is empowered to construct the figurative significance of the written."

35. "Bilder wollen nur ihren Fluss, denen ist alles gleich." Walter Benjamin, *Über Haschisch* (Frankfurt am Main: Suhrkamp, 1972), p. 118. Bruno Schulz also speaks of his difficulty in resisting the movement of images: see *Sanatorium under the Sign of the Hourglass* (New York: Walker and Co., 1978), pp. 172–73.

36. Cf. Ezra Pound, *Gaudier-Brzesca* (London: John Lane, 1916), p. 106; and Wordsworth's "Spots of Time" in *The Prelude,* bk. 12.

37. This reference to *Hamlet* (3.1.615) and all subsequent citations are from the edition by G. B. Harrison, *23 Plays and the Sonnets* (New York: Harcourt, Brace and Co., 1948). On the "unthanked" level in thinking, Brian Caraher comments: "It struck me that the German word 'Gedanke' lurks etymologically and philosophically behind the word 'unthanked' in your teacrate image. A thought is a thanking of an image for what it helps us to do, but the image can

also remain behind, unthanked and unthought. Cf. Heidegger's lectures on 'What is Called Thinking?' "

38. In this area of dream investigation, Freud is of little help. Convinced that dreams rest upon the image, in the specular dimension, with all its evil connotations, he has relatively little to say about sound and language in dream. Roy Schafer's work represents the *reductio ad absurdum* of Freudian iconoclasm. On the general topic of specularity in Freud, see Patrick Lacoste, *Il écrit* (Paris: Galilée, 1981).

39. See Charles Altieri, "Motives in Metaphor," *Genre* 11 (Winter 1978): 653–87.

40. *Genre* 10 (Fall 1977): 395–411. The *Hamlet* section of the present chapter was first delivered at the Modern Language Association meeting in 1978 before Don Parry Norford's " 'Very Like a Whale': The Problem of Knowledge in *Hamlet*," *English Literary History* 46 (Winter 1979): 559–76, appeared. It also addresses the disjunction of image from language in the play; but, while using many of the same examples, it sets them in a different philosophical context. Another good essay on the detached image in *Hamlet* (especially in the "Mousetrap" scene) is Thomas Pison's "A Lacanian Reading of Shakespeare's *Hamlet*" (typescript).

41. Cf. Ralph Norrman and Jon Haarberg, *Nature and Language* (London, Boston, and Henley: Routledge and Kegan Paul, 1980), pp. 170, 5–8, and passim, on the natural meaning of flora. This book, although not very successful, represents a step toward redressing the balance in contemporary critical theory. It reminds us that the mystery is not (as the Derrideans would have it) why one finds traces of previous writing in all writing, but how one recognizes and understands that which is *not* merely repetition of previous writing.

42. Cf. The King's call for a cannonade in honor of Hamlet, 1.2.124–28.

Notes to Chapter 2: The Ethics of Particularity

1. James L. Calderwood, "Hamlet: The Name of Action," *Modern Language Quarterly* 39 (December 1978): 331–62; George T. Wright, "Hendiadys and *Hamlet*," *PMLA* 96 (March 1981): 168–93; Richard Fly, "Accommodating Death: The Ending of *Hamlet*," *Studies in English Literature* 24 (1984): 257–74. All three essays mention a number of passages in *Hamlet* that I have also pointed out, but to a different purpose.

For more on the subject of particularity in literature, see M. L. Rosenthal's review of Alan Williamson's *Introspection and Contemporary Poetry, New York Times Book Review,* September 23, 1984, p. 34. The approach has also been renewed in the field of historiography by Paul Ricoeur, with his revival of the term *événement* ("event"): see *Temps et récit,* 2 vols. (Paris: Seuil, 1983), 1:289–313.

2. In Nerval's variant, "La treizième revient: c'est la première encore" ("Artémis.")

3. See Rodolphe Gasché, *System und Metaphorik in der Philosophie von Georges Bataille* (Bern: Peter Lang, 1978), pp. 184ff. Goux's critique of exchange values (interchangeability) also has a bearing on my argument here. See *Les Iconoclastes,* chap. 8ff, as well as Michael Sprinker's review of Hans Robert Jauss, *Toward an Aesthetic of Reception,* in *Modern Language Notes* 97 (December 1982), 1205–12 (especially p. 1209, on Walter Benjamin's conception of the historical event as monad).

4. Freud, of course, tries to deal with some of these problems in "The Unconscious." See the *Standard Edition,* 24 vols. (London: Hogarth Press, 1957), 14: 159–215.

5. We may remember that, long before Derrida, Vico, in the *New Science* (#429) argued that writing must have preceded spoken language. See also Jacob Böhme, *Sämtliche Schriften,* 11 vols. (Stuttgart: Fr. Frommanns, 1958), 7: 334–35, on mental language's preceding speech.

6. See P. F. Strawson, *Individuals,* p. 120, for an inconclusive encounter with this problem.

7. My difference from Heidegger derives partly from the fact that Heidegger doesn't set up a category of the experiential—only of Being, in nature itself, as it were. On the general theme of language and Difference in Heidegger, see *Identität und Differenz,* passim.

8. I use this term only partly in its philosophical acceptance; rather, as a broadening of "particulars," the connotations of which are too concrete for my purpose.

9. "The Dis-articulated Image," MS, p. 40.

10. Ibid., p. 17. Despite my objections to some details, I still find this to be one of the most important essays on *Alice.*

11. Richard Fly has taken me to task for simplifying *Hamlet* and giving the impression both that Hamlet himself is incapable of personal statement, and that the language of the play as a whole is trapped in echo and analogy. Much of Calderwood's essay would support Fly's objections, as would another article that Fly has also pointed out to me: Heather Asals's " 'Should' and 'Would,' " in *Genre* 13 (Winter 1980): 431–39.

12. On maternal silence vs. patriarchal noise, see Jerry McGuire's dissertation, "Shakespeare's Gaps" (State University of New York at Buffalo, 1981), especially the chapters on *Hamlet* and *The Tempest.*

13. I had written on this passage before reading David Leverenz's fine essay, "The Woman in *Hamlet,*" in Murray Schwartz and Coppelia Kahn, eds., *Representing Shakespeare* (Baltimore: Johns Hopkins University Press, 1980), pp. 291–308. He makes the same point: "So much for Hamlet's 'golden couplets,' the fledgling poetry of the self he has tried to 'disclose' " (p. 305).

14. Edward A. Snow, "Sexual Anxiety and the Male Order of Things in *Othello,*" *English Literary Renaissance* 10 (Autumn 1980): 384–412, esp. 393. T. G. A. Nelson and Charles Haines speak of Othello's inability even to imagine himself as having sexual intercourse with Desdemona, in "Othello's Unconsummated Marriage," *Essays in Criticism* 33 (January 1983): 1–18.

On women's individualistic opposition to the social order, see also Hegel, *Phänomenologie,* chap. C.BB.b.

15. Cf. Irving Massey, *The Gaping Pig* (Berkeley: University of California Press, 1976), p. 215.

16. Material on scoptophilia is neither abundant nor enlightening. "The most striking thing about the literature on voyeurism is the relative lack of material in print." R. Spencer Smith, "Voyeurism: A Review of Literature," *Archives of Sexual Behavior* 5 (1976): 585–608, esp. 585. For an important exception, see the article on voyeurism in relation to textuality and reading by E. B. Sivert, "Narration and Exhibitionism in *Le Rideau cramoisi*," *Romanic Review* 70 (March 1979): 146–58, esp. n. 1.

17. Charles Bernheimer has recalled to me the story "La Vengeance d'une femme" by Barbey d'Aurevilly, which concerns a woman who achieves orgasms of extraordinary intensity by imagining her husband's watching her as she makes love to another man. See the discussion of the imagination in Taylor Stoehr, "Pornography, Masturbation and the Novel," *Salmagundi* 2 (Fall 1967–Winter 1968): 28–56. On the inherently voyeuristic masochism of sexuality see Leo Bersani, "Representation and its Discontents," in Stephen J. Greenblatt, ed., *Allegory and Representation* (Baltimore and London: Johns Hopkins University Press, 1981), pp. 145–62 (especially pp. 145–48), and Charles E. May, "Perversion in Pornography: Male Envy of the Female," *Literature and Psychology*, no. 31 (1981), pp. 66–74.

18. I might quote Allen Grossman, from a reading: "There is no subject of love except jealousy." Alphonse de Waelhens cites Lacan: "Human jealousy thus appears as the archetype of all social feelings." *Schizophrenia* (Pittsburgh: Duquesne University Press, 1978), p. 78.

19. *Monadology* #19; see also David Wiggins, *Sameness and Substance* (Oxford: Basil Blackwood, 1980), pp. 55–56.

20. Lovejoy has, of course, gone over much of this ground in *The Great Chain of Being*. For an interesting application of Leibniz to literature, see Antoine Compagnon, *La seconde Main* (Paris: Seuil, 1979), pp. 373ff.

21. Robert McRae, *Leibniz* (Toronto and Buffalo: University of Toronto Press, 1976), p. 139.

22.   Alan Williamson, "Introspection and Contemporary Poetry," MS, p. 218.

23.   There are some analogies, though not very close ones, in the fifth "Chant" of Lautréamont's *Les Chants de Maldoror.*

24.   John Erwin, "Spectacularity of the Universe," MS.

25.   Leibniz, *Nouveaux Essais sur l'entendement humain,* 2.1.1.

26.   Cf. the ejection from the mirror in Hawthorne's "Feathertop." The horse's pied saddle recalls the tradition of the Pseudo-Dionysius, according to which the dappled horse can become the symbol of unification. See Dionysius the Areopagite, *The Mystical Theology and the Celestial Hierarchies* (Letchworth: Garden City Press, 1965), p. 66. I will not now attempt to deal with the iconography of the leopard or of the hunt in the background. See also Gerard Manley Hopkins, "Pied Beauty." (Compare the flecks on the fur robe of the figure in another Parmigianino painting in Vienna, the "Bildnis eines Mannes.")

27.   Cf. Friedrich Schlegel, "Idyll of Idleness," from *Lucinde:* "Then, with the greatest indignation, I thought of those evil people who want to subtract sleep from life." *Friedrich Schlegel's* Lucinde *and the* Fragments (Minneapolis: University of Minnesota Press, 1971), p. 65.

28.   Cf. Yeats, "The Phases of the Moon": "and all / Deformed because there is no deformity / But saves us from a dream."

Notes to Chapter 3: Escape from Fiction

1.   Some of the issues discussed in this paper are touched on in T. R. Henn, *The Harvest of Tragedy* (New York: Barnes & Noble, 1966), pp. 43–58, "The Shadow of the Pleasure." I am indebted to Rick Abrams for the reference. For further background see William Nelson, *Fact or Fiction: The Dilemma of the Renaissance Storyteller* (Cambridge, Mass.: Harvard University Press, 1973).

2.   See Aileen Kelly, "Justice to Mrs. Tolstoy," *New York Review of Books,* 28, no. 16, October 22, 1981, p. 10. (The review extends over pp. 3, 6, 8, 10.)

A *locus classicus* for the debate on the morality of the artist's personal life is Plutarch's *Life of Pericles,* chap. 2, secs. 1–2.

3.   On fiction as postponement, see Patricia A. Parker, *Inescapable Romance* (Princeton: Princeton University Press, 1979); and, on the difficulty in making a sharp distinction between thinking and reading (an issue of importance in this chapter), Neil Hertz, "The Notion of Blockage in the Literature of the Sublime," in Geoffrey Hartman, ed., *Psychoanalysis and the Question of the Text* (Baltimore and Houston: Johns Hopkins University Press, 1978).

4.   On literature as a device for tormenting the reader see Charles Baxter, "In the Suicide Seat," *Georgia Review* (Winter 1980), pp. 871–885.

5.   If we are to be entirely honest with ourselves, we must admit that Ivan Ilyich is such a vapid character that it is sometimes hard to take his sufferings seriously. The personality with the greatest presence in the story is undoubtedly that of his wife, especially in the opening scenes, although she has no pretensions to moral perfection and has certainly undergone no conversion.

6.   Edward Pechter's powerful essay "On the Blinding of Gloucester" (*English Literary History* 45 [1978]: 181–200) presents a view of *King Lear* that is very similar to my own (for instance, p. 198: "whatever the meaning of the experience for Gloucester, the importance of the scene is primarily in what it makes us come to feel, recognize, understand"). I am grateful to Rick Abrams for bringing this article to my attention after this chapter was first published in essay form.

7.   In terms of Peter M. Daly's *Literature in the Light of the Emblem* (Toronto: University of Toronto Press, 1979), p. 39, the emblem has a special ontological status as "res significans," combining the functions of representation and interpretation, like body and soul together.

8.   Spivak, "Thoughts on the Principle of Allegory," *Genre* 5 (1972): 337.

9.   C. J. G. Turner, "The Language of Fiction," *Modern Language Review* 65 (1970): 120.

10.   "Die Möglichkeit der Selbstbegrenzung ist die Möglichkeit

aller Synthesis, alles Wunders. Und ein Wunder hat die Welt angefangen." Quoted in Walter Benjamin, *Gesammelte Schriften*, 1:35.

11. "Die Beschränktheit ist nicht bloss ein matter Widerschein des Ichs, sondern ein reelles Ich; kein Nicht-Ich, sondern ein Gegen-Ich, ein Du." Quoted in Walter Benjamin, *Gesammelte Schriften*, 1:36.

12. Walter Benjamin, *Ursprung des deutschen Trauerspiels*, in *Gesammelte Schriften*, 1:296–97. (Al Cook has recalled to me Benjamin's source in Nietzsche, *Die Geburt der Tragödie*, chaps. 14, 19).

13. When I wrote the above, I had not yet seen Vincent Descombes's *L'Inconscient malgré lui* (Paris: Minuit, 1977), which takes up these problems in great detail. On the unconscious element in language see also Alphonse de Waelhens, *Schizophrenia*, pp. 165–69, 180, 199–200.

14. Benjamin, *Gesammelte Schriften*, 1:358–59; (see also the whole chapter on allegory, 1:336ff.) As Benjamin describes it, at least in this passage, allegory is in constant conflict with the decline or decay of time and history; and, being a perpetual rearguard action, it is inherently immediate, local, and transitory, without permanent beauty, whereas symbol contains the sense of transcendence right within it. Allegory, then, would be artistic temporality itself. The connections of Paul de Man's work with Benjamin's on this subject are apparent, and fully acknowledged. One might add that there is a strong affinity between Geoffrey Hartman's early work, especially *The Unmediated Vision*, and Benjamin's *Ursprung* (although Hartman had not yet read Benjamin), in the principle that modern literature seeks among the fragments of a submerged world the signs of a new apocalypse.

15. Cf. Brian Caraher and Irving Massey, eds., *Literature and Iconoclasm* (Buffalo: State University of New York, 1976), pp. 1–3. Benjamin sees the iconoclastic principle as a refusal to deal with morality through representation: the ethical essence of man is not subject to description (*Ursprung*, pp. 284, 407). By implication, there can be no such thing as a moral story, at least not in a realistic mode. (Cf. the essay on Leskov, "Der Erzähler.")

16. Similar observations, but to a less "deconstructive" purpose

than the early Derrida's, are made by Johann Wilhelm Ritter, in *Fragmente aus dem Nachlasse eines jungen Physikers* (Heidelberg, 1969; reprint of 1810 edition), 2:229: "Wort und Schrift sind gleich an ihrem Ursprunge eins. . . . " ("Word and script are one at their very origin"); or, 2:242: "Das Wort schreibt, der Buchstabe tönt; beydes in seiner Unzertrennbarkeit ist das Seyn, das Bewussteyn, das Leben" ("The word writes, the letter sounds: the combination in its inseparability is Being, Consciousness, Life").

17. *The Gaping Pig: Literature and Metamorphosis,* p. 197.

18. Cf. Edward Young, "The Complaint, or Night Thoughts," 1, ll. 372–74:

> In human hearts what bolder thought can rise
> Than man's presumption on tomorrow's dawn?
> Where is to-morrow? In another world.

Notes to Chapter 4: Yiddish Poetry of the Holocaust

1. *At the Mind's Limits* (Bloomington: Indiana University Press, 1980), pp. 5–6, 16. Améry seems to suggest that the most inhuman victimizer still has the potential for humanization, but only if he, in turn, becomes a victim: then the "anti-man" can "once again become a fellow man" (p. 70). Cf. text above n. 4 below.

2. Lawrence L. Langer, *The Age of Atrocity* (Boston: Beacon Press, 1978), p. 52.

3. *A Sentimental Journey,* p. 163.

4. I should like to thank A. Sutzkever for permission to translate several of his poems. I am also grateful to Irving Feldman and to Ruth Wisse for assistance in the preparation of this chapter; Ruth Wisse has further permitted me to use part of her translation from Sutzkever's "Green Aquarium." The remaining translations are my own, with the exception of the following: 66 lines from "The Book of Job" by H. Leivick, translated by Leonard Woolf; 5 lines from "I Believe" by Aaron Zeitlin, translated by Robert Friend;

29 lines from "In the Beginning" by Jacob Glatstein, translated by Etta Blum; "Reb Levi Yitzhok" by Itzik Manger, translated by Leonard Woolf; "Good Night, Wide World" by Jacob Glatstein, translated by Marie Syrkin, from *A Treasury of Yiddish Poetry*, edited by Irving Howe and Eliezer Greenberg. Copyright 1969 by Irving Howe and Eliezer Greenberg. Reprinted by permission of Holt, Rinehart and Winston, Publishers.

5.   Alfred Kazin emphasizes the priority of experience to literature for Jews. See Kazin's introduction to S. de K. Ezrahi, *By Words Alone* (Chicago and London: University of Chicago Press, 1980), pp. x–xi, and the author's *The Uncreating Word* (Bloomington: Indiana University Press, 1970), p. 93.

6.   Here I differ with Lois Rosen, "Sylvia Plath's Poetry About Children," *Modern Poetry Studies* 10 (1981): 98–115, esp. 113.

7.   Ruth Wisse, "Aesthetics as a Form of Resistance: the Ghetto Poetry of Abraham Sutzkever," typescript.

8.   Cary Nelson, "Whitman in Vietnam," *Massachusetts Review* 16 (Winter 1975): 55–71, esp. 68. The whole question whether there can be an appropriate or an adequate Holocaust literature is intelligently reexamined by Barbara Foley in "Fact, Fiction, Fascism," *Comparative Literature* 34 (Fall 1982): 330–60.

9.   Cf. introduction and chap. 3 above, on parable.

10.   David Edelstadt was born in Russia in 1866. After the Kiev pogrom of 1881 he emigrated to the United States. He worked in the sweat shops, became an anarchist, and was editor of the Yiddish periodical *Die Freie Arbeiter Shtimme* (*The Voice of Free Labour.*) Edelstadt died of tuberculosis at age 26.

I am obliged to the late Professor Marvin Duchow of the McGill Conservatorium of Music for his transcription of the two melodies.

Notes to Chapter 5: The Effortless in Art and Ethics
(A) Meditations on "The Frog King, or Iron Henry"

1. Franz Niemetschek, *W. A. Mozarts Leben nach Originalquellen*
(Prague: I. Taussig, 1905; facsimile of 1798 edition edited by E.
Rychnovsky), pp. 54–55. For a different view of Mozart's experience
as a composer see Robert Craft, "B-flat Movie," *New York Review of
Books* 32, April 11, 1985, pp. 11–12, esp. p. 11. On Coleridge, see the
"Preface" to "Kubla Khan": "The Author continued for about three
hours in a profound sleep, at least of the external senses, during
which time he has the most vivid confidence, that he could not
have composed less than from two to three hundred lines if that
indeed can be called composition in which all the images rose up
before him as *things*, with a parallel production of the correspond-
ent expressions, without any sensation or consciousness of effort."
Concerning the unprepared character of the dream-melody, cf.
Edmund Husserl on what he calls the "primal impression." "Sie . . .
entsteht nicht als Erzeugtes, sondern durch *genesis spontanea*. . . . Sie
erwächst nicht (sie hat keinen Keim). . . . " ("It . . . does not arise as
something begotten, but through spontaneous genesis. . . . It does
not grow [it has no bud]. . . . ") *The Phenomenology of Internal Time-
Consciousness*, pt. 2, appendix 1.

2. Kant, however, is emphatic in his assertion that the mind
never operates without effort; see "Versuch den Begriff der negativen
Grössen in die Weltweisheit einzuführen," in Kant, *Werke in Sechs
Bänden*, 6 vols. (Wiesbaden: Insel-Verlag, 1960), 1:779–819, especially pp. 802–4. For a contrary view in the eighteenth century, cf.
the associationist Abraham Tucker's *Light of Nature Pursued*, 1:3.

Charles Rycroft says: "We do not make up or construct our
dreams; they occur or happen to us." *The Innocence of Dreams* (New
York: Pantheon, 1979), p. 163.

Also cf. Emmanuel Levinas, *De l'existence à l'existant* (Paris: Vrin,
1978), chap. 2, "La Fatigue et l'instant."

3. One can hardly avoid quoting Wordsworth's "Expostulation
and Reply" here:

The eye—it cannot help but see;
We cannot bid the ear be still;
Our bodies feel, where'er they be,
Against or with our will. . . .

Cf., again, Husserl, *The Phenomenology of Internal Time-Consciousness* on the spontaneous "primal impression." The notion of "empty" protentions in chapter 24 further suggests a background of pure preparatory consciousness, active though as yet without content.

4. Jean Laporte, *La Doctrine de Port-Royal* (Paris: Presses Universitaires de France, 1923), 2:419. One might also think of Keats: "And he's awake who thinks himself asleep." ("What the Thrush Said.")

5. The association between labor and the misguided aspiration to personality is one of the themes in F. Schlegel's "Idylle über den Müssiggang" ("Idyll of Laziness") in *Lucinde*. See also Philippe Lacoue-Labarthe, "Typographie," in Sylviane Agacinski et al., *Mimésis: des Articulations* (Paris: Aubier-Flammarion, 1975), pp. 165–270, especially pp. 180–86. For Keats, identity is "a fog-born elf" or "noisy nothing" (quotes in an unpublished essay by Richard Macksey).

6. John Updike, by the way, suggests that myths, the basic thoughts, unlike literature, are effortless. "Bruno Schulz, Hidden Genius," *New York Times Book Review,* Sept. 9, 1979, pp. 1 and 36–39, esp. p. 36. For some insight into the extraordinary achievements of minds unburdened by abstract reasoning see Oliver Sacks, "The Twins," *New York Review of Books,* 32, no. 3, February 28, 1985, pp. 16–20.

7. "Métamorphosant sans cesse l'imprévisible en imprévu." Hubert Aquin, *Neige noire* (Montreal: La Presse, 1974), p. 165. On virtuality and generative space in Mallarmé see Raphaël Célis, ed., *Littérature et musique* (Brussels: Publications des facultés universitaires Saint-Louis, 1982), p. 85.

8. The essay on jokes only makes obvious a theme that runs through all of Freud's work, culminating in the belief that the death wish is basic to human desire: namely, that what the organism seeks above all is the avoidance of effort. Note also that Freud speaks of

thought itself as "without quality and unconscious" ("an sich qualitätslos und unbewusst") in "The Unconscious," in 5:14 of the *Standard Edition* (London: Hogarth Press, 1957), pp. 159–215, esp. p. 202.

9. "De déployer en temporalité visible ce qui n'est pas et n'a jamais été un avenir qui va au passé en venant au présent." *Discours, Figure*, p. 154.

10. Perhaps children's fantasies and play result from the surplus, the overflow of thought from the unworking mind, which has to be dealt with by the working mind, and falls into patterns.

11. There is a reference to after-images of berries in the psychological literature. See Mardi J. Horowitz, *Image Formation and Cognition* (New York: Appleton-Century-Crofts, 1978), p. 95. Cf. Chatterton, "Aella" (ll. 304–5):

> When . . . berries of black die
> Do daunce yn ayre, and call the eyne arounde.

12. Coleridge, *Biographia Literaria*, chap. 13; cf. the quotations in E. S. Shaffer, *'Kubla Khan' and the Fall of Jerusalem* (Cambridge: Cambridge University Press, 1975), p. 89. In the *Logic*, as in *Biographia Literaria*, chap. 13, Coleridge seems to be trying to reconcile a principle of totally unconscious, spontaneous creation with the action of the "combinatory and judicial powers." *Logic* (Princeton: Routledge and Kegan Paul, Princeton University Press, 1981), p. 8. For Schelling, as for Shelley, poetry has no necessary dependence on consciousness or will. See respectively the *System des Transzendentalen Idealismus*, passim, and *A Defence of Poetry* (Indianapolis: Bobbs-Merrill, 1965), pp. 76–77 and 72.

13. "En eux sans eux." M. Merleau-Ponty, *L'Oeil et l'Esprit* (Paris: Gallimard, 1964), p. 29.

14. Lyotard, *Discours, Figure*, p. 156, remarks that the mind makes patterns for the purposes of perception where the eye itself could not possibly have seen any pattern.

15. On sacred space, see Goux, *Les iconoclastes*, p. 44. The notion of sacred and/or creative space is also to be found, of course, in Eliade and Heidegger.

16. See appendix for the story itself. The history of the text is extraordinarily intricate; some clues to it will be found in Heinz Rölleke, *Die älteste Märchensammlung der Brüder Grimm* (Cologny-Geneva: Fondation Martin Bodmer, 1975), pp. 144–53 and 365–67. I am indebted to Professor Rölleke for sharing his thorough knowledge of the Grimm corpus with me. John M. Ellis, in *One Fairy Story Too Many* (Chicago: University of Chicago Press, 1983), stresses the inauthentic elements in the Grimms' collection.

17. Cf., to a different purpose, Jean-Luc Nancy, *Le Discours de la syncope* (Paris: Aubier-Flammarion, 1976).

(B) Myth, Fiction, and Ethics (A Response to Girard and Lyotard)

1. E. J. Sweeney has suggested a different reading. He sees the frog as a metaphor that is rejected (killed) and driven back to its prior inauthentic condition (in a reversal of the sequence found in "Ivan Ilyich").

2. Cf. Stevie Smith: "I have been a frog now / For a hundred years / And in all this time / I have not shed many tears." *The Frog Prince* (London: Longmans, 1966).

3. Keats found himself in this predicament, caught between an obsolescent myth and a half-formed ethical choice, but still had the courage to reject fiction (what he sometimes called Romance, at other times merely dream). See especially "The Fall of Hyperion."

4. See chap. 5 (A), n. 15 above.

5. See the quotation from Peirce in chap. 1, n. 20 above.

Notes to Chapter 6: Toward the Rehabilitation of the Image

1. *Phaedrus* #259. They live on, not only in the grasshoppers, but in the Muses' affection for dancers, lovers, and philosophers alike.

2. But cf. Kant, "Versuch," *Werke* 1; 802, on the unconscious labor involved in reading.

3. David Pierson Haney, "The Rhetoric of Wordsworth's *Prelude:* Figural Aspects of Poetic Autobiography," Ph.D. diss., State University of New York at Buffalo, 1980. See chap. 3, esp. pp. 15–26.

4. Lyotard, *Discours, Figure,* p. 270; "Discussions, ou: phraser après Auschwitz," pp. 283–315, in *Les Fins de l'homme* (Galilée: Paris, 1981), p. 308: "Et peut-être toute phrase, même 'bien connue,' reconnaissable, récèle-t-elle la force de ce qui tombe (*fallen*), de ce qui vous court dessus (*occur*)." For more on modern iconophobia, see W. J. T. Mitchell, "The Politics of Genre," *Representations* 2 (Spring 1984): 98–115. See also my introduction, text above n. 15. On the basically visual character of deception for Plato, see Antoine Compagnon, *La seconde Main* (Paris: Seuil, 1979), pp. 118–20.

5. See pp. 290–92 of the author's "Two Types of Visual Metaphor." David H. Hirsch has reminded me that in any case the extrapolation from graven images to verbal images is by no means self-imposing, even though it occurs commonly in iconoclastic doctrine. And, of course, as I have mentioned, the Old Testament itself is by no means consistent in its iconoclasm: see especially 1 Kings 6–7, on the statuary in Solomon's house and in the Temple.

6. From Thomas de Quincey, as quoted by D. D. Devlin, *De Quincey, Wordsworth and the Art of Prose* (London: Macmillan, 1983), p. 79. Cf. the quotations from Paul Klee's journal in Lyotard, *Discours, Figure,* pp. 229–30. Or, following Lacoue-Labarthe, I could quote Pascal again: "The image was modeled on the truth and truth was recognized through the image" (*Pensées* #673). Sacher-Masoch points out that it is the embodiment of a work that reveals his problem to the artist, rather than vice versa; see Gilles Deleuze, *Présentation de Sacher-Masoch* (Paris: Minuit, 1967), p. 291, as well as

Bruce Clarke on the "Idea/Affect Ratio" in "Metamorphic Romance" (unpublished paper.)

7. Lyotard, *Discours, Figure*, p. 179. On the inadequacies of abstract perception, see Schopenhauer, *The World as Will and Idea*, #36; also Jacques Garelli, *La Gravitation poétique* (Paris: Mercure de France, 1966), pp. 132–33.

About being in love with trees, I should mention that my epigraph from Ruskin for chapter 5 comes from a longer passage about a tree in *Praeterita*, a passage that formed the center of discussion at Albert Cook's 1979 MLA panel on images. Convalescing from an illness, the young Ruskin, though still very weak, went out for a walk. He lay down on a bank by the roadside, "to see if I could sleep." But he couldn't. He says: "But I couldn't, and the branches against the blue sky began to interest me, motionless as the branches of a tree of Jesse on a painted window. Feeling gradually somewhat livelier . . . I took out my book, and began to draw a little aspen tree, on the other side of the cart-road, carefully. . . . Languidly, but not idly, I began to draw it; and as I drew, the languor passed away: the beautiful lines insisted on being traced, — without weariness. . . . With wonder increasing every instant, I saw that they 'composed' themselves, by finer laws than any known of men. At last the tree was there, and everything that I had thought before about trees, nowhere . . . " (Ruskin, *Praeterita*, vol. 35 of *The Complete Works of John Ruskin*, 39 vols. [London: George Allen, 1908], pp. 313–14).

8. (Toronto: McClelland and Stewart, 1977), p. 172. As for the question, "What's so wrong with that?", it is taken up again in chap. 7 below, in connection with the possibility that erotic love is always a "Blendwerk"; that woman, for man, is always necessarily Bild, or a *blinding* "annunciation." (For references on the Annunciation theme, and on the subtle interaction between the angel and Mary, see Mary Ann Caws, *The Eye in the Text* [Princeton: Princeton University Press, 1981], chap. 7).

9. "La figure ne peut mentir." Lyotard, *Discours, Figure*, p. 269. The whole question of iconoclasm is thoughtfully reviewed in Adélie and Jean-Jacques Rassial, eds., *L'Interdit de la représentation* (Paris: Seuil, 1984).

10.   Goux, *Les Iconoclastes* p. 130, quotes Malevich on nonrepresentation: "la vie et l'infini sont pour l'homme dans le fait qu'il ne peut rien représenter" ("life and the infinite reside, for man, in the fact that he cannot represent anything").

11.   E.g., Justice, or the Divine Will. See the references to St. Thomas in Gombrich, *Symbolic Images,* p. 175; also Battista Fiera, *De Justicia Pingenda* (London: Lion and Unicorn Press, 1957), pp. 35–37.

12.   Susan Handelman, "On Interpreting Sacred and Secular Scripture: The Relation of Biblical Exegesis to Literary Criticism," Ph.D. diss. State University of New York at Buffalo, 1979.

13.   Gombrich, *Symbolic Images,* p. 165.

14.   Philippe Lacoue-Labarthe, *Le Sujet de la philosophie* (Paris: Aubier-Flammarion, 1979), pp. 283–84.

George Landow has pointed out to me that the visual part of many "images" is not their principal feature at all; in fact, in some cases there may be no visual element. For instance, if we say that a happy relationship between two people of different temperaments is like counterpoint, we do not have a strong visual experience of the analogy. The same may be said of my own final illustration in this chapter, the "Minsk-Pinsk" joke (see below).

15.   Geoffrey Hartman, "Psychoanalysis: the French Connection," pp. 86–113, in Geoffrey Hartman, ed., *Psychoanalysis and the Question of the Text* (Baltimore: The Johns Hopkins University Press, 1978), pp. 107–8.

16.   From the MS of John W. Erwin's essay, "Proust and Venice."

17.   Goux, p. 24 and passim.

18.   Hartman, *Psychoanalysis,* p. 106. The ambiguity of Proust's dependence on images is also searchingly examined in chapter 4 of Carol Jacobs's *The Dissimulating Harmony* (Baltimore and London: The Johns Hopkins University Press, 1978).

Robert A. Brinkley takes a position on Wordsworth's "spots of time" that is similar to Erwin's on the involuntary memory in Proust. Brinkley concludes his analysis of the "Simplon Pass" episode in *The Prelude* with the remark, "Through revision, the epiphany of the Imagination becomes its memorial." See "The Incident in the Simplon Pass," *The Wordsworth Circle* 12 (Spring 1981): 122–25, esp. 124.

19. *"Er* [the poet] *weiss jene geheimen Kräfte in uns nach Belieben zu erregen....* " *Heinrich von Ofterdingen,* in Novalis, *Schriften,* ed. P. Kluckhohn and R. Samuel, 3 vols. (Stuttgart: Kohlhammer Verlag, 1960), 1:209–10. Also cf. "Fragmente und Studien 1799–1800": "Poésie = Gemütherregungskunst" and "Das Symbolische afficirt nicht unmittelbar, es veranlasst Selbstthätigkeit." References are on pp. 639 and 393 of Novalis, *Schriften,* vol. 3, ed. R. Samuel, H.-J. Mähl, and G. Schultz. I am most grateful to Prof. Erika Metzger for researching these quotations.

On metonymy vs. metaphor (or grammar vs. rhetoric), Erwin's concern, see also Paul de Man, *Allegories of Reading* (New Haven and London: Yale University Press, 1979), chap. 1.

20. Cf. Francis Jacques, "Les Conditions dialogiques de la référence," *Les Études philosophiques* 32 (1977): 267–305. I am obliged to Newton Garver for bringing this essay to my attention. On the centrality of the dialogic condition in language, see also M. M. Bakhtin, *The Dialogic Imagination* (Austin and London: University of Texas Press, 1981), especially chap. 4, "Discourse in the Novel." John W. Erwin's *Lyric Apocalypse* (Chicago: Scholars Press, 1984) is a large-scale defense of dialogic and communitarian functions in the arts.

I am inclined to believe that there are semantic elements in speech that are in principle not translatable into writing. The tape of a lecture may make perfectly good sense, when the same sentences in typed transcription may be quite incomprehensible. In fact, I am inclined to think that there is an error implicit in the very act of distinguishing between language and people using language: they form a single entity, "person-speaking," from which "meaning" cannot be fully isolated. Another approach to this problem is offered by Mallarmé, who suggests that writing is only "la fixation du chant immiscé au langage et persuasif du sens" ("the fixing of song mingled with language and persuasive of meaning"). See Raphaël Célis, ed., *Littérature et musique,* p. 82.

On the role of metaphor in dialogue, cf. with my views those of

Ted Cohen in "Metaphor and the Cultivation of Intimacy," in Sheldon Sacks, ed., *On Metaphor* (Chicago and London: University of Chicago Press, 1979), pp. 1–10.

21. See Israel Scheffler, *Beyond the Letter,* pp. 128–30, "Metaphor and Exploration." "The utterance itself serves as an invitation, to himself and to others, to explore the context for significant shared predicates ... " (p. 129). On destabilization and prevention of closure as characteristics of Jewish discourse, see Philippe Boyer, "Le Point de la question," *Change* 22 (February 1975): 41–72. Cf. Hans-Georg Gadamer, *Truth and Method* (New York: Seabury Press, 1975), pt. 2, 2.3.C, and *Dialogue and Dialectic* (New Haven and London: Yale University Press, 1980), pp. 52–53, n.8.

22. Quoted by Stanley Cavell as the epigraph to *The Claim of Reason* (Oxford: Clarendon Press, 1979).

23. Maurice Merleau-Ponty, "Le Primat de la perception et ses conséquences philosophiques," *Bulletin de la société française de philosophie* 41 (Oct.–Dec. 1947): 119–53; the relevant references are on pp. 123 and 126.

24. See n. 22 above.

25. Cf. P. E. More as quoted in Elizabeth Merrill, *The Dialogue in English Literature* (New York: Henry Holt, 1911), p. 3: "The real Platonism, then, is not a dogmatic statement of the truth, but continuous approximation thereto, which, for us as we are constituted, is more veracious than truth."

26. Cf. Husserl, *Ideas* #138, on the weighing of alternatives.

Some analogies to my Minsk-Pinsk sequence may be found in Descombes's *L'Inconscient malgré lui,* pp. 24–26, 62–65, 76–77. See also Wendy Steiner, *The Colors of Rhetoric,* pp. 123–24, 138. Descombes quotes a relevant passage from Heidegger: "the essential can never be reached except by passing through something else" (p. 159). There are excellent passages on the importance of maintaining instability or fluidity in thought in David Simpson, *Irony and Authority in Romantic Poetry* (Totowa: Rowman and Littlefield, 1979), pp. 181–90; see also Elrud Ibsch, "Historical Changes of the Function of Spatial Description," *Poetics Today* 3 (Autumn 1982): 97–113, p. 97, and, on the idea of "hovering" mentioned above, the chapter entitled "Ventriloquus Interruptus" in the dissertation by David S. Ferris, "Transfigurations" (S.U.N.Y.A.B., 1985).

Notes to Chapter 7: Orpheus and Eurydice

1. See, for instance, Peter J. McCormick, *Heidegger and the Language of the World* (Ottawa: University of Ottawa Press, 1976), pp. 181–82.

2. "Woman and Metaphor", *Enclitic* 2, no. 1 (Spring 1978): 27–37, esp. 35.

3. See the Iginla quotations for n.2 above. Robbe-Grillet's images are widowed images masquerading as phenomenological reductions or "bracketed" percepts. (Robbe-Grillet has told me of the influence that Husserl has exerted on his thinking.)

4. Cf. the beginning of my introduction.

5. *Journals and Papers* (London: Oxford University Press, 1959), pp. 193–94. See also Robert Rogers, "Hopkins' 'Carrion Comfort' ", *The Hopkins Quarterly* 8 (Winter 1981): 143–65. For a different view of "widowhood" in Hopkins, see Sandra M. Gilbert and Susan Gubar, *The Madwoman in the Attic* (New Haven and London: Yale University Press, 1979), p. 11.

6. As in Longinus, "On the Sublime", 10.7 and 43.5.

Perhaps Roland Barthes need not have worried so much, after all, about the signifier's (Orpheus's) condemning Eurydice (the signified) to eternal death by looking back at her.

7. I am following Frank Bisher's reading of the story, in an unpublished essay.

8. Orpheus and Rumpelstiltskin, like Zagreus, Adonis, and Osiris, are never fully reassembled; they never achieve organic form again in the sense in which Sappho, in "On the Sublime", 10.2, is said by Longinus to reassemble her scattered members, as she seals her "cracks" and resumes control of her audience.

Incidentally, Plato's reading of the Orpheus myth is similar in intent to the one I offer above. See *Symposium* #179.

A useful outline of recent positions in feminist criticism may be found in Louis A. Renza, *"A White Heron"* (Madison: University of Wisconsin Press, 1984), chap. 2 and passim.

9. Cf. Nietzsche, *Jenseits von Gut und Böse*, sec. 194: "keine Mutter zweifelt im Grunde ihres Herzens daran, am Kinde sich ein Eigentum geboren zu haben" ("no mother doubts at the bottom of her heart that the child she has borne is thereby her property"), *Werke in drei Bänden* (Munich: Carl Hanser Verlag, 1955), 2:652.

10. Rudolf Geiger, *Mit Märchen im Gespräch* (Stuttgart: Urachhaus, 1972), p. 257, from version 2: "Liebes Kindlein, ach, ich bitt / Bet für Rumpelstilzchen mit."

11. *The Complaint of Nature* (New York: Henry Holt and Co., 1908), trans. Douglas M. Moffat, p. 51.

Cf. André Leroi-Gourhan's *Préhistoire de l'art occidental* (Paris: L. Mazenod, [1965]), which argues that the female elements of cave art are central, the masculine peripheral. (I am indebted to Geoffrey Harpham for the reference).

12. Cf. chap. 6, n. 10 above.

13. On the distinction between mimesis (weak) and representation (strong), see Aristotle, *La Poétique* (Paris: Seuil, 1980), p. 20; Göran Sörbom, *Mimesis and Art* (Bonniers: Svenska Bokförlaget, 1966), pp. 14–18; Philippe Lacoue-Labarthe, "Typographie," in *Mimesis: des articulations;* and, for general background, Wilhelm Worringer, *Abstraktion und Einfühlung.*

14. G. W. H. Schubert, *Die Symbolik des Traumes* (Bamberg: C. F. Kunz, 1814), pp. 201–2, suggests that our communication with the divine takes place through images because the real world was itself once that communication.

15. B.-H. Lévy, *Le Testament de Dieu* (Paris: Grasset, 1979), p. 163. See also chap. 6, text following n. 12.

16. Lévy does not commit this error when dealing with analogous materials. In the Old Testament there is no form (male) and matter (female) to receive the imprint of form. The rock is God, form and material. See Lévy, *Testament*, p. 144.

17. "L'éternel devient une place non métaphorisable...." " "[Le judaïsme] soustrait un site infigurable (l'Éternel) à toute la richesse bigarrée des productions de l'imaginaire." Goux, *Les Iconoclastes,* p. 44.

18. André Schwartz-Bart, as quoted in Lawrence Langer, *The Holocaust and the Literary Imagination* (New Haven: Yale University Press, 1975), p. 261.

19. Jewish sources on the whole support the King James reading of this much-disputed verse (7:9). I am grateful to Kenneth Dauber for researching this reference.

Notes to Chapter 8: Brahms's Deconstruction of a Text by Goethe: Of Honesty in Music.

1. This chapter was written before the article by Aubrey S. Garlington, Jr., *"Harzreise als Herzreise:* Brahms's Alto Rhapsody," appeared in *The Musical Quarterly* 69 (Fall 1983): 527–42. I am in broad agreement with Garlington's essay in seeing the Rhapsody as a strenuous attempt to confront erotic failure rather than as testimony to Brahms's serene intellectual transcendence of his emotional pain; I also share Garlington's opinion (as does Dr. Otto Biba of the Gesellschaft der Musikfreunde in Vienna) that Brahms never did actually offer to marry Julie Schumann. My chapter differs from Garlington's essay in interpreting Goethe's poem, and the episode that gave rise to it, as reflecting a more troubled and ambiguous state of mind in the young Goethe than Garlington would admit, as well as in setting both Goethe's and Brahms's problem in the wider philosophical perspective of the relation between music and desire.

It is important, by the way, to be aware that Brahms studied Goethe thoroughly in his youth. See Annegret Kockegey, *Brahms und Goethe* (Berlin: Humboldt-Universität, 1949), p. 3.

2. I am grateful to Peter Heller for a close critique of this

translation, but remain entirely responsible for errors of omission and commission.

3.   *A Vindication of the Rights of Woman,* chap. 5, sec. 1. For a detailed study of Rousseau's attitudes toward women, see Joel Schwartz, *The Sexual Politics of Jean-Jacques Rousseau* (Chicago and London: University of Chicago Press, 1984).

Anne Robinson Taylor, *Male Novelists and their Female Voices* (Troy: Whitston, 1981), attempts to explore male authors' efforts to project themselves into female roles.

4.   Richard A. Baer, Jr., *Philo's Use of the Categories Male and Female* (Leiden: Brill, 1970), pp. 51, 98.

5.   *Goethe* (Harmondsworth: Penguin Books, 1964), p. 109. A propos Christiane Vulpius and Goethe, I am reminded of Anna Magdalena Bach's scandalous last word on that monument to chaste tenderness and aesthetic exaltation, the *Little Notebook for Anna Magdalena Bach.* Building (com-posing?) is all very well, but, Cupid reminds us, holes must still be bored. "Cupido, der vertraute Schalk, / Lässt keinen ungeschoren, / Zum Bauen braucht man Stein und Kalk, / Die Löcher muss man bohren," etc. It is something of a relief to know that Bach himself could sometimes rise to the occasion and join in a bawdy *quodlibet.*

On the peculiar status of the language used to express sexual desire, see Sandor Ferenczi, *Sex in Psycho-Analysis* (New York: Dover, 1956), chap. 4, and Steven Marcus, *The Other Victorians* (New York: Basic Books, 196[6]), pp. 240–41.

6.   *Campagne in Frankreich 1792,* pp. 1–271 in *Goethes Werke* 55 vols. (Weimar: Hermann Böhlaus Nachfolger), vol. 33 (1898); the relevant pages are 208–29. The work dates from 1821–22. The "Harzreise" is also discussed by Goethe in "Über Goethe's [*sic*] Harzreise im Winter. Einladungsschrift von Dr. Kannegiesser . . . ," vol. 41 (1902) of the Weimar ed., pp. 328–39, dated 1820.

7.   "La raison s'aliène dans le mouvement même où elle prend possession de la déraison." Michel Foucault, *Histoire de la folie* (Paris: Gallimard, 1972), p. 366; cf. the preface to Rousseau's "Discourse on the Origins of Inequality."

8.   Barker Fairley, *A Study of Goethe* (London: Oxford Univer-

sity Press, 1961), p. 101. The quotation from Shelley that follows in my text is understood by Richard Holmes, in *Shelley: the Pursuit* (New York: Dutton, 1975), p. 627, as referring to bladder surgery rather than to any form of Liebestod!

9. "Young Goodman Brown." Cf. John Clare, "Song:" "Love lives beyond / The tomb, the earth, which fades like dew—"

10. Bernard Jacobson argues, convincingly, that Brahms deliberately avoided "expressive" melodies that simply reinforce the obvious meanings of individual words. *The Music of Johannes Brahms* (London: Tantivy Press, 1977), pp. 134ff. Lawrence Kramer tries to show that the music of the "Rhapsody" actually "interrogates" the text in clearly definable ways. See his valuable book *Music and Poetry* (Berkeley: University of California Press, 1984), pp. 136–39 (including a cross-reference to an earlier essay of Kramer's on the same subject).

11. As quoted by Philippe Lacoue-Labarthe in *Le Sujet de la philosophie*, p. 279. This nonspecificity is not to be confused with the practice of abstract generalization repudiated in chap. 2 above, and passim.

12. "Die Musik . . . den innersten aller Gestaltung vorhergängigen Kern gibt." Nietzsche, *Die Geburt der Tragödie*, p. 91.

13. Neil Hertz, "Lecture de Longin," *Poétique* 15 (1973): 292, 306. See also chap. 7, n.9 above.

14. Nietzsche, *Die Geburt der Tragödie*, pp. 116–19. For an attempt to demystify Nietzsche's Dionysus, see Paul de Man, *Allegories of Reading* (New Haven and London: Yale University Press, 1979), e.g. pp. 116–18. For further controversy on this subject, see Stanley Corngold, "Error in Paul de Man," *Critical Inquiry* 8 (Spring 1982): 489–507, and de Man's reply on pp. 509–13.

15. "The Sublime of Edmund Burke," *Glyph* 8 (1981): 62–78.

16. For more on prospective art, see chap. 1 above.

17. Cf. Arnold Schoenberg's essay, "Brahms the Progressive," as well as Jonathan Dunsby, *Structural Ambiguity in Brahms* (Ann Arbor: UMI, 1981).

18. Siegfried Kross, *Die Chorwerke von Johannes Brahms* (Berlin-Halensee: Max Hesse, 1963), pp. 296–97. See also the notes by Kross for the Deutsche Grammophon recording.

19.   I am obliged to Peter Heller for identifying the reference.

20.   Annelise Liebe, "Zur Rhapsodie aus Goethes Harzreise im Winter," *Musa-Mens-Musici* (Leipzig: Deutscher Verlag für Musik, [1969]), 233–42. Cf. n.1 above.

21.   As quoted in Edwin Evans, *Handbook to the Vocal Works of Brahms* (London: William Reeves, 1912), p. 235.

22.   When I wrote this chapter, I had not yet read Lacoue-Labarthe's "Typographie" in *Mimesis: des articulations.* Of "la vie mimétique," Lacoue-Labarthe says (p. 260): "le 'sujet' y dé-siste, et doublement quand il s'agit de l'homme (du mâle), puisque les rôles, qui sont eux-mêmes fictifs, sont en outre passivement enreg-istrés, reçus de la bouche des femmes." ("The 'subject,' especially the male subject, has no consistency under mimetic conditions, for the roles, which are themselves fictive, are, further, passively registered, received from the mouths of women.") Cf. the introduc-tion to Plato's "Menexenus" on mimetic roles being assigned by women. Very similar ideas are to be found in Jean-Louis Cornille, "Medusina: La voix, l'opéra," pp. 173–92 in Célis, ed., *Littérature et musique,* pp. 181, 183. In a recent paper on Barbey d'Aurevilly, Charles Bernheimer seems to suggest that the narrative impulse itself is a defense against the authority of female sexuality.

23.   "Was dem Wortdichter nicht gelungen war ... ihm als schöpferischer Musiker in jedem Augenblick gelingen konnte." Nietzsche, *Die Geburt der Tragödie,* p. 94.

24.   *Sämmtliche Werke,* 1:350–51. Of course, there is a historical dimension to Schopenhauer's remark that should not be overlooked: early nineteenth-century music was still in the process of emanci-pating itself from its previous subordination to text. On the other hand, as Charles Rosen shows (*The Classical Style* [New York: Norton, 1972], p. 378), Friedrich Schlegel insisted that there was a textual element even in purely instrumental music.

25.   Nietzsche, *Die Geburt der Tragödie,* pp. 117–18.

26.   "Mais dans l'art dionysiaque, malgré tout, sauf aux moments d'extrême vigilance, il pourrait arriver que la nature parlât avec sa 'vraie voix,' 'sa voix non dissimulée'. . . . " Philippe Lacoue-Labarthe, *Le Sujet de la philosophie,* p. 62. In the chapter entitled "L'Écho du

sujet," p. 284, Lacoue-Labarthe envisages an a-rhythmic chaos more extreme than the emotional state I attribute to Brahms, which is still organized by desire. I encountered this remarkable essay only after having completed this chapter. See above, chap. 6, n. 14.

27.   " . . . dass sie alle Regungen unseres innersten Wesens wieder-giebt, aber ganz ohne die Wirklichkeit und fern von ihrer Qual." *Sämmtliche Werke,* 1:354. For a brief comment on the general subject of ethics in music see Peter Kivy, *The Corded Shell: Reflexions on Musical Expression* (Princeton: Princeton University Press, 1980), pp. 42–43.

Notes to Chapter 9: Conclusion

1.   To change fields of reference entirely: in its own way, even John Cheever's "The Enormous Radio" casts doubt on the integrity and the adequacy of classical music.

2.   *Groundwork of the Metaphysic of Morals,* trans. H. J. Paton (New York and Evanston: Harper and Row, 1964), p. 63. For the German text, see Kant, *Werke in sechs Bänden,* 4:20–21.

3.   See end of chap. 2 above.

4.   For scientific opinions about the imposition of order on a random universe, see the works of Ilya Prigogine, Edgar Morin, and other theorists of asymmetry. I am indebted to Cesareo Bandera for these references. See also my quotation from Schelling in chap. 1, text for n. 7.

5.   See chap. 6, n. 21.

6.   On the child as the "hidden third," see Julia Kristeva, *Desire in Language* (New York: Columbia University Press, 1980), pp. 271, 279, and chap. 4 above: Sutzkever's "To the Child."

7.   Quoted from Novalis by Simpson, *Irony and Authority,* p. 33. See also V. P. Suransky, *The Erosion of Childhood* (Chicago and London: University of Chicago Press, 1982). Neil Postman's *The*

Disappearance of Childhood (New York: Delacorte Press, 1982) is a more advanced treatment of the same subject.

8.   I think it no accident that children were used to double the major parts in Yossi Yizraeli's summer production of *Lear* (Buffalo, 1983). Richard Abrams has now developed the notion that Cordelia's return is only a fantasy, in a splendid essay: "The Double Casting of Cordelia and Lear's Fool" (forthcoming in *Texas Studies in Literature and Language.*)

Bibliography

Abrams, Richard. "The Double Casting of Cordelia and Lear's Fool." *Texas Studies in Literature and Language.* Forthcoming.

Aeschylus. *Eumenides.* In Volume 2 of *Aeschylus in Two Volumes.* Loeb Classical Library, 1921–26.

Aleichem, Sholem. "The Pair." In *Selected Stories of Sholem Aleichem.* New York: Random House, 1956.

Alexander, Edward. *The Resonance of Dust: Essays on Holocaust Literature and Jewish Fate.* Columbus: Ohio State University Press, 1979.

Alter, Robert B. "Sacred History and the Beginnings of Prose Fiction." *Poetics Today* 1 (Spring 1980): 143–62.

Altieri, Charles. "Motives in Metaphor: John Ashbery and the Modernist Long Poem." *Genre* 11 (Winter 1978): 653–87.

Alvarez, A. *Beyond All This Fiddle: Essays, 1955-67.* London: A. Lane, 1968.

Améry, Jean. *At the Mind's Limits: Contemplations by a Survivor, or Auschwitz and its Realities.* Translated by Sidney Rosenfeld and Stella P. Rosenfeld. Bloomington: Indiana University Press, 1980.

Aquin, Hubert. *Neige noire.* Montréal: La Presse, 1974.*

*follows foreign titles

Arendt, Hannah. "Reflections: Thinking." *The New Yorker,* Nov. 21, Nov. 28, Dec. 5, 1977, 65–140, 114–63, 135–216.

Aristotle. *The Complete Works of Aristotle.* 2 vols. The Revised Oxford Edition of 1912–52, revised and edited by Jonathan Barnes. Bollingen Series 70:2. Princeton: Princeton University Press, 1984.

———. *La Poétique.* Paris: Seuil, 1980.

Arnheim, Rudolf. "Space as an Image of Time." In *Images of Romanticism,* edited by Karl Kroeber and William Walling. New Haven: Yale University Press, 1978.

Asals, Heather. " 'Should' and 'Would': *Hamlet* and the Idioms of the Father." *Genre* 13 (Winter 1980): 431–39.

Ashbery, John. *Self-Portrait in a Convex Mirror.* New York: Viking Press, 1975.

———. *Shadow Train: Poems.* New York: Viking Press, 1981.

Babel, Isaac. "Crossing into Poland." In *Collected Stories,* edited and translated from the Russian by Walter Morison. New York: Criterion Books, [1955].

Bach, Johann Sebastian. *Little Note Book for Anna Magdalena Bach Complete.* Kalmus Piano Series, no. 3055. Melville, New York: Belwin Mills Publishing Corporation, n.d.

Baer, Richard A., Jr. *Philo's Use of the Categories Male and Female.* Leiden: Brill, 1970.

Bakhtin, M. M. *The Dialogic Imagination: Four Essays.* Translated from the Russian by Caryl Emerson and Michael Holquist. Austin: University of Texas Press, 1981.

Barbey-d'Aurevilly, Jules-Amédée. "La Vengeance d'une femme." In *Les Diaboliques: les six premières.* Paris: Éditions Garnier frères, 1963.*

Baxter, Charles. "In the Suicide Seat: Reading John Hawkes's *Travesty.*" *Georgia Review* 34 (Winter 1980), 871–85.

Begg, Ian, Douglas Upfold, and Terrance D. Wilton. "Imagery in Verbal Communication." *Journal of Mental Imagery* 2 (Fall 1972): 165–86.

Benjamin, Walter. *Gesammelte Schriften.* 5 vols. to date. Frankfurt am Main: Suhrkamp Verlag, 1974–.*

——. *Reflections: Essays, Aphorisms, Autobiographical Writings.* Translated from the German by Edmund Jephcott, and edited by Peter Demetz. New York: Harcourt Brace Jovanovich, 1978.

——. *Über Haschisch.* Frankfurt am Main: Suhrkamp, 1972.*

——. *Versuche über Brecht.* Frankfurt am Main: Suhrkamp, 1966.*

Bergson, Henri. *Matière et mémoire: essai sur la relation du corps à l'esprit.* Paris: Presses Universitaires de France, 1965.*

Bersani, Leo. "Representation and its Discontents." In *Allegory and Representation,* edited by Stephen J. Greenblatt. Baltimore: Johns Hopkins University Press, 1981.

Bertrand, Aloysius. *Gaspard de la nuit: fantaisies à la manière de Rembrandt et de Callot.* Paris: Flammarion, 1972.*

Blanchot, Maurice. "L'Écriture du désastre." *La Nouvelle Revue française,* 330–31 (July–August 1980): 1–33.*

Block, Ned, ed. *Imagery.* Cambridge: M.I.T. Press, 1981.

Böhme, Jacob. *Sämmtliche Schriften.* 11 vols. Stuttgart: Fr. Frommans, 1958.*

Bonnefoy, Yves. *Le Nuage rouge: Essais sur la poétique.* Paris: Mercure de France, 1977.*

Borowski, Tadeusz. *"This Way for the Gas, Ladies and Gentlemen," and Other Stories.* New York: Viking Press, 1967.

Boyer, Philippe. "Le Point de la Question." *Change* 22 (February 1975): 41–72.*

Brahms, Johannes. *Sämtliche Werke.* 26 vols. Edited by H. Gál and E. Mandyczewski. Wiesbaden: Breitkopf and Härtel, [1965]. (Reprint of Leipzig edition, 1926–27).

Brinkley, Robert A. "The Incident in the Simplon Pass: A Note on Wordsworth's Revisions." *The Wordsworth Circle* 12 (Spring 1981): 122–25.

Brown, Merle. "Poetic Listening." *New Literary History* 10 (Autumn 1978): 125–39.

Bruss, Elizabeth W. *Beautiful Theories: The Spectacle of Discourse in Contemporary Criticism.* Baltimore: Johns Hopkins University Press, 1982.

Buber, Martin. *Ich and Du.* Leipzig: Insel Verlag, 1923; Köln: Hegners, 1966.*

Bucher, Gérard. "De la vision et de l'énigme: éléments pour une analytique du logos." Ph.D. diss., University of Paris, in progress.*

Burke, Edmund. *A Philosophical Enquiry into the Origin of our Ideas of the Sublime and the Beautiful.* London: Routledge and Kegan Paul, 1958.

Burke, Kenneth. *Rhetoric of Religion: Studies in Logology.* Boston: Beacon Press, 1961.

Burns, Robert. *Poems and Songs of Robert Burns.* Edited by James Kinsley. New York: Oxford University Press, 1968.

Calderwood, James L. "Hamlet: The Name of Action." *Modern Language Quarterly* 39 (December 1978): 331–62.

Calvino, Italo. *The Castle of Crossed Destinies.* New York: Harcourt Brace Jovanovich, 1977.

Caraher, Brian and Irving Massey, eds. *Literature and Iconoclasm.* Buffalo: State University of New York, 1976.

Carroll, Lewis. *Alice's Adventures in Wonderland, and Through the Looking-Glass and What Alice Found There.* Edited by Roger Lancelyn Green. London: Oxford University Press, 1971.

Cavell, Stanley. *The Claim of Reason: Wittgenstein, Skepticism, Morality and Tragedy.* Oxford: Clarendon Press, 1979.

Caws, Mary Ann. *The Eye in the Text: Essays on Perception, Mannerist to Modern.* Princeton: Princeton University Press, 1981.

Célis, Raphaël, ed. *Littérature et musique.* Brussels: Publications des facultés universitaires Saint-Louis, 1982.*

Char, René. Epigraph to Nathaniel MacKey, "Gassire's Lute: Robert Duncan's War Poems." MS. Private Collection.

Chatterton, Thomas. *The Complete Works of Thomas Chatterton.* 2 vols. Edited by Donald S. Taylor and Benjamin B. Hoover. Oxford: Clarendon Press, 1971.

Chaucer, Geoffrey. "The Miller's Tale." In volume 2 of *A Variorum Edition of the Works of Geoffrey Chaucer,* edited by Thomas W. Ross. Norman: University of Oklahoma Press, 1983.

Cheever, John. "The Fourth Alarm" and "The Enormous Radio." In *The Stories of John Cheever.* New York: Alfred A. Knopf, 1978.

Chekhov, A[nton]. "Palata no. 6" ("Ward no. 6"). In *Izbrannie Proizvedeniya.* Moscow: Izdatielstvo "Khoodozhestvennaia Litieratoora," 1967.*

Church, Philip. "Editorial." *Kenyon Review* (Fall 1983): 119–21.

Churchland, Paul M. and Clifford A. Hooker eds. *Images of Science: Essays on Realism and Empiricism.* Chicago and London: University of Chicago Press, 1985.

Clare, John. *The Poems of John Clare.* Edited by J. W. Tibble and Anne Tibble. London: Routledge and Kegan Paul, [1951].

Clarke, Bruce. "Metamorphic Romance." MS. Private Collection.

Cohen, Ted. "Metaphor and the Cultivation of Intimacy." In *On Metaphor,* edited by Sheldon Sacks. Chicago: University of Chicago Press, 1979.

Coleridge, Samuel Taylor. *Biographia Literaria.* Edited by J. Shawcross. Oxford: Oxford University Press, 1969.

———. Collected Letters. 6 vols. Edited by Earl Leslie Griggs. Oxford: Clarendon Press, 1956–71.

———. *Logic.* Volume 13 of *Collected Works.* London: Routledge and Kegan Paul; Princeton: Princeton University Press, [1981].

———. *Notebooks.* 3 vols. Edited by Kathleen Coburn. Princeton: Princeton University Press, 1957–73.

———. *Poetical Works.* Edited by Ernest Hartley Coleridge. London: Oxford University Press, 1969.

Compagnon, Antoine. *La Seconde main: ou, le Travail de la citation.* Paris: Seuil, 1979.*

Corngold, Stanley. "Error in Paul de Man." *Critical Inquiry* 8 (Spring 1982): 489–507.

Craft, Robert. "B-Flat Movie." Review of *Amadeus,* a film written by Peter Shaffer and directed by Milos Forman. *New York Review of Books* (11 April 1985): 11–12.

Creuzer, Georg F. *Symbolik und Mythologie der alten Völker, besonders der Griechen.* Leipzig and Darmstadt: Heyer und Leske, 1819–23.*

Daly, Peter M. *Literature in the Light of the Emblem: Structural Parallels between the Emblem and Literature in the Sixteenth and Seventeenth Centuries.* Toronto: University of Toronto Press, 1979.

Dante Alighieri. *The Divine Comedy.* Translated by Charles S. Singleton. 6 vols. Princeton: Princeton University Press, [1970–75].

de Insulis, Alanus. *The Complaint of Nature.* Translated from the Latin by Douglas M. Moffat. Yale Studies in English, edited by A. S. Cook, no. 36. New York: Henry Holt and Co., 1908.

Deleuze, Gilles. *Présentation de Sacher-Masoch, le froid et le cruel.* Paris: Minuit, 1967.*

de Man, Paul. *Allegories of Reading: Figural Language in Rousseau, Nietzsche, Rilke, and Proust.* New Haven: Yale University Press, 1979.

Descombes, Vincent. *L'Inconscient malgré lui.* Paris: Minuit, 1977.*

Devlin, D. D. *De Quincey, Wordsworth and the Art of Prose.* London: Macmillan, 1983.

Diderot, Denis. *Oeuvres complètes.* 20 vols. Edited by J. Assézat. Paris: Garnier Frères, 1875–77.*

Dillon, George L. *Language Processing and the Reading of Literature: Toward a Model of Comprehension.* Bloomington: Indiana University Press, 1978.

Dionysius the Areopagite. *The Mystical Theology and the Celestial Hierarchies.* Letchworth: Garden City Press, 1965.

Dostoyevsky, Fyodor. *The Double: A Poem of St. Petersburgh.* Translated by George Bird. Bloomington: Indiana University Press, 1966.

Dummet, Michael. *Frege: Philosophy of Language.* London: Duckworth, [1973].

Dunsby, Jonathan M. *Structural Ambiguity in Brahms: Analytical Approaches to Four Works.* British Studies in Musicology, no. 2. Ann Arbor: UMI Research Press, 1981.

Duverlie, Claud. "Beyond the Image: An Interview with Alain Robbe-Grillet." *New Literary History* 11 (Spring 1980): 527–34.

Eco, Umberto. *The Name of the Rose.* Translated by William Weaver. New York: Harcourt Brace Jovanovich, 1983.

Ellis, John M. *One Fairy Story Too Many: The Brothers Grimm and their Tales.* Chicago: University of Chicago Press, 1983.

Erwin, John. *Lyric Apocalypse.* Chicago: Scholars Press, 1984.

———. "Proust and Venice." MS. Private Collection.

———. "Spectacularity of the Universe." MS. Private Collection.

Evans, Edwin. *Handbook to the Vocal Works of Brahms.* London: William Reeves, 1912.

Fairley, Barker. *A Study of Goethe.* London: Oxford University Press, 1961.

Ferenczi, Sandor and Otto Rank. *Sex in Psycho-Analysis (Contributions to Psycho-Analysis)* and *The Development of Psycho-Analysis.* Translated by Ernest Jones. New York: Dover Books, 1966.

Ferguson, Frances. "The Sublime of Edmund Burke, or The Bathos of Experience." *Glyph* 8 (1981): 62–78.

Ferris, David S. "Transfigurations." Ph.D. diss., State University of New York at Buffalo, 1985.

Fiera, Battista. *De Iusticia Pingenda. On the Painting of Justice. A Dialogue between Mantegna and Momus.* Translated by James Wardrop. London: Lion and Unicorn Press, 1957.

Flaubert, Gustave. *Oeuvres,* edited by A. Thibaudet and R. Dumesnil. Paris, Gallimard, 1958–9.*

Fly, Richard. "Accommodating Death: The Ending of *Hamlet.*" *Studies in English Literature* 24 (1984): 257–74.

Foley, Barbara. "Fact, Fiction, Fascism; Testimony and Mimesis in Holocaust Narratives." *Comparative Literature* 34 (Fall 1982): 330–60.

Foucault, Michel. *Histoire de la folie.* Paris: Gallimard, 1972.*

French, Marilyn. *Shakespeare's Division of Experience.* New York: Summit Books, 1981.

Freud, Sigmund. *The Standard Edition of the Complete Psychological Works of Sigmund Freud.* 24 vols. Edited by James Strachey in collaboration with Anna Freud. London: Hogarth Press and the Institute of Psychoanalysis, [1953], 1964–74. (Reprint of 1957 edition).

Fry, Paul. *The Reach of Criticism.* New Haven: Yale University Press, 1983.

Gadamer, Hans-Georg. *Dialogue and Dialectic: Eight Hermeneutical Studies on Plato.* Translated by P. Christopher Smith. New Haven: Yale University Press, 1980.

———. *Truth and Method.* Translation edited by Garrett Barden and John Cumming. New York: Seabury Press, 1975.

Gardner, Martin. "The Charms of Catastrophe." *New York Review of Books* (15 June 1978): 30–34.

Garelli, Jacques. *La Gravitation poétique.* Paris: Mercure de France, 1966.*

Garlington, Aubrey S., Jr. "*Harzreise als Herzreise:* Brahms's Alto Rhapsody." *The Musical Quarterly* 69 (Fall 1983): 527–42.

Gasché, Rodolphe. *System und Metaphorik in der Philosophie von Georges Bataille.* Bern: Peter Lang, 1978.

Geiger, Rudolf. *Mit Märchen im Gespräch.* Stuttgart: Urachhaus, 1972.*

Gilbert, Sandra M. and Susan Gubar. *The Madwoman in the Attic: The Woman Writer and the Nineteenth Century Literary Imagination.* New Haven: Yale University Press, 1979.

Girard, René. *Violence and the Sacred.* Baltimore: Johns Hopkins University Press, 1977.

Glatstein, Jacob. *The Selected Poems of Jacob Glatstein.* New York: October House, 1972.

Goethe, Johann Wolfgang von. *Goethes Werke.* 55 vols. Weimar: Hermann Böhlaus Nachfolger, 1887–1918.*

———. *Goethe: Selected Verse.* Translated by David Luke. Harmondsworth: Penguin Books, 1964.

Gombrich, E. H. *Symbolic Images: Studies in the Art of the Renaissance.* London: Phaidon, 1972.

———. *The Sense of Order: A Study in the Psychology of Decorative Art.* Ithaca: Cornell University Press, 1979.

Goux, Jean-Joseph. *Les Iconoclastes.* Paris: Seuil, 1978.*

Grimm, Jakob Ludwig Karl and Wilhelm Karl Grimm. *Kinder- und Hausmärchen gesammelt durch die Brüder Grimm.* 7th ed. 3 vols. Göttingen: Dietrich, 1856–57.*

Gross, David. "Space, Time, and Modern Culture." *Telos* 50 (Winter 1981–82): 59–78.

Hampshire, Stuart. *Morality and Conflict.* Oxford: Basil Blackwell, 1983.

Hanay, Alastair. *Mental Images: A Defence.* London: Humanities Press, 1971.

Handelman, Susan. "On Interpreting Sacred and Secular Scripture: The Relation of Biblical Exegesis to Literary Criticism." Ph.D. diss., State University of New York at Buffalo, 1979.

Haney, David Pierson. "The Rhetoric of Wordsworth's *Prelude:* Figural Aspects of Poetic Autobiography." Ph.D. diss., State University of New York at Buffalo, 1980.

Hartman, Geoffrey, ed. *Psychoanalysis and the Question of the Text.* Baltimore: Johns Hopkins University Press, 1978.

——. *The Unmediated Vision: An Interpretation of Wordsworth, Hopkins, Rilke, and Valéry.* New York: Harcourt, Brace, and World, 1966.

Hawthorne, Nathaniel. *The Centenary Edition of the Works of Nathaniel Hawthorne.* 16 vols. to date. Ohio: Ohio State University Center for Textual Studies, [1962]– .

Hazlitt, William. *The Complete Works of William Hazlitt.* 21 vols. Edited by P. P. Howe after the edition of A. R. Waller and Arnold Glover. London: J. M. Dent and Sons, 1930–34.

Hegel, Georg Wilhelm. *Phänomenologie des Geistes.* Volume 2 of *Sämmtliche Werke.* Stuttgart: F. Fromman, [1958].*

Heidegger, Martin. *Identität und Differenz.* Pfullingen: G. Neske, [1957].*

——. *What Is Called Thinking?* New York: Harper and Row, 1968.

Henn, Thomas Rice. *The Harvest of Tragedy.* New York: Barnes and Noble, 1966.

Hertz, Neil. "Lecture de Longin." *Poétique* 15 (1973): 292–306.*

Hirsch, E. D., Jr. "Writing and Reading: Toward a Model of Comprehension." *Cornell Review* 4 (Fall 1978): 115–26.

Holmes, Richard. *Shelley: The Pursuit.* New York: Dutton, 1975.

Homer. *The Odyssey.* 2 vols. Loeb Classical Library, 1919.

Hopkins, Gerard Manley. *Journals and Papers.* Edited by Humphrey House. London: Oxford University Press, 1959.

——. *The Poems of Gerard Manley Hopkins.* Edited by W. H. Gardner and N. H. MacKenzie. London: Oxford University Press, 1967.

Horowitz, Mardi J. *Image Formation and Cognition*. New York: Appleton-Century-Crofts, 1978.

Howe, Irving. "Beyond Bitterness." Review of *Kolyma Tales*, by Varlam Shalamov. *New York Review of Books* (14 August 1980): 36–37.

Howe, Irving and Eliezer Greenberg, eds. *A Treasury of Yiddish Poetry*. New York: Holt, Rinehart and Winston, 1972.

Husserl, Edmund. *Ideas: General Introduction to Pure Phenomenology*. Translated by W. R. Boyce Gibson. New York: Collier, 1972.

———. *Zur Phänomenologie des inneren Zeitbewussteins*. 's–Gravenhage: Martinus Nijhoff, 1966. Translated by James S. Churchill, as *The Phenomenology of Internal Time-Consciousness*. Edited by Martin Heidegger. Bloomington: Indiana University Press, 1964.

Ibsch, Elrud. "Historical Changes of the Function of Spatial Description in Literary Texts." *Poetics Today* 3 (Autumn 1982): 97–113.

Iginla, Biodun. "Woman and Metaphor." *Enclitic* 2:1 (Spring 1978): 27–37.

Jackson, Laura Riding. *The Poems of Laura Riding*. Manchester: Carcanet New Press, 1980.

Jacobs, Carol. *The Dissimulating Harmony: The Image of Interpretation in Nietzsche, Rilke, Artaud and Benjamin*. Baltimore: Johns Hopkins University Press, 1978.

Jacobson, Bernard. *The Music of Johannes Brahms*. London: Tantivy Press, 1977.

Jacques, Francis. "Les Conditions dialogiques de la référence." *Les Études Philosophiques* 32 (1977): 267–305.*

Jakobson, Roman. "Quest for the Essence of Language." *Diogenes* 51 (Fall 1965): 21–37.

James, Henry. *The Novels and Tales of Henry James*. 26 vols. Prefaced by Henry James. New York: Charles Scribner's Sons, 1907–17.

Jauss, Hans Robert, ed. *Die Nicht mehr schönen Künste: Grenzphänomene des Ästhetischen. Poetik und Hermeneutik*, 3. Munich: Wilhelm Frank Verlag, 1968.*

Jenny, Laurent. "Il n'y a pas de récit cathartique." *Poétique* 41 (February 1980): 1–21.*

Johnson, D. Barton. "Spatial Modeling and Deixis." *Poetics Today* 3 (Winter 1982): 81–98.

Kant, Immanuel. *Groundwork of the Metaphysics of Morals.* Translated by H. J. Paton. New York: Harper and Row, 1964.

———. *Kritik der Urteilskraft.* Leipzig: F. Meiner, 1948.*

———. *Prolegomena to any future Metaphysics.* With an introduction by Lewis W. Beck. The Little Library of Liberal Arts, no. 27. New York: Liberal Arts Press, [1950].

———. *Werke in sechs Bänden.* Wiesbaden: Insel-Verlag, 1960–64.*

Kazin, Alfred. Introduction to *By Words Alone: The Holocaust in Literature,* by Sidra DeKoven Ezrahi. Chicago: University of Chicago Press, 1980.

Keats, John. *Complete Poems.* Edited by Jack Stillinger. Cambridge: Belknap Press of Harvard University Press, 1982.

Kelly, Aileen. "Justice to Mrs. Tolstoy." Review of *Sonya: The Life of Countess Tolstoy,* by Anne Edwards. *New York Review of Books* (October 22 1981): 3, 6, 8, 10.

Kestner, Joseph A. *Spatiality of the Novel.* Detroit: Wayne State University Press, 1978.

Kivy, Peter. *The Corded Shell: Reflexions on Musical Expression.* Princeton: Princeton University Press, 1980.

Kockegey, Annagret. *Brahms und Goethe.* Berlin: Humboldt-Universität, 1949.*

Kramer, Lawrence. *Music and Poetry: The Nineteenth Century and After.* Berkeley: University of California Press, 1984.

Kristeva, Julia. *Desire in Language: A Semiotic Approach to Literature and Art.* Translated by Thomas Gora, Alice Jardine, and Leon S. Roudicz. New York: Columbia University Press, 1980.

Kroeber, Karl and William Walling. *Images of Romanticism.* New Haven: Yale University Press, 1978.

Kross, Siegfried. *Die Chorwerke von Johannes Brahms.* Berlin-Halensee: Max Hesse, 1963.*

Kundera, Milan. *The Book of Laughter and Forgetting.* Translated by Michael Henry Heim. Harmondsworth, Middlesex, England: Penguin Books, 1981.

Lacoste, Patrick. *Il écrit: une mise en scène de Freud.* Paris: Galilée, 1981.*

Lacoue-Labarthe, Philippe. *Le Sujet de la philosophie.* Paris: Aubier-Flammarion, 1979.*

——. "Typographie." In *Mimesis: des Articulations,* edited by Sylviane Agacinski, et al. Paris: Aubier-Flammarion, 1975.*

Laforgue, Jules. *Moralités légendaires.* Volume 3 of *Oeuvres complètes.* Paris: Mercure de France, 1924.*

Lane, John. "Waking in the Blue Ridge." *Harvard Magazine* 83, no. 4 (March–April 1981): 10.

Langer, Lawrence L. *The Age of Atrocity: Death in Modern Literature.* Boston: Beacon Press, 1978.

——. *The Holocaust and the Literary Imagination.* New Haven: Yale University Press, 1975.

Laporte, Jean. *La Doctrine de Port-Royal.* 2 vols. Paris: Presses Universitaires de France, 1923.*

Lautréamont, comte de [Isidore Ducasse]. *Les Chants de Maldoror.* Paris: Presses de la Renaissance, 1977.*

Leibniz, Gottfried Wilhelm. *Die Hauptwerke.* Stuttgart: Alfred Kröner, 1958.*

——. *Monadology, and Other Philosophical Essays.* Translated by Paul Schrecker and Anne Martin Schrecker. Indianapolis: Bobbs-Merrill Co., 1965.

——. *Die philosophischen Schriften.* 7 vols. Edited by C. J. Gerhardt. Hildesheim: Georg Olms, 1960–61. (Reprint of 1890 edition).*

Leivick, Halper. *In the Days of Job* (in Yiddish). New York: Tsiko, 1953.*

——. *In Treblinka bin Ich nicht gewesen 1940–45, Lieder un Poemen.* New York: Tsiko, 1945.*

Leroi-Gourhan, André. *Préhistoire de l'art occidental.* Paris: L. Mazenod, 1965.*

Leverenz, David. "The Woman in *Hamlet.*" In *Representing Shakespeare: New Psychoanalytic Essays,* edited by Murray M. Schwartz and Coppelia Kahn. Baltimore: Johns Hopkins University Press, 1980.

Levinas, Emmanuel. *De l'existence à l'existant.* Paris: Vrin, 1978.*

Lévy, Bernard-Henri. *Le Testament de Dieu.* Paris: B. Grasset, 1979.*

Liebe, Annalise. "Zur Rhapsodie aus Goethes Harzreise im Winter." *Musa-Mens-Musici.* Leipzig: Deutscher Verlag für Musik, 1969.*

Longinus, Cassius. *Longinus' 'On the Sublime.'* Edited by D. A. Russell. Oxford: Clarendon Press, 1964.*

Lovejoy, Arthur O. *The Great Chain of Being: A Study of the History of an Idea.* New York: Harper and Row, 1960.

Lyons, John D. "Speaking in Pictures, Speaking of Pictures: Problems of Representation in the Seventeenth Century." In *Mimesis, From Mirror to Method, Augustine to Descartes,* edited by John D. Lyons and Stephen G. Nichols, Jr. Hanover: University Press of New England, 1982.

Lyotard, Jean François and Jean-Loup Thébaud. *Au Juste: conversations.* Paris: Christian Bourgois, 1979.

Lyotard, Jean François. *Discours, Figure.* Paris: Klincksieck, 1978.*

——. *Les Fins de l'homme.* Paris: Galilée, 1981.*

——. "Jewish Oedipus." *Genre* 10 (Fall 1977): 395–411.

McCormick, Peter. *Heidegger and the Language of the World.* Ottawa: University of Ottawa Press, 1976.

McGuire, Jerry. "Shakespeare's Gaps: Essays in Psychosexual Rhetoric and Poetics." Ph.D. diss., State University of New York at Buffalo, 1981.

MacIntyre, Alisdair D. *After Virtue: A Study in Moral Theory.* Notre Dame, Indiana: University of Notre Dame Press, 1981.

MacPhail, Sir Andrew. *The Master's Wife.* Toronto: McClelland and Stewart, 1977.

McRae, Robert. *Leibniz: Perception, Apperception, and Thought.* Toronto: University of Toronto Press, 1976.

Mahler, Gustav. *Briefe, 1879–1911.* Hrsg. von Alma Maria Mahler. Berlin: P. Zsolnay, 1924.*

Marcus, Steven. *The Other Victorians: A Study of Sexuality and Pornography in Mid-Nineteenth Century England.* New York: Basic Books, 1966.

Marvell, Andrew. *Poems and Letters of Andrew Marvell.* 3rd ed., revised. 2 vols. Edited by H. M. Margoliouth. Oxford: The Clarendon Press, 1971.

Massey, Irving. *The Gaping Pig: Literature and Metamorphosis.* Berkeley: University of California Press, 1976.

——. "Two Types of Visual Metaphor." *Criticism* 19 (Fall 1977): 285–295.

——. *The Uncreating Word: Romanticism and the Object.* Bloomington: Indiana University Press, 1970.

May, Charles E. "Perversion in Pornography: Male Envy of the Female." *Literature and Psychology* 31, no. 2 (1981): 66–74.

Mayanowa, M. R. "Verbal Texts and Iconic-Visual Texts." In *Image and Code,* edited by Wendy Steiner. Ann Arbor: Michigan Studies in Humanities, 1981.

Maze, Ida. *A Mame.* Montreal: Jewish Cultural Society, 1931.*

Mehlman, Jeffrey. "Cataract: Diderot's Discursive Politics, 1744–1751." In *Glyph* 2 (1977): 37–63.

Merleau-Ponty, Maurice. *L'Oeil et l'esprit.* Paris: Gallimard, 1964.*

——. "Le Primat de la perception et ses conséquences philosophiques." *Bulletin de la société française de philosophie* 41 (October–December 1947): 119–53.*

Merrill, Elizabeth. *The Dialogue in English Literature.* New York: Henry Holt, 1911.

Meschonnic, Henri. "Il n'y a pas de judéo-chrétien." *La Nouvelle Revue Française* 326 (March 1980): 80–89.*

Miall, David S., ed. *Metaphor: Problems and Perspectives.* Brighton, Sussex: Harvester Press; Atlantic Highlands, New Jersey: Humanities Press, 1982.

Mill, John Stuart. *The Essential Works of John Stuart Mill.* Edited by Max Lerner. New York: Bantam Books, 1965.

Miller, Arthur I. "Visualization Lost and Regained: The Genesis of the Quantum Theory in the Period 1913–27." In *On Aesthetics in Science,* edited by Judith Wechsler. Cambridge: M.I.T. Press, 1978.

Mitchell, W. J. T. "The Politics of Genre: Space and Time in Lessing's *Laocoön.*" *Representations* 2 (Spring 1984): 98–115.

Molino, J. "Métaphores, modèles, et analogie dans les sciences." *Langages* 54 (June 1979): 83–102.*

Monnoyer, Jean-Maurice. "Ludwig Wittgenstein." *Nouvelle Revue française* 330–31 (July–August 1980): 218–223.*

Musil, Robert. *Gesammelte Werke.* 9 vols. Reinbek bei Hamburg: Rowohlt, 1978.

Nancy, Jean-Luc. *Le Discours de la syncope.* Paris: Aubier, 1976.*

Nashe, Thomas. *The Unfortunate Traveller, or the Life of Jack Wilton.* Edited by John Berryman. New York: G. P. Putnam's Sons, 1960.

Nelson, Cary. "Whitman in Vietnam: Poetry and History in Contemporary America." *Massachusetts Review* 16 (Winter 1975): 55–71.

Nelson, T. G. A. and Charles Haines. "Othello's Unconsummated Marriage." *Essays in Criticism* 33 (January 1983): 1–18.

Nelson, William. *Fact or Fiction: The Dilemma of the Renaissance Storyteller.* Cambridge: Harvard University Press, 1973.

Nerval, Gérard de. *Sylvie; les chimères; Aurélia.* [Paris]: Bordas, 1967.*

Niemetschek, Franz. *W. A. Mozarts Leben, nach Originalquellen beschrieben.* Facsimile of the 1798 edition, edited by Ernst Rychnovsky. I. Taussig, 1905.*

Nietzsche, Friedrich. *Die Geburt der Tragödie aus dem Geiste der Musik.* Stuttgart: Reclam, 1966.

———. *Werke in Drei Bänden.* Munich: Carl Hanser Verlag, 1955.

Norford, Don Parry. " 'Very Like a Whale.' The Problem of Knowledge in *Hamlet.*" *English Literary History* 46 (Winter 1979): 559–76.

Norrman, Ralph and Jon Haarberg. *Nature and Language.* London: Routledge and Kegan Paul, 1980.

Novalis. *Schriften.* 3 vols. Edited by Paul Kluckhohn, Richard Samuel, et al. Stuttgart: Kohlhammer Verlag, 1960.*

Nozick, Robert. *Philosophical Explanations.* Cambridge: Harvard University Press, 1981.

Packard, William, ed. *The Craft of Poetry.* Interviews from *The New York Quarterly.* New York: Doubleday, 1974.

Parker, Patricia A. *Inescapable Romance: Studies in the Poetics of a Mode.* Princeton: Princeton University Press, 1979.

Pascal, Blaise. *Oeuvres complètes.* Texte établi et annoté par Jacques Chevalier. Paris: Gallimard, 1964.*

Pechter, Edward. "On the Blinding of Gloucester." *English Literary History* 45 (1978): 181–200.

Pison, Thomas. "A Lacanian Reading of Shakespeare's *Hamlet.*" Typescript. Private Collection.

Plath, Sylvia. *Collected Poems.* New York: Harper and Row, 1981.

Plato. *The Dialogues of Plato.* Translated by B. Jowett. New York: Random House, n.d.

Plutarch. *Plutarch's Lives.* Translated by Bernadette Perrin. London: W. Heinemann, 1928.

Pope, Alexander. *Poems of Alexander Pope.* Edited by John Butt. New Haven: Yale University Press, 1963.

Postman, Neil. *The Disappearance of Childhood.* New York: Delacorte Press, 1982.

Pound, Ezra. *Gaudier-Brzeska: A Memoir.* London: John Lane, 1916.

Prigogine, Ilya. *From Being to Becoming: Time and Complexity in the Physical Sciences.* San Francisco: W. H. Freeman, 1980.

Proust, Marcel. *À la recherche du temps perdu.* Paris: Gallimard, 1954.

———. "John Ruskin." In *Pastiches et Mélanges.* Paris: Gallimard, 1949.

Rapaport, Herman. "The Dis-Articulated Image." MS. Private Collection.

Rassial, Adélie and Jean-Jacques Rassial, eds. *L'Interdit de la représentation: colloque de Montpellier.* Paris: Seuil, 1984.*

Rawicz, Piotr. *Blood from the Sky.* New York: Harcourt, Brace and World, 1964.

Renza, Louis A. *"A White Heron" and the Question of Minor Literature.* Madison: University of Wisconsin Press, 1984.

Ricoeur, Paul. *Temps et récit.* 2 vols. Paris: Seuil, 1983.*

Ritter, Johann Wilhelm. *Fragmente aus dem Nachlasse eines jungen Physikers.* Heidelberg: L. Schneider, 1969.*

Rogers, Robert. "Hopkins' 'Carrion Comfort.'" *The Hopkins Quarterly* 7 (Winter 1981): 143–165.

Rölleke, Heinz. *Die älteste Märchensammlung der Brüder Grimm.* Cologny-Genève: Fondation Martin Bodmer, 1975.*

Rosen, Charles. *The Classical Style: Haydn, Mozart, Beethoven.* New York: Norton, 1972.

Rosen, Lois. "Sylvia Plath's Poetry about Children." *Modern Poetry Studies* 10 (1981): 98–115.

Rosenthal, M. L. Review of *Introspection and Contemporary Poetry,* by Alan Williamson. *New York Times Book Review* (September 23 1984): 34.

Rousseau, Jean-Jacques. *Oeuvres complètes.* 4 vols. Paris: Gallimard, 1959–69.*

Ruskin, John. *The Complete Works of John Ruskin.* 39 vols. Edited by E. T. Cook and Alexander Wedderburn. London: George Allen, 1908.

Rycroft, Charles. *The Innocence of Dreams.* New York: Pantheon, 1979.

Sacks, Oliver. "The Twins." *New York Review of Books 32* (28 February 1985): 16–20.

Sartre, Jean-Paul. *L'Imaginaire: psychologie phénoménologique de l'imagination.* Paris: Gallimard, 1940.

Scheffler, Israel. *Beyond the Letter: Philosophical Inquiry into Ambiguity, Vagueness, and Metaphor in Language.* London: Routledge and Kegan Paul, 1979.

Schelling, Friedrich Wilhelm Joseph. *System des transzendentalen Idealismus.* Hamburg: Felix Meiner Verlag, 1957.*

Schlegel, Friedrich. "Idyll of Idleness." In *Lucinde and the Fragments.* Minneapolis: University of Minnesota Press, 1971.

Schoenberg, Arnold. "Brahms the Progressive." In *Style and Idea: Selected Writings of Arnold Schoenberg.* Translated by Leo Black. London: Faber and Faber, 1975.

Schopenhauer, Arthur. *Sämmtliche Werke.* Grossherzog Wilhelm Ernst Ausgabe. 5 vols. Leipzig: Insel Verlag, 1905–10.*

Schubert, G. W. *Die Symbolik des Traumes.* Bamberg: C. F. Kunz, 1814.

Schulz, Bruno. *Sanatorium under the Sign of the Hourglass.* Translated by Celina Wieniewska. New York: Walker and Co., 1978.

Schwartz, Joel. *The Sexual Politics of Jean-Jacques Rousseau.* Chicago: University of Chicago Press, 1984.

See, Fred G. "The Kinship of Metaphor." *Structuralist Review* 1:2 (Winter 1978): 55–81.

Shaffer, Elinor S. *"Kubla Khan" and the Fall of Jerusalem: The Mythological School in Biblical Criticism and Secular Literature.* Cambridge: Cambridge University Press, 1975.

Shakespeare, William. *23 Plays and the Sonnets,* Edited by G. B. Harrison. New York: Harcourt, Brace and Co., 1948.

Shelley, Percy Bysshe. *A Defence of Poetry.* Edited by John E. Jordan. Indianapolis: Bobbs-Merrill, 1965.

Shklovsky, Victor B. *A Sentimental Journey.* Translated by Richard Sheldon. Ithaca: Cornell University Press, 1970.

Simpson, David. *Irony and Authority in Romantic Poetry.* Totowa: Rowman and Littlefield, 1979.

Sivert, Eileen Boyd. "Narration and Exhibitionism in *Le Rideau cramoisi.*" *Romanic Review* 70 (March 1979): 146–158.

Smith, R. Spencer. "Voyeurism: A Review of Literature." *Archives of Sexual Behavior* 5 (1976): 585–608.

Smith, Stevie. *The Frog Prince, and Other Poems.* London: Longmans, 1966.

Smitten, Jeffrey R. and Ann Daghistany. *Spatial Form in Narrative.* Ithaca: Cornell University Press, 1981.

Snow, Edward A. "Sexual Anxiety and the Male Order of Things in *Othello.*" *English Literary Renaissance* 10 (1980): 384–412.

Sörbom, Göran. *Mimesis and Art: Studies in the Origin and Early Development of an Aesthetic Vocabulary.* Bonniers: Svenska Bokförlaget, 1966.

Spivak, Gayatri. "Thoughts on the Principle of Allegory." *Genre* 5 (December 1972): 337–352.

Sprinker, Michael. Review of *Toward an Aesthetic of Reception,* by Hans Robert Jauss. *Modern Language Notes* 97 (December 1982): 1205–1212.

BIBLIOGRAPHY

251

Steiner, Wendy. *Colors of Rhetoric: Problems in the Relation Between Modern Literature and Painting.* Chicago: University of Chicago Press, 1982.

Stevens, Wallace. *The Necessary Angel: Essays on Reality and the Imagination.* New York: Random House, 1965.

Stoehr, Taylor. "Pornography, Masturbation and the Novel." *Salmagundi* 2 (Fall 1967–Winter 1968): 28–56.

Strawson, P. F. *Individuals: An Essay in Descriptive Metaphysics.* London: Methuen and Co., 1959.

Suransky, Valerie Polakow. *The Erosion of Childhood.* Chicago: University of Chicago Press, 1982.

Sutzkever, Abraham. *Geistige Erd* (*Spiritual Soil*). New York: Der Kval, 1961.*

——. *Lider fun Yam-Hamoves* (*Dead Sea Poems*). Tel-Aviv: Bergen-Belsen Memorial Press, 1968.*

Taylor, Anne Robinson. *Male Novelists and their Female Voices: Literary Masquerades.* Troy: Whitston, 1981.

Tolstoi, L. N. *Sobranie Sotchinenii.* 20 vols. Moscow: Gosoodarstvennoie Izdatielstvo Khoodozhestvennoi Litieratoori, 1960–65.*

Tucker, Abraham. *Light of Nature Pursued.* 2nd ed. 7 vols. New York: Garland, 1977.

Turner, C. J. G. "The Language of Fiction: Word Clusters in Tolstoy's 'The Death of Ivan Ilyich'." *Modern Language Review* 65 (January 1970): 116–121.

Updike, John. "Bruno Schulz, Hidden Genius." *New York Times Book Review* (9 September, 1979): 1, 36–39.

Valéry, Paul. *Oeuvres.* 2 vols. Paris: Gallimard, 1957–60.*

Vico, Giovanni Battista. *The New Science of Giambattista Vico.* Translated by Thomas Goddard Bergin and Max Harold Fisch. Ithaca: Cornell University Press, 1948.

Vigny, Alfred de. *Les Destinées.* Edited by V. L. Saulnier. Geneva: Droz; Paris: Minard, 1967.*

Virgil. *Georgics.* In volume 1 of *Virgil in Two Volumes.* Loeb Classical Library, 1935.*

Waelhens, Alphonse de. *Schizophrenia: A Philosophical Reflection on

Lacan's Structuralist Interpretation. Translated by W. ver Eecke. Pittsburgh: Duquesne University, 1978.

Werner, Heinz. *Die Ursprünge der Metapher.* Leipzig: W. Engelman, 1919.*

Wiggins, David. *Sameness and Substance.* Oxford: Basil Blackwell, 1980.

Williams, Bernard. *Descartes: The Project of Pure Enquiry.* New York: Penguin Books, 1978.

Williamson, Alan. *Introspection and Contemporary Poetry.* MS. Private Collection.

Wisse, Ruth. "Aesthetics as a Form of Resistance: The Ghetto Poetry of Abraham Sutzkever." Typescript. Private Collection.

Wittgenstein, Ludwig. *On Certainty.* Edited by J.E.M. Anscombe and G. H. von Wright. New York: J. and J. Harper, 1969.

——. *Tractatus logico-philosophicus.* Translated by D. F. Pears and B. F. McGuiness. London: Routledge and Kegan Paul; New York, The Humanities Press, 1966.

Wollstonecraft, Mary. *A Vindication of the Rights of Woman.* Edited by Carol H. Poston. New York: Norton, 1975.

Wordsworth, Dorothy. *Recollections of a Tour Made in Scotland.* Edited by J. C. Shairp. Edinburgh: David Douglas, 1894.

Wordsworth, William. *The Poetical Works of William Wordsworth.* Boston: Houghton Mifflin, 1982.

——. *The Prelude: 1799, 1805 and 1850.* Edited by Jonathan Wordsworth et al. New York: Norton Critical Editions, 1979.

Worringer, Wilhelm. *Abstraktion und Einfühlung.* Munich: R. Piper Verlag, 1959.*

Wright, George T. "Hendiadys and *Hamlet.*" *Publications of the Modern Language Association of America* 96 (March 1981): 168–93.

Yeats, W. B. *The Poems.* Edited by Richard J. Finneran. New York: Macmillan, 1983.

Young, Edward. *The Complete Works, Poetry and Prose.* 2 vols. Edited by James Nichols. Hildesheim: Georg Olms, 1968.

Zavarzadeh, Mas'ud. "The Critic as Conservator." MS. Private Collection.

Index

Abstraction. *See* Art: and representation
Aeschylus, 126, 129, 155
Aesop, 132
Aesthetics, xii
Aleichem, Sholem, 97
Allegory, 60, 63–65, 139, 157; and science, 65–66; time
    (metaphoric and abstract) in, 64–66
Alvarez, Alfred, 101
Améry, Jean, 80
Aquin, Hubert, 117
Aquinas, Saint Thomas, xii
Arendt, Hannah, 6
Aristotle, 1, 8
Arnheim, Rudolf, 17–18
Art, xiii–xiv, xvii, xx–xxi, 58, 63, 64, 119, 154, 162, 184,
    188–189; and creative act, 60–63, 101, 114–117; and
    representation, 153, 156–158. *See also* Effortless: and
    aesthetic organization
Ashbery, John, 45, 46, 50; "No Way of Knowing," 23, 46–47;
    "Self-Portrait in a Convex Mirror," 32, 48–52, 183